it is essential to have *absolute* clarity *about what you are
liver and how you are going to do it. Let* How to be a CEO
rify your plan."

Jan Smits, CEO and Deputy Chair, APAC, Pro-invest Group

*orn a CEO. However, with the right preparation and
you can become a CEO. Let this book show you how."*

Javier Echave, CFO, Heathrow

*y people who could make brilliant CEOs. Use this book
potential and give yourself the best chance to succeed."*

John Holland-Kaye, CEO, Heathrow

*important to believe in your ability to succeed so that
n authentic way. Let* How to be a CEO *strengthen
and accelerate your success."*

John Murray, President and CEO, Sonesta International
Hotels Corporation

urehead of an organization. Use How to be a
*he example you want to set leading the business
e."*

Jonathan Akeroyd, CEO, Burberry

*coach plays an important role in supporting a
ok is similar to having him as your own coach
ing and ability to build a high-performing*

Jonathan Mills, CEO, EMEA, Choice Hotels

*day's age of uncertainty and transformation
nt to a meaningful mission both personally
ow to be a* CEO *help define what is most
hip."*

ustin Basini, CEO and co-founder, ClearScore

*hat there are certain things only you can do
nvolves strategy, capability, talent and cul-
actical guide to discipline your approach."*

Keith Barr, CEO, IHG

Praise for *Ho*

"It is super important for CEOs today to make sure they are getting the value out of business data. Reading How to be a CEO is another valuable source of data. Read it!"

Laura Miller, CIO, Macy's

"There is no such things as a perfect CEO. It takes different skills to be highly relational and commercial. However, reading How to be a CEO will make you better in building relationships and driving performance."

Mike Mathieson, Chairman, NED, advisor, founder and former CEO, Cake

"A primary mission for a CEO is to find their replacement. How to be a CEO is an insightful guide for CEOs wanting to develop others, or for anyone aspiring to the top job."

Paul Dupuis, CEO and Chairman, Randstad Japan

"A great CEO creates energy and enthusiasm about the future of an organization. Let this book inspire you to translate your vision in reality."

Paula Stannett, Chief People Officer, Heathrow

"As a CEO you need to be visionary and have the ambition to change the world. This book shows you how."

Phil Bayliss, Chairman, Inspired Villages and CEO, Infinium

"Nothing fully prepares you for the step up to CEO. It is a job like no other. What will help your preparation is to read How to be a CEO and apply the lessons to your own career journey."

Richard Solomons, Chairman, Rentokil Initial plc

"Focus on determining your own sense of purpose and use this to motivate, guide and inspire you. Combining this with the wealth of advice and experience to be found in this book will help you to establish your own identity as a CEO and maximise your potential as a leader."

Dr Sam Barrell CBE, Deputy CEO, The Francis Crick Institute

"One of the main ways to make things happen as a CEO is communication. Use this book to develop your compelling CEO story to engage others."

Simon Baugh, Chief Executive, Government Communication Service

"Once you have made a conscious decision to become a CEO revisit your original attributes and learn to make them better. Let this book inspire you along the way."

Sneh Khemka, former CEO, Simplyhealth

"About to move into a CEO role or aspiring to move into the position? This book is the perfect primer. Read How to be a CEO to speed up your readiness for the role."

Sophie Devonshire, CEO, The Marketing Society

"Be intentional in developing your career towards becoming a CEO. Let this book show you how."

Sophie Moloney, CEO, Sky NZ

"As a CEO you need to have a point! It is hard to build your presence in a business unless you stand for something. Let this book develop your core CEO identity."

Stephen McCall, CEO, edyn

"How to be a CEO by Ben Renshaw provides the essential 'runway' for all those who aspire to C-Suite roles. The book is packed with real world case studies and hard-won expert guidance. It skilfully balances the challenge of the CEO role with the encouragement and practical next steps leaders need to take. Highly recommended."

Steven D'Souza, Senior Client Partner, Korn Ferry, author of the award-winning Not Knowing trilogy

"Be open about your ambition to become a CEO. This book will help translate your focus and put it into action."

Viviane Paxinos, CEO, AllBright

"Be intentional about how you are going to become an excellent CEO and create a plan to get there. Use How to be a CEO to accelerate your process."

Will Stratton-Morris, CEO, Caffè Nero UK

"The role of a CEO is to be the guardian of the business and culture. Your job is to leave it in a better place. How to be a CEO gives you the framework to make this happen."

Wim Dejonghe, Senior Partner, Allen & Overy LLP

How to Be a CEO

Ben Renshaw

How to Be a CEO

Purpose – People – Performance

Ben Renshaw

NICHOLAS BREALEY
PUBLISHING
London • Boston

First published by Nicholas Brealey Publishing in 2023
An imprint of John Murray Press

1

Copyright © Ben Renshaw 2023

A CIP catalogue record for this title is available from the British Library

Hardback ISBN 978 1 39980 979 5
ebook ISBN 978 1 39980 980 1

Typeset by KnowledgeWorks Global Ltd.

Printed and bound in Great Britain by Clays Ltd, Elcograf S.p.A.

John Murray Press policy is to use papers that are natural, renewable and recyclable products and made from wood grown in sustainable forests. The logging and manufacturing processes are expected to conform to the environmental regulations of the country of origin.

John Murray Press
Carmelite House
50 Victoria Embankment
London EC4Y 0DZ

Nicholas Brealey Publishing
Hachette Book Group
Market Place, Center 53, State Street
Boston, MA 02109, USA

www.nicholasbrealey.com

John Murray Press, part of Hodder & Stoughton Limited
An Hachette UK company

For my children, India, Ziggy and Zebedee, who inspire my passion for Purpose, People and Performance.

May you (and the next generation of those who will enter the world of leadership) discover your own sense of purpose and use it to fulfil your potential.

Contributors

The following people gave their insight and time with incredible generosity, providing in-depth interviews or insightful quotes. They will be referenced by name and title in the book:

Amber Asher, Chief Executive Officer, Standard International

Amy C. Edmondson, Novartis Professor of Leadership and Management, Harvard Business School

Andy Cosslett CBE, Chair ITV plc and Kingfisher plc

Andy Mitchell CBE, Chief Executive Officer, Tideway

Chris Annetts, Chief Strategy Officer, Heathrow

Emily Chang, Chief Executive Officer, Wunderman Thompson West

Emma Gilthorpe, Chief Operating Officer, Heathrow

Francesca Lanza Tans, Chief Executive Officer, The Alexander Partnership

Graham Alexander, Founder, The Alexander Partnership

Helen Tupper, Chief Executive Officer, Amazing If

Jamie Bunce, Chief Executive Officer, Inspired Villages

Jan Smits, Chief Executive Officer and Deputy Chair, APAC, Pro-invest Group

Javier Echave, Chief Financial Officer, Heathrow

Joel Burrows, Chief Executive Officer, Ghirardelli Chocolate Company

John Holland-Kaye, Chief Executive Officer, Heathrow

John Murray, Chief Executive Officer, Sonesta International Hotels Corporation

Jonathan Akeroyd, Chief Executive Officer, Burberry

Jonathan Mills, Chief Executive Officer, EMEA, Choice Hotels

Justin Basini, Chief Executive Officer and co-founder, ClearScore

Justin Reese, President and Chief Executive Officer, Lindt & Sprüngli Canada

Keith Barr, Chief Executive Officer, IHG Hotels & Resorts

Laura Miller, Executive Vice President, Chief Information Officer, Macy's

Mike Mathieson, Chairman, NED, advisor and former founder and Chief Executive Officer, Cake

Neil Jowsey, Chief Executive Officer, Cromwell

Paul Dupuis, Chief Executive Officer and Chairman, Randstad Japan

Paula Stannett, Chief People Officer, Heathrow

Phil Bayliss, Chairman, Inspired Villages and Chief Executive Officer, Infinium

Richard Solomons, Chairman, Rentokil Initial plc

Dr Sam Barrell CBE, Deputy Chief Executive Officer, The Francis Crick Institute

Simon Baugh, Chief Executive, Government Communication Service

Sneh Khemka, former Chief Executive Officer, Simplyhealth

Sophie Devonshire, Chief Executive Officer, The Marketing Society

Sophie Moloney, Chief Executive Officer, Sky New Zealand

Stephen McCall, Chief Executive Officer, edyn

Viviane Paxinos, Chief Executive Office, AllBright

Will Stratton-Morris, Chief Executive Officer, Caffè Nero UK

Wim Dejonghe, Senior Partner, Allen & Overy LLP

Contents

Foreword

The role of a CEO is to create the conditions for people to thrive while working together to serve a worthy purpose in pursuit of performance. In my book *The Fearless Organization*, I looked at how organizations often fail to create sufficient psychological safety for learning, innovation and growth – essential ingredients for organizational performance in the modern economy. My research shows that psychological safety is essential to help unlock an organization's potential to do great things, and that CEO leadership plays a vital role in building psychological safety. With so much riding on people's ability to think differently, adapt to change and work in fast-paced, challenging, uncertain contexts, a CEO's approach is vital for setting the right tone. In uncertain contexts, people must be willing to voice half-finished thoughts, ask questions from left field and brainstorm out loud. This creates a culture that supports a continuous influx of new ideas and critical thought, and where the interpersonal climate does not suppress, silence, ridicule or intimidate. Not every idea is great; there *are* stupid questions, and dissent can indeed slow things down. But having a voice and talking things through is an essential part of the creative process. Sometimes, it's vital to slow a conversation down to prevent avoidable costly failures. And any time a company faces uncertainty and high stakes, the quality of information and reasoning matters for effective decision making.

An effective CEO understands that building a psychologically safe environment does not mean people will always agree with one another for the sake of being nice. In fact, quite the opposite. It also does not mean that people offer unequivocal praise or unconditional support for everything said. Psychological safety is not an 'anything goes' environment where people are not expected to adhere to high standards or meet deadlines. It is not about being 'comfortable' at work. Learning is rarely entirely comfortable, and learning is more vital than ever in a fast-changing world. Psychological safety enables candour and openness, which thrive in an environment of mutual respect. All organizations today want to attract and retain quality talent – but hiring talent when no one feels able to speak up doesn't help. The traditional culture of 'fitting in' and 'going along' spells doom in the knowledge economy.

To be clear, psychological safety is *not* the fuel that powers the car. That, I believe, comes from a worth purpose and from the intrinsic motivation to excel that talented people bring to your organization. To continue with the metaphor, psychological safety is what takes off the brakes that otherwise keep people from achieving what is possible. And so, in any challenging industry setting, CEOs have two vital tasks: one, they must build an organization of psychological safety to enable learning and avoid preventable failures; two, they must emphasize a worthy purpose and set high standards to inspire and enable people to feel excited about pursuing excellence.

Are CEOs born with an ability to lead a fearless organization? In a word: no. Leadership consists of a set of skills and mindsets that must be learned. And in my role as Novartis Professor of Leadership and Management at the Harvard Business School, I have found that CEOs and other leaders can indeed learn how to create the environment where people can thrive – as is essential to sustained organizational performance. Ben Renshaw's book, *How to Be a CEO*, aligns with my work and offers a powerful methodology for taking steps to develop your leadership potential. Its seven formative ideas provide a roadmap for achieving a senior leadership role. Whatever the outcome of your CEO journey, what matters is getting started with adopting the growth mindset that allows you to stretch yourself to become smarter and better. The combination of challenging yourself to improve while developing a deep interest in other people and what they bring is how you make progress towards ambitious goals that may have been previously cited as impossible.

In today's complex and ambiguous world, continuous learning and agility are vital to your success. The best leaders are those who are aware of their limitations, have the humility to admit their mistakes, accept when they are wrong, and place more importance in understanding reality than in being right. Their courage and curiosity enable them to create meaningful and open connections with others. They build inclusive team climates where everyone has a sense of belonging and can do their best work. Perhaps the most important aspect of learning how to be a CEO is to practise self-reflection. This book will help you do just that.

Amy C. Edmondson
Novartis Professor of Leadership and Management,
Harvard Business School
January 2023

There is no CEO school. Nothing can prepare you fully for the responsibility of leading an organization. Attending a business course won't get you there and whatever discipline you excelled in on the way up, whether it be operations, marketing or finance, the majority of organizations are not set up, even at the most senior level, to give you the necessary exposure to hit the ground running.

The horizon of a CEO is far reaching and continues to broaden and deepen all of the time. There is an extraordinary level of detail you need to learn in an unfamiliar environment with people who assume your expertise. Knowing the language of the boardroom, navigating its various committees and being the lead spokesperson for the business are all new challenges that will hit you at the same time. On top of this you need to review the company strategy within six months, build your leadership team and set up the company to perform. The net outcome will be a steep and fast learning curve as soon as you step up. One way to accelerate your CEO preparation is to join a public company board as a non-executive. This will help you understand the breadth of what a board director deals with in the modern world and gets you tuned in to the often arcane language of the boardroom and various committees.

There are multiple factors expanding the CEO role, including technology and complex stakeholder requirements. Change is constant, but the speed of change now is dramatic. Sitting down with Ben on a cold December day in London to discuss his new book,

I remarked on how few people were around. Traditionally the crowds are out in the run-up to Christmas. Working from home is just one of the many new developments in our society which have emerged post Covid. CEOs need to be on top of them all; however, the changes taking place in less familiar areas such as corporate governance and reporting are likely to create the biggest challenges. Public companies in the UK have strict regulation in place governed by bodies like the Financial Reporting Council and the Financial Conduct Authority. As politicians seek to move into the arena of corporations to ensure they are 'good citizens', the power and reach of these regulatory authorities are growing all the time. The demands placed on business today are blurring the previous distinctions between the role of the Board and executive team. To fulfil their responsibilities, boards and chairs need to be all over the detail on multiple areas as companies are required to disclose and report in a granular way on their governance, risk profile and key social issues. Equality, diversity, inclusion, purpose and sustainability are examples of this change. At the same time, technology and the advance of social media are creating a compression within businesses to bring the front line of operations more closely in touch with the leadership population. This has the power to align organizations; however, it requires the CEO to make sure all stakeholders are receiving the right messages in a consistent way. As a result, internal and external communications are essential skills for CEOs to master.

Given the varied agendas CEOs face, they need to combine adaptability with focus. For example, moving into a CEO role in private equity will require a very different prioritization of needs and demands than with a large corporate monolith. The ownership of these companies is entirely different and therefore the time horizons and expectations of the CEO will be equally different. Your approach as CEO depends on 'the gig'. When assessing opportunities, it is important to fully understand the organizational and owner requirements. Some CEOs are better suited to the world of private equity, while others prosper better in corporate environments with larger, slower-moving, heavily governed companies with the weight of their structure, decision making and reporting. As a CEO you need to be clear about the difference and where you fit best.

As a chair looking at executive leaders there are some truths that remain. The need for CEOs to be great leaders is timeless. Attributes such as humility, courage, integrity and judgement are always at the top of my list. Without these key characteristics it doesn't matter how good you are at managing tasks, everyone who becomes a CEO will be tested. It's difficult to anticipate or predict the nature of the test; however, when it comes, these enduring elements of leadership differentiate companies that navigate adversity successfully from those that do not.

Upon reflection, one of the hardest things about being a CEO is to understand the relationship between authenticity and visible leadership. It has been well documented that the best leaders have a large degree of humility. However, when taken to an extreme this can cause CEOs to stay in the shadows, to let others dominate the floor and to shun the limelight. This is not the right thing for the organization. Like it or not, a CEO is the figurehead of the business. They are the leader to whom everybody looks for vision and hope as the chief communications officer. I have learned that one of the true tests of a CEO is to be humble and visible. I wish you well on your CEO journey and I am sure this book will help you along the way.

Andy Cosslett CBE
Chair ITV plc and Kingfisher plc
January 2023

There are many people who could make brilliant CEOs but never get the chance. You might have the right mindset, skills, knowledge, experience and network to be a highly effective CEO, but the opportunity to land the position has not yet arisen. You can try to create your own luck – if you aspire to be a CEO in three years, don't go to work for a company which has just appointed a new CEO – but there are multiple factors involved in landing the role.

Different circumstances require different types of CEO. In a financial crisis, a Board will look for a different skillset than when they are planning for growth. The broader the skillset you can develop early on in your career, the more chance you will have. If you are a finance specialist, you may have the right skills to become CEO in a company with a portfolio of investments or one in financial crisis, but to increase your chances, you might want to broaden your experience and leadership skills by taking on a big operational role.

I started my career in strategy consulting and after a few years realized that I enjoyed making things happen more than advising. I went to work at Bass plc, a FTSE25 international hotel, leisure and brewing business which had a brilliant management development programme. Bass gave me big operational responsibilities and I was soon managing a sales and marketing team with £1 billion of revenues. That was when I started to think that I might have a chance of becoming a CEO. In my next company, Taylor Wimpey, I took on roles that broadened my experience, such as HR, procurement, investor relations, operations and finance. These were not my areas of expertise, but they helped to develop my general management skills and understanding of how a company worked.

While being a generalist is a great background for a CEO, it can be hard to find the right opportunities earlier in your career, when companies often want functional expertise. I was fortunate when I joined Heathrow as commercial director that they were looking for someone with experience in retail and property who could also be effective in a matrix organization which requires an understanding of how other functions work. After a few years I was asked to lead the Development team responsible for delivering the new Terminal 2 on time and on budget. Having been successful in two of the three main functions in the organization made me a credible candidate for CEO when the opportunity came up.

I am often asked how to be a CEO. I can now give people Ben Renshaw's book. The three stages he has mapped out on Purpose, People and Performance fit with my leadership approach. On a personal note, my purpose is to *make things better – today*. I have a deep sense of urgency to make change happen, which you really need as a CEO. Your time in the role can feel very short, and you need to deliver improvements for your stakeholders.

From an organizational perspective, Heathrow's purpose is *Making every journey better*. We have partnered with Ben over many years where he has coached my executive committee, as well as delivering our major leadership development and cultural programmes such as *Leading with Purpose and Values* and *Leading Sustainable Growth*. The insight and practical steps in *How to Be a CEO* will help individuals and organizations unlock their potential and make every outcome better.

John Holland-Kaye
CEO, Heathrow
January 2023

INTRODUCTION

• • •

One of the first times I encountered a CEO I had high anxiety. A chemistry meeting had been scheduled to test if I would be the right fit to coach this FTSE 100 leader. I couldn't find an available parking space in the company office parking lot so I tentatively parked in a reserved bay to announce my arrival on time. It was an unusual initial meeting as we were going to play a game of tennis at the CEO's health club as part of getting to know each other. The CEO, who I shall call William, came out to meet me ready for our game. I had been referred to him through a mutual acquaintance. As we were about to depart, one of the security guards approached us about my car being parked in the wrong bay. I explained the reason for doing so and was asked to move. I had a modest car and felt embarrassed driving it in front of the CEO. When I got back into the passenger seat of William's luxury SUV he commented on the small size of my car. It didn't seem like a great start, both in terms of having aligned values and creating a favourable first impression.

Thankfully, on the tennis court I was able to hold my own. Tennis is a big passion of mine and although I'm not a great player, I never give up. The harder William hit the ball, the more I was able to get it back in. The game broke the ice. Over lunch I asked introductory questions to understand William's background, current reality and future aspirations. It was a compelling story. He had grown up with a modest background, attending state education in the UK, without any of the trappings of a privileged upbringing of private schooling or an Oxbridge education. His family struggled financially and William had seen the effect of money worries, as well as both parents being at the beck and call of others. This had planted seeds about desiring autonomy, as well as wanting to help others succeed.

As is the case with many of the CEOs I interviewed for *How to Be a CEO*, mapping out a deliberate plan to become CEO had not been on William's agenda. He started his career journey in sales and marketing. William's drive and negotiation skills had led him to become top salesperson in his company, enabling him to move into a chief commercial role early in his tenure. It was a steep learning curve, requiring him to contribute to the company strategy, ensure the right commercial capability to deliver the plan, develop talent and navigate the organizational culture. The experience ignited a spark to become a CEO. William stepped back to seek counsel about the mindset and skillset required to become a CEO and how best to go about it. He had initial conversations with his own CEO, who was highly supportive. Together they mapped out a pathway, which included taking on projects outside William's area to broaden his experience, attending an accelerator programme for leadership development at Harvard Business School, acquiring an external CEO mentor and gaining increased exposure to the Board. One of the primary gaps identified for William's progression was strategic thinking. Although at full capacity in his role, the opportunity to become Chief Strategy Officer emerged at the right time. The serendipity of being in the right place at the right time meant that he could take on a dual role. This forced him to reorganize his commercial team so that he had the bandwidth to dedicate to strategy as well. William quickly learned one of the most important lessons to succeed as CEO – do what only you can do.

It was a steep learning curve to let go of the day-to-day running of the commercial function and to act as the enabler for others to perform. But it was the vital leadership development required in preparing William for the next step to CEO. Once again this happened sooner than expected. Following a Christmas break, the existing CEO took William into his confidence. After seven years in role it was time to move on and they wanted to know if William would like to be put forward for the CEO role. William was aware of the enormity of the task so asked for time to speak with his family and mentor to ensure clarity and alignment. William described the complexity of the decision making because although his aspiration to become a CEO had grown over the years, the actual reality of it happening was new and potentially now. However, the selection process for CEO is not straightforward for a public limited company. There is stringent governance, as well as internal and external selection. William committed fully to each step of the journey and eventually achieved a successful outcome. Having started in role, he now wanted an executive coach to help him fulfil the manifesto he had promised the business.

I loved working with William. It was an extraordinary experience not only to observe the varied opportunities, challenges and responsibilities of a CEO but to have the privilege of helping a CEO deliver on their complex agenda. Delving into the world of CEOs became the initial catalyst for writing *How to Be a CEO*. I was surprised to see that there was no book by the same title and although there are various executive education courses focused on leadership, the route to becoming a CEO is such a unique journey. I committed to doing my own research and to creating a practical framework to accelerate the learning and development of future CEOs. *How to Be a CEO* is not an A–Z encyclopedia of every insight, competence or technical skill to become a CEO. However, the seven steps that sit within the three stages of **Purpose, People** and **Performance** are universal to all CEOs and relevant to small-, medium- or large-scale organizations. When I thought about the best way of writing the book and evidencing my ideas, I realized there was no better way than drawing upon the insight and experience of people who live and breathe the reality of being a CEO every day. Therefore, each idea is brought to life through the authentic voice of CEOs, C-suite leaders supporting CEOs, and supported by Amy C. Edmondson, Novartis Professor of Leadership and Management, Harvard Business School, who was ranked the number one management thinker in 2021 by the biannual Thinkers50 global ranking.

In Amy's words: 'There are variables which will have a major impact for becoming a CEO, such as sector, size, public, private. However, at the highest level being a great CEO blends humility and determination together. Determination is essential because there will be setbacks, challenges and sometimes devastation, which will require your deepest endurance. You will need to be dedicated to a greater cause which impacts humanity. Focusing on your own bank account will not get you to where you want to go. Your contribution must add value to customers' lives and to society as a whole. Your drive and dedication will need to be married to humility. As CEO you won't have all the answers. It is important to take a stance of not knowing as this enables others to step up and contribute. The role of CEO requires you to create the conditions where others are willing to take the risk of doing what is needed for the company to succeed.'

Richard Solomons, Chairman, Rentokil Initial plc, shared his experience: 'What prepares you to become a CEO is to get a grounding in the business. When I became CEO at IHG I am sure that I was the right person at the time because I had a detailed understanding of the company. I had never set out to be CEO. However, I did want to help the business and made sure I got the relevant experience. My background was in finance, but at one point I stepped in to take an interim role as COO of the Americas. Operations was not my strength, however I learned a lot on the ground which helped me to understand the mechanics of the business. I then also looked after strategy, which informed what needed to be done in the organization.'

It was great to reconnect with my co-author of *LoveWork*, Sophie Devonshire, CEO, The Marketing Society. We had our conversation as Sophie was taking a much-needed walk to get some air. Reflecting upon her experience stepping into a CEO role, Sophie shared: 'There are different flavours as CEO. In preparation to become a CEO, think about what type of CEO is required for the particular organization and shareholders you are focused on and compare it with the type of CEO you want to be. In order to define a sweet spot it is vital to understand what the organization needs from the CEO, what the leadership team needs, and to combine it with what you are best at.'

Sophie went on to say: 'Know what you can do and where you will need support. The buck stops with the CEO. You are the ultimate decision maker and therefore you must know how your Board will support you. If you are fortunate enough to secure a CEO role, spend time soaking up and understanding the context. Make sure you have a strategic pause before jumping into action. As with any leadership role, success is often a question of timing. When I started, people were constantly asking me for my vision and what I was going to make happen. For somebody who loves speed, I made sure that I didn't rush. I took time to not jump in with my vision before getting the team on board.'

Helen Tupper is a fellow author of the brilliant book *The Squiggly Career* and transitioned into the CEO of Amazing If. She shared: 'Being an effective CEO is a culmination of collecting great experiences from other roles. I learned how to create a compelling company vision from my marketing background. My ability to drive performance came from sales. My future focus was derived from a role in innovation. To be a CEO you need to connect the dots from your collection of knowledge, skills and experience to maximize the role. Ask yourself, "How does everything I have done equip me to be a great CEO?"'

Helen is also a big advocate of learning from others: 'I have a strong network of people with diverse skills. When I started in role, I met a different CEO each month for a mentoring conversation to understand what they did in a day, what advice they had for me, what challenges they faced and who they turned to for guidance. This helped me curate a CEO mindset.' She also challenges aspiring CEOs to seize the moment: 'CEOs lead people, projects and organizations into the future. However, you don't have to wait to be a CEO to put it into action. You can exercise these muscles in multiple ways. If you need to become more strategic, think about the future. If you want to develop others, stop having all the answers and ask better questions. Think about how you can demonstrate the skills of a CEO today, such as asking more questions, challenging the status quo and conducting scenario planning. You don't need a title to do it.'

Amber Asher, CEO, Standard International, reinforced the need to be open minded: 'Being curious is a vital ingredient as CEO. I have always wanted to understand more and have cultivated a learning mindset.'

I appreciated the perspective of Jonathan Akeroyd, CEO, Burberry: 'Don't make the CEO tag the driver for being a CEO. You must love what you do. I can genuinely say I love my job. I love the brand and I get to manage an incredible business. If I didn't have a passion for the project, it is not for me. Throughout my 30-year career I have only had four main jobs. I have turned down many interesting things because I didn't think I could add value. It is critical to know that you can make a tangible difference to the company you are leading.'

Jonathan went on to say: 'There's no real or direct route to becoming a CEO. My journey has focused on performance and results balanced with humility, openness and being a team player.' Jonathan was also clear about the role of a CEO: 'The CEO is the figurehead of an organization. The bigger the business, the more the CEO needs to lead by example, manage the business and motivate people.'

John Murray, CEO, Sonesta International Hotels Corporation, made the transition from the world of finance into the CEO role: 'To be a CEO it is important to believe in your ability to succeed so that you can lead in an authentic way. Don't try to make others think you are something you are not.' John went on to say: 'The way to prepare yourself is hard work! I was influenced by my parents, who had some family sayings including "You are the company you keep". As CEO, surround yourself with smart people to bring out the best in you. Be aware, watch people, listen. You don't necessarily need to have a formal mentor, however constantly looking at others who are doing well and learning how they behave makes a big difference.'

John also highlighted: 'Focus on growing your business. Recognize that if you're not growing, you are falling behind. Motivating people to make the company stronger and bigger creates success.'

Researching for this book would have been a great opportunity to see Sophie Moloney, CEO, Sky New Zealand, in person as I love the country; however, getting her valuable perspective online was the next best thing. In terms of her journey to becoming CEO, she shared: 'Nothing beats experience to round you out in preparation for becoming a CEO. From a personal perspective, law was a useful way to frame my thinking. I worked hard and learned my craft as a commercial lawyer. However, I started to recognize that I didn't just want to advise on corporate or commercial decisions, I wanted to be part of the decision making. I was fortunate to be selected for a year-long leadership development programme while at Sky UK. I became obsessed with leadership and learning about how to get the best out of people. The reality is you can only achieve so much with one person, but the sky is the limit when leading a high-performing team.

'Be intentional in developing your career. You will never have the perfect suite of experience for a CEO role, however put your hand up for new opportunities. Don't shy aware from stuff that has never been done before. Sometimes you will need to take a lead. For instance, I drove my career forward and went to Abu Dhabi to be part of a team that launched a news channel called Sky News Arabia. I learned how to influence decision making and work with different people in different cultures. I then took a step back from the executive table when I returned to New Zealand. However, a senior stakeholder who knew my career helped me transition from the legal sphere to a commercial role where I was able to take bigger strategic decisions. A year later I started to visualize myself leading the company and thinking about how I would do things differently. I needed to round out my career and found opportunities to become versed with investors and financial metrics. I started to have conversations with recruitment firms about CEO roles. They say that getting your first gig as a CEO is the hardest. However, when the opportunity presented itself with Sky NZ, I spoke with the chair of the Board and showed my interest in being considered to lead the company. I had been at the Board table, delivered on some significant projects and was humbled to land the role.'

Sophie concluded: 'Be the editor-in-chief of your own career. As I came through the ranks, I remember thinking that senior leaders must know how hard I worked and cared. However, unless you have a sponsor taking a specific interest in you, it is essential to own your own career. When moments present themselves, don't wait to be tapped on the shoulder. At the same time don't be in a rush. Prepare yourself for the next opportunity. For instance, go for job interviews to practise and refine your skills. Pull together your story and what you want to land. Go have conversations with people in different roles. Be curious about how other people have shaped their careers. There is no set path for getting there.'

Graham Alexander, founder of The Alexander Partnership and one of the originators of executive coaching, gave his advice: 'The most important thing of all to become CEO is to make sure you really, really, really, really want the role when you stare into the reality of it. You have probably come up a ladder which has conditioned you to think onward and upward is better and that the ultimate prize is to be a CEO. I have encountered leaders who, when they finally reach the door of being a CEO, realize it's not what they want. Educate yourself on all facets of being a CEO. There are multiple dimensions to the role and it's vital to understand each aspect of the role, including having responsibility for:

1. Setting overall vision and strategy.
2. Managing the company capability and operations.
3. Developing talent and culture.
4. Being accountable to the main stakeholders and shareholders of the business for results.'

Sneh Khemka, former CEO of Simplyhealth, reinforced Graham's experience of people reaching the CEO door: 'I never thought about whether I wanted to be a CEO. I had success as my most important metric, which I marked by status, power, influence and finance. Therefore, becoming a CEO appeared to be a natural path for someone driven like myself. However, I believe you need to stop and think about it. It needs to be a conscious decision because sacrifices will be made. I am fortunate to balance my work and life, however it is a constant challenge.'

Sneh went on to say: 'Once you have taken a conscious decision to become a CEO, revisit your original attributes and learn how to make them better. For instance, you need an education in areas like strategy, compliance, regulation, P&L, communication, operations and commercial. I did an MBA on the job; however, if you need structured learning, make sure that you arm yourself with the tools first as they will be tested. Have critical friends along the way such as executive coaches, mentors, colleagues, Board members and external advisors to help and guide you. It is lonely at the top, therefore you need to go to people with whom you can have the honest conversations which go deep into your soul.'

Another valuable point of view about the pursuit of becoming a CEO came from Francesca Lanza Tans, a highly experienced CEO coach and CEO of The Alexander Partnership: 'There are five key points to set yourself up for success on the journey to becoming a CEO:

1. Be clear on your own sense of purpose. The role of CEO is multi-faceted, with numerous demands on your time. It becomes more complicated to make the right trade-offs, so having a strong sense of purpose will define your focus. Taking the time to understand your driving force is the number one requirement to succeed.

2. Unlearn some of the behaviours which enabled you to become a CEO in the first place. For instance, letting go of the need to control outcomes, or to be the subject matter expert in the room. As CEO, it's no longer your job to have all the answers, your job is to set the vision and then inspire those around you to come along on that journey with you.

3. Be comfortable making decisions, even when they don't make some people happy. You are there to do what is right for the organization, not what makes you popular. Have the courage to trust your instinct and do what's right – a CEO doesn't need to please everyone all the time.

4. Do less and be more. Be a human being, not a human doing. Your ability to influence is not driven by how much you do. It is primarily driven by your presence, the way you engage and show up, the environment you create around you.

5. Connect with those who will keep you honest. Being CEO can be lonely, and it can be tempting to surround yourself with yes-men and supporters, but being challenged is just as important. Engage the help of a formidable coach. Invite those who know you best to challenge you and force you out of your own inner narrative.'

Jonathan Mills, CEO, EMEA, Choice Hotels, also had five big ideas for becoming a CEO. In our conversation he shared: 'You need to set the context around the role of a CEO as the scope varies subject to the type of company. As the CEO for a region within the context of a global publicly listed company, the responsibility of our global CEO covers multiple stakeholder interactions, such as investors and Wall Street, which is very different to a CEO of a new start-up. However, when you distil the role down to its core requirements, I believe they remain the same, irrespective of the scope, based on five core needs:

1. The need to be a great leader, which involves providing inspiration, direction and creating a culture where everyone wants to work.

2. The need to have a real thirst, inquisitiveness and passion for the business and the customer experience.

3. The need to set a vision, strategy and to execute a plan.

4. The need to build high-performing teams and to develop talent.

5. The need to build and develop organizational capability, including enablers like products, systems and technology.'

Due to our post-Covid world I met most contributors online. However, when I could meet in person it was a welcome respite from the digital world. I was fortunate to see Keith Barr, CEO, IHG, at their InterContinental Hotel London overlooking Hyde Park. Over a cup of tea Keith shared a profound truth about being a CEO: 'Having high self-awareness is a vital ingredient for being a CEO. If you are self-aware of your strengths and gaps, it helps you build your team. The CEOs that stumble think they are the smartest in the room. You need high drive, but you need to know when to pull back and to keep yourself in check. Recognize there are people out there who are better at things than you and leverage their skills accordingly.'

Keith went on to say: 'To succeed as a CEO, it's vital to understand what gives you energy. I have found that what people often miss is having a better understanding of who they are, what gives them energy and what helps them to have a sense of purpose and accomplishment. If you are taking the job of CEO for the title or for the money, it won't be sustainable in the long run.'

Andy Mitchell, CEO, Tideway, reinforced this point: 'I hadn't realized the reality of quite how much I would have to give to the role. It is essential to give all of me, but I have found the emotional impact more draining than I had originally thought. It has been a learning about how much I can give.' In our conversation Andy reflected on a significant observation: 'If I could go back and do it again, I would have been more ambitious. Why have a limit? I believe we could have done more as an organization if I had thought bigger, bolder and been prepared to do more radical things.'

In terms of being a CEO I concur with the experience of Phil Bayliss, CEO, Infinium: 'No one in the world is born to be a CEO. It is a combination of experience, learned skills and behaviour. I developed specific skills by getting on the steepest learning curve I could. I was a hard-working academic and got scholarships for university, but quickly saw that in the workplace I would use approximately 10 per cent of my academic learning. Progress at work was about the application of EQ, a strong work ethic, and gaining the most diverse and challenging job training and experience I could. I covered numerous roles and treated each job as an apprenticeship. I set myself the target to expand into as many different roles and meet as many high-quality people as possible. The leaders that have mentored and challenged me allowed me to grow my skills quickly.'

When I caught up with Sam Barrell, Deputy CEO, The Francis Crick Institute, she gave a rounded view to set the tone: 'To succeed and thrive as a CEO you need energy, passion and a clear sense of purpose. It's also really important to care about those around you. You need to understand challenges, not only from your own perspective but also from the viewpoints of your colleagues, so that you can reach consensus or influence appropriately.'

Sam continued: 'Having a vision, an understanding of the "big picture", and a strong strategic focus is obviously essential in a CEO role, but you also need to remain close enough to the coal face so that you can delve into and understand the detail when needed. You need to be proactive, imaginative in the face of barriers and challenges, and resilient. It is also important to remain solution focused – sitting on a problem is highly unlikely to resolve it, so find ways to address it. Finally, to be successful you must be able to develop people and create cohesive teams; recruiting well is an essential element of this.'

Wim Dejonghe, Senior Partner, Allen & Overy LLP, shared his specific lens from leading one of the world's top law firms: 'I had the opportunity to make many mistakes before taking the top job. You need the opportunity to learn combined with being streetwise. To be eligible for the role you need to have been a successful practitioner (in law) where your peers recognize that she or he knows how to do it.

This involves having been seen as an equal peer within the partnership, having built a big practice, and having been visible in the marketplace.'

Wim went on to say: 'I think the best way to succeed as CEO is to surround yourself with the best people. Allow and encourage others to challenge you. Don't interfere. Trust people to get on with it. Treat everyone equally. Being a CEO is all about teamwork. I believe that genuine influence develops as a result of your credibility to do a great job, be inclusive and make more of the right decisions than the wrong ones.'

About the Book: Thinking About Becoming a CEO, Accelerating Your Pathway to CEO, Enabling Others to Become CEO

This book is for you if you're looking at the haloed CEO role and assessing whether it is right for you; wanting to fast track your CEO or leadership journey; or supporting others to becoming CEO from the role of chair, non-executive director, CEO, executive mentor or coach. *How to Be a CEO* is a crystallization of my experience partnering and coaching CEOs across a variety of sectors, including aviation, banking, construction, fashion, FMCG (fast-moving consumer goods), government, hospitality, insurance, legal, marketing, media, medical, property, retail, technology and transportation. By synthesizing key insights and referencing relevant research, I have created a clear and practical model to use. There are three pivotal stages in the process and across those, seven tangible steps to follow:

Stage 1: Purpose focuses on the foundational phase of being a CEO to understand your own sense of purpose, to clearly define how the company will serve all stakeholders through a compelling vision and robust strategy.

Stage 2: People recognizes that the quality of talent will determine the quality of the business and challenges you to genuinely put people first.

Stage 3: Performance is a call to deliver results today, alongside the ultimate goal of a CEO which is to build a sustainable organization for the future.

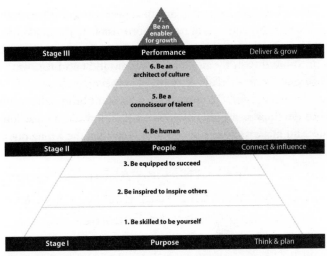

Figure 0.1 Overview of the 3P framework

Figure 0.1 shows a high-level overview of the 3P framework to be a CEO.

STAGE 1 – PURPOSE

1. **Be skilled to be yourself** places self-awareness centre stage for being a CEO. As Socrates said, 'To know thyself is the beginning of wisdom.' There are three provocations to improve your skills:
   - **Purpose matters** invites you to understand your sense of personal purpose. In the absence of having a clear 'why', you are at risk of following others' agendas or being distracted by external factors which take you away from your 'True North'. In the words of Stephen McCall, CEO, edyn, 'It is essential to know when to be your own person as you'll always have someone telling you what to do.' Being anchored in your big 'why' enables you to make an authentic linkage with the organizational purpose, or to help redefine it, providing energy, meaning and impact for all stakeholders.

13

- **Take a stand** challenges you to be clear and deliberate about living your core values and to evidence them in consistent ways. People want to understand your 'CEO brand'. Bringing it to life through your values is the simplest and strongest way to help others decide if they resonate with who you are and want to follow. The quality of your leadership is determined by the quality of your followership. It will not be possible to be an effective CEO if you don't have people helping you to deliver on your promise.

- **Play to strengths** enables you to maximize your impact for the company. There is no such thing as the 'perfect CEO'. I like the straight-talking approach of Andy Mitchell, CEO, Tideway: 'Yes, it's tough at the top, but don't whinge about it. The truth is that you get paid to give everything you can. Be open with your innermost self. Earning a lot of money means you need to do everything to justify it. You have to recognize that the difficult stuff in the role impacts your heart and soul. You need to be as giving and committed as you can in the waking hours you have.' Playing to your strengths means focusing on activities that energize and stretch you to be at the top of your game.

2. **Be inspired to inspire others** recognizes that the lifeblood of a CEO is inspiration. It is the number one characteristic that employees look for in a CEO:

   - **Clear vision** requires the clarification of a compelling future picture for the organization. From an individual perspective, this enables you to decide how to spend your time by using a simple criterion that unless an activity is moving you in the direction of the vision, don't do it. Helping the company clarify the vision sets the organizational context for prioritization and decision making.

   - **Big strategy** highlights the critical need for CEOs to create and deliver the roadmap for organizational success. Research shows that CEOs who make the right bold moves early in their tenure drive economic profit. However, in an ongoing turbulent environment, using a potent mix of data and facts to clarify your big bets takes a high dose of judgement and courage.

- **Energize the organization** encourages CEOs to step out of their comfort zone and engage the hearts and minds of stakeholders by linking ideas and information with energy and emotion through telling compelling stories. A CEO needs to understand that they set the climate and creating a great place to work unlocks the energy of those serving the company.

3. **Be equipped to succeed** suggests that no matter how self-aware and inspiring you are, to lead it is essential to be rigorous about setting up the organization for sustainable success:

   - **Preparation is everything** demands you to be thoughtful about every step you take to becoming a CEO, ensuring a seamless transition into role, setting the right tone in the precious first 90 days in role, and ring-fencing critical preparation time as you move forward to prioritize, delegate and protect your own time.

   - **Build capability** demonstrates the vital need to develop the right organizational machine to deliver the plan, including data, technology, procurement, process and systems. You will not be an expert in all these areas; however, you will need to bring intense curiosity to ask the right questions, seek to understand the right solutions and make the necessary investments to protect and grow the business.

   - **Unlock potential** illustrates one of the most important jobs a CEO has, which is to remove interference to drive performance. CEOs have to navigate multiple blockers. From an internal perspective this can include factors like unclear priorities and plans, silo ways of working, broken systems and technology, turnover, lack of productivity or limited innovation. External factors can be political instability, market conditions, recession or global pandemics. You will need to set up the right conditions for the organization to respond in agile and effective ways.

STAGE 2 – PEOPLE

4. **Be human** puts forward a fundamental proposition. The quality of people in the company determines the quality of the business.

You can have a shining strategic framework, a well-manicured organizational structure and flawless systems, but without great people working together you will fail:

- **Psychological safety** is about creating an environment where everyone has a voice and can contribute fully without the fear of negative consequences. A CEO needs to model the way by orchestrating opportunities so that people can be open and transparent in sharing their viewpoints and responding with appreciation and encouragement for ongoing learning and innovation.

- **Belonging** means that a CEO deeply understands and embraces equity, diversity and inclusion (EDI), creating a place to work where everyone has a sense of belonging and can be themselves. We live in an age of humanity where everyone needs to feel valued to be able to add value.

- **Thrive** highlights the vital need for CEOs to champion the health and wellbeing agenda. This involves being clear about your position and messaging on issues as varied as hybrid working, working from home, flexible working, mental health, absenteeism, presenteeism (working when ill), leaveism (using holiday entitlement to work), digital technologies, financial wellbeing, bereavement and trauma.

5. **Be a connoisseur of talent** acknowledges that people are the greatest asset of an organization. It is the role of a CEO to build high-performing teams, drive succession and ignite a hunger for learning and development which will be paramount for success:

- **Teaming** suggests a number one priority as CEO is to build an 'A' team. Every CEO I spoke to reinforced the message that their success is dependent on the success of their team. Therefore, CEOs need to surround themselves with brilliant and diverse people, develop an exciting plan collectively and let them get on with delivering it.

- **Succession** challenges a CEO to identify at least two, preferably three, internal successors who they champion from their early days in role. This sends a powerful message to their own team about the importance of building a deep and broad talent pipeline. The best CEOs obsess about succession plans and having the right people in the right roles.

- **Learning and development** is a fundamental ingredient to attract and retain top talent and goes beyond the workplace. Great CEOs recognize that people want to integrate their work and lives with personal and professional development running as a golden thread, ensuring that they can achieve their goals across all areas.

6. **Be an architect of culture** emphasizes the impact of culture on strategy. When Patrick Cescau, former CEO of Unilever and Chairman of IHG, spoke at one of my senior leadership development programmes he delivered a clear message: 'When culture and strategy collide, culture will always win.':

- **Climate** sets the environment for the way things are done in the company. A CEO casts a big shadow and therefore needs to have heightened awareness about their intention and impact. Great CEOs have a feedback loop in place to ensure their behaviours do not get lost in translation.
- **Relationship** recognizes the fact that better connections lead to better business. In the absence of strong relationships with multiple stakeholder groups, CEOs will fail to deliver strong performance. Relationships are emotional bank accounts. It is essential to invest in them on a continuous basis, giving the currency to lead.
- **Influence** brings to life one of the biggest shifts that CEOs need to make – from control to influence. On the way to the top many people succeed because of their ability to drive agendas and get stuff done. However, at the top it is a different proposition. The role of the CEO is to create the highest-performing organization possible. The move from control to influence requires CEOs to adopt different approaches with different people and starts by understanding where others are coming from. This means that as a CEO you need to meet people where they are and take them on a journey to where the business needs them to be.

STAGE 3 – PERFORMANCE

7. **Be an enabler for growth** is the most significant role a CEO plays – to set an organization up for long-term success. Unless a CEO delivers high performance, they will not be in role, which requires having the right conditions in place:

   - **Deliver results** shows that just telling people to hit targets is not enough. There are some essential elements needed to enable great results, including clear prioritization and metrics so that everyone is aligned about what needs to be delivered and having the right organizational capability in place, such as data, technology, procurement, systems and resources. A basic requirement as CEO is to invest sufficient analysis and planning to have your finger on the performance pulse in real time and to drive it forward when needed.

   - **Lead today** paints the picture of the complex, ambiguous and challenging world that a CEO has to navigate and translate for an organization. With new, unpredictable and unplanned scenarios arising at rapid pace on a continuous basis, CEOs are required to apply thinking big and acting small. Thinking big focuses on creating future possibilities in a sustainable way. Acting small means dropping into detail to ensure the business is on track and operating to the best of its ability.

   - **Develop tomorrow** is the execution of the commitment to building a better company. It is not just talk. The best CEOs live by a one-to-one say/do ratio, meaning they do what they say. This can include developing and providing amazing customer service, building robust organizational capability, delivering environmental, societal and governance promises, driving diversity, inclusion and talent commitments, and ensuring financial and shareholder results. The biggest impact a CEO has is to leave an organization and the world in a better place.

How to Be a CEO is structured to apply insight and learning with immediate effect. There is no such thing as the 'perfect' CEO. The best CEOs have intense curiosity, operate at pace and generate momentum through continuous improvement. To make the book as accessible as possible, each chapter breaks down into three big ideas. At the end of each idea there is a CEO note to nudge your thinking forward. Every chapter concludes with an Exec summary for those who like to keep it brief.

My hope is that whatever the outcome of your CEO pursuit, the philosophy and approach in *How to Be a CEO* will help you become a better leader and, in turn, will help others. Ultimately, leadership is not a role, position or title. It is a mindset and way of being that helps our world be a better place for the next generation.

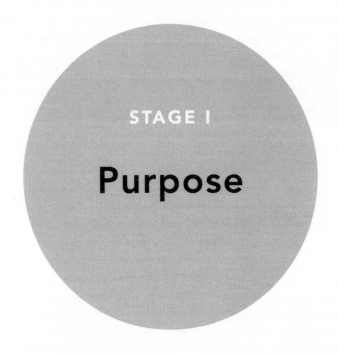

STAGE I

Purpose

Welcome to the first, foundational phase of being a CEO: Purpose. One of the fundamental roles of a CEO is to engage all stakeholders, including colleagues, customers, investors, suppliers, communities and governments, with a compelling reason about why a company exists to improve our world. However, if a CEO fails to authentically define, reset or embody an organizational purpose, they will lack credibility and followership may decline. Your ability to use purpose as a North Star to guide your thinking, decisions and actions is critical to increase clarity, strengthen energy, deepen meaning and unlock the impact that being purpose-led brings.

The power of purpose is here to stay. On 19 August 2019, the Business Roundtable in Washington announced the release of a new Statement on the Purpose of a Corporation signed by 181 CEOs who committed to lead their companies for the benefit of all stakeholders. In the opening statement it says: 'Americans deserve an economy that allows each person to succeed through hard work and creativity and to lead a life of meaning and dignity. We believe the free-market system is the best means of generating good jobs, a strong and sustainable economy, innovation, a healthy environment, and economic opportunity for all.'

As the world continues to evolve following the impact of a global pandemic, the role of purpose has gone up the agenda. In the McKinsey & Company 2021 Environmental, Social and Governance (ESG) Report, Bob Sternfels, Global Managing Partner, shared: 'At McKinsey, we believe the future belongs to those who can drive growth that is both sustainable and inclusive – and we are working with purpose, on issues from decarbonization to diversity, in order to make that future a reality.'

Placing purpose at the heart of your proposition as a CEO increases your accountability to serve all stakeholders and to help the world become a better place. It will help shape what you stand for as CEO, which is a prerequisite for providing the focus required to succeed in a complex world. The Purpose stage also embraces the need to develop a compelling vision to lift up an organization and provide the context for the creation of a clear strategic plan, critical decision making, and energizing a business to deliver superior performance.

CHAPTER 1

Be Skilled to be Yourself

● ● ●

Purpose Matters

Paul was a reluctant leader. He was on the succession plan to become CEO for a major company. As the existing CFO, Paul was well known in the finance sector. His insight and expertise were sought after, and he was highly trusted in the investor community. As good organizations do, the company had put Paul through a rigorous CEO assessment process, including a variety of psychometric and personality tests, as well as a personalized 360-feedback exercise. The messages were clear and consistent. The tests demonstrated that he had the aptitude to be a CEO. The feedback showed that everyone admired and respected Paul's technical capability, which was second to none. But people wanted to know who he was as a person. Paul tended to come across as aloof and distant. It appeared that the only people who knew the real Paul were a few trusted colleagues in his inner circle.

I was introduced to Paul by the company HR director for an initial chemistry meeting. It was a tense encounter. Paul was not an advocate of executive coaching and when I asked him about his aspiration as a future CEO, he swiftly remarked that he was 'not a leader'. He perceived himself as a 'technocrat' and had never considered himself in the CEO mould. Early on in the conversation I asked him about his sense of purpose and specifically, beyond making profit, why he did what he did. Paul did not have an immediate answer. However, he did become curious about the question, which formed

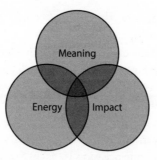

Figure 1.1 Purpose: the three main criteria

the start of our work together. Before continuing with Paul's story, let's look at what purpose is.

I define purpose as the reason for existence. It is the deepest intrinsic motivation for being. A purpose is changeless in a changing world. A purpose provides direction, focus and inspiration. It acts as a North Star, guiding the way forward. There are three main criteria to help discover and develop purpose for individuals, teams and organizations (Figure 1.1)

ENERGY

What energizes you? Where does a team get its energy from? What fuels an organization? In a *Harvard Business Review* article by Emma Seppälä and Kim Cameron (2022) entitled 'The best leaders have a contagious positive energy' the authors state: 'Numerous studies show that positive energizers produce substantially higher levels of engagement, lower turnover and enhanced feelings of well-being among employees. In organizations, superior shareholder returns occur, and in some studies, outcomes exceeded industry averages in profitability and productivity by a factor of four or more.'

They go on to say: 'There is a botanical term for these results: the heliotropic effect. That's the phenomenon whereby plants naturally turn toward and grow in the presence of light. In nature, light is the life-giving force; photosynthesis occurs only in its presence. Human beings have the same inherent attraction toward life-giving and life-supporting energy. This form of energy is what you receive – and give – in relationships with others.'

Once you have discovered and become fuelled by your own sense of purpose, it will sustain your energy and will enable you to show up in a consistent way as the sun, radiating warmth and positivity and nourishing those around you. Contrast this to showing up as a black cloud, engendering a climate of fear, anxiety and negativity. Although it might activate performance in the short term, it is not a formula for long-term success. On one occasion I was invited to meet with the HR director in a company that was driving hyper-growth. It transpired that the organization recruited some of the brightest talent around; however, the average tenure of people was 18 months. The company was haemorrhaging talent. People were literally having breakdowns in the office as a consequence of being driven so hard. The CEO's response was a public declaration that he didn't care and if people couldn't keep up, they would be quickly replaced. The HR director was in a minority in trying to shift the culture. My perspective was not welcome. However, it was interesting to see that the company had ongoing issues with the regulatory body governing its affairs and eventually the CEO got fired.

Contrast this with the sense of purpose at the UK's national airport. I was fortunate to coach the Heathrow leadership team responsible for the delivery of Terminal 2, The Queen's Terminal. As John Holland-Kaye, Heathrow CEO, says, 'Heathrow is Hollywood' – in other words, anything related to Heathrow gets high media coverage – so it was critical that the organization got Terminal 2 right. Brian Woodhead was Terminal 2's Programme and Operations Director. John put Brian in role as he was purpose-led. One of Brian's first acts in role was to schedule a team offsite, which I facilitated to define the leadership team's shared sense of purpose. People were busy. The idea of taking 24 precious hours out of their diaries did not appeal. Unperturbed, Brian stayed focused on the discovery of purpose, and we used a simple process to get under the skin of what it could mean for the team. We framed the session by indicating that it was an exploratory process. This meant not making any immediate decisions or actions to implement. The steps involved asking team members to:

1. Generate adjectives to describe why the team existed and what they aspired to be like as a team.
2. Select the adjectives, once shared, that had the greatest impact.

The team came up with multiple adjectives and aligned on some unified themes, including growth, inspiration, delivery, people and opportunity. I then challenged the team to create a statement that best represented their shared sense of purpose, beyond the immediate goal of opening the terminal on time and on budget. Following considerable probing they alighted on 'To inspire people to go beyond what they think is possible'. Going forward, this intent became an energizer, reminding the team about their collective reason for existence beyond hitting their delivery goal.

Sitting down with Paula Stannett, Chief People Officer, Heathrow, she clearly articulated the impact of purpose for an organization: 'Being purpose led provides a clear mindset for CEOs to make necessary business trade-offs. A vital leadership component in our current societal and environmental climate is to leave the company in a better place. Leading with purpose gives a framework for everything CEOs look at and enables them to deploy consistent decision making to deliver better outcomes.'

MEANING

In the McKinsey article 'Increasing the meaning quotient of work', authors Susie Cranston and Scott Keller (2013) write that their focus has been on creating work settings that promote high energy, self-assurance, and personal productivity. When inquiring with leaders about the missing element they find most challenging to provide for themselves and their colleagues, they consistently point to one crucial factor: a profound sense of meaning. 'Meaning' here refers to a sentiment that what is happening holds genuine significance, that the tasks at hand are novel or impactful to others.

This insight is reinforced by a Great Place To Work article. Author Roula Amire (2022) shared that many people consider the importance of purpose in their work, as it can lead to job satisfaction or prompt them to seek new opportunities elsewhere. The organizations listed as the Best Workplaces for Millennials™ recognize the significance of meaning for Generation Y, the largest generation in the current workforce. These successful workplaces, spanning different company sizes, actively strive to provide their younger employees with a sense of purpose. Consequently, they enjoy higher retention rates, greater pride in their work, and increased endorsements from their millennial workforce. However, only 79 percent of millennials feel their work has a special meaning, in contrast to 90 percent of baby boomers. For millennials and Generation Z, a sense of purpose profoundly influences their perception of the future, making them more inclined to leave jobs that they don't find meaningful.

Michael C. Bush, CEO of research and analytics firm Great Place To Work, says that millennials can teach companies valuable lessons about work. If a company can help them find meaning and pride in their work, they'll stay committed to your organization.

Sitting down with Stephen McCall, CEO, edyn, in the company's beautiful office space which reflects the company purpose, he spoke passionately about the linkage between purpose and meaning: 'As a CEO you need to have a point. Start with purpose. It is hard to build your presence in the business unless you stand for something meaningful. At edyn we asked colleagues what they wanted the company to be and how to pursue what they cared about, which included humanity, beauty, experiences and love. We conducted multiple listening groups to deeply understand why people loved edyn and what they thought made it precious. Through an iterative process we arrived at the company purpose, 'Soulful hospitality'. Importantly, we asked our colleagues to dream of a better way and what that might look like, rather than simply to describe a slightly better version of their current reality. This allowed us to be more radical and transformational with the changes we wanted to implement.'

Stephen went on to say: 'It is vital to know what you are striving for so that you can make sure it becomes embedded in the culture. The company purpose needs to become the True North and narrative of the business so that people reference it and use it as a lens for decision making. For instance, if someone is having a bad day, we can ask them what they need to be more soulful. When making business trade-offs we will use our purpose to establish the pros and cons to arrive at the right answer. Every business will have to make choices between their ambition and, for example, economic reality, but the trade-offs are often opaque and being clear on your deeper purpose helps you gauge where you can compromise or where you should stand firm.'

What is most meaningful for you? It is vital to understand your own sense of meaning in order to be able to help people, teams and the organization to be aligned about what matters most. This could include:

- Individually – for example, fulfilling potential, enjoying autonomy, mastering skills or helping others.

- Teams – for instance, having a sense of belonging, playing to strengths, working collaboratively or delivering passion projects.

- Customers – for example, making life easier, providing a superior service or product, or creating memorable experiences.

- Society – for instance, making a better world, contributing to the community, reducing carbon emissions or stewarding resources.

IMPACT

When you ask most people what they want to be remembered for they answer with some version of wanting to make a difference, add value, help others or have a positive impact. In the *Harvard Business Review* article 'From purpose to impact' by Nick Craig and Scott A. Snook (2014) the authors write that in effective purpose-to-impact plans, language is personalized to resonate with each individual, avoiding corporate terminology. These plans concentrate on future, overarching ambitions and gradually delve into specific details by working backward. Furthermore, they prioritize the individual's strengths and advocate for a balanced perspective on both work and family life.

Focusing on impact is a powerful tonic when the permanent busyness takes over. Laura Miller, Executive Vice President, Chief Information Officer, Macy's, gave her perspective: 'Whether it's trying to make a difference to a company, team or individual, there are some days that you feel caught up on the hamster wheel and you are spinning so hard that it's hard to recognize the impact you can make. When this happens, I have to remember that what makes the difference for me is to enhance the lives of others. If I can help one person's work become easier or make them more successful, I have fulfilled my purpose that day.'

I am fortunate to work with Diageo, a global leader in premium drinks. As a purpose-led organization the company articulates its purpose as 'Celebrating life, every day, everywhere'. The company states: 'Our accessible purpose provides a platform for us to be the best we can be at work, at home and in our communities – it's about *celebrating life* in its broadest sense. Our purpose goes hand in hand with performance – never one without the other.'

An example of moving from purpose to impact was an event I helped facilitate with Diageo Reserve, the luxury portfolio of Diageo. The Reserve leader came up with the title 'Let's Dance'. The event was held in Barcelona and the team gathered from around the world for the first time post Covid. We used dance as a metaphor for how to succeed in the business and had amazing Spanish dance instructors guide us through a series of dances to provoke curiosity. We debriefed the learning and the team arrived on the acronym FLOW as the way to work together. The impact of FLOW is:

- **Feeling** brings together emotion and performance. Everyone in Reserve is encouraged to speak up about how they feel in order to help unlock the potential to perform. Line managers will ask team members how they are feeling in performance conversations to ensure everyone feels safe to share what is going on and get the help they need to succeed.

- **Learning** invites a growth mindset where everyone sees challenges as opportunities, understands how to make better decisions when navigating between choices, removes right and wrong to find the power in different perspectives, and recognizes setbacks and red flags earlier to course correct.

- **Owning** creates the conditions where everyone feels ownership of the Reserve Strategy, Performance and Culture. It means everyone takes accountability for what is going on, thinks about Reserve as one team, brings all their ideas to the table, and seeks sufficient data and insights that quickly move the team to action.

- **Winning** is about building a sustainable future. It requires everyone to think differently, be innovative and creative to take risks, push boundaries and deliver brilliant results. It means being prepared to fail fast, drive progress not perfection, and enjoy the journey!

Bringing together energy, meaning and impact becomes a tangible way of defining purpose and brings it to life in multiple ways.

Back to Paul's story – the reluctant leader who was in line to become CEO. The provocation about purpose led him on a journey where he genuinely wanted to discover his own purpose and explore what it could mean in terms of the company and role as CEO. We scheduled an afternoon to discuss. I introduced Paul to a timeline exercise which is a reflective process focused on three key steps:

1. Identify times when you have experienced peak moments, you have been in flow and truly fulfilled, to understand when you have been at your best.
2. Make meaning of these times to recognize why these experiences were so significant and highlight some stand-out themes.
3. Distil this learning and insight into a statement representing your personal purpose.

The personal purpose process is shown in Table 1.1.

TABLE 1.1 PERSONAL PURPOSE PROCESS

Step 1 Identify peak moments or memorable chapters when you were at your best	Step 2 Highlight key themes associated with each experience and why they were so meaningful	Step 3 Recognize the links between key themes to help clarify personal purpose
When have you been at your best? What was happening when you experienced peak moments or memorable chapters? When have you been most energized?	Why were these experiences so impactful for you? What did they mean? Why were they so significant?	What do your big themes have in common? What is most meaningful for you? What impact do you want to have in the world?

Paul took this insight and we embarked on an inquiry:

Ben: What does 'going beyond what you think is possible' mean to you?

Paul: It means overcoming any hurdles and perceived limitations.

Ben: What massive value would you like to ultimately add?

Paul: Making things better for others so that they have opportunity to flourish.

Ben: Why does being a catalyst for change ignite you?

Paul: I love making big things happen and in particular helping others unlock their potential.

Ben: What stands out for you when you reflect upon these different elements?

Paul: Helping others, making things better and creating new things.

Ben: If you brought these ideas together, what would it mean?

Paul: Being a creator of opportunity.

Guiding Paul on this inquiry was enlightening and is best captured in Table 1.2.

TABLE 1.2 PAUL'S PURPOSE PROCESS

Step 1 Identify peak moments or memorable chapters when you were at your best	Step 2 Highlight key themes associated with each experience and why they were so meaningful	Step 3 Recognize the links between key themes to help clarify personal purpose
Competing in road bicycle racing	• Winning – love the feeling of stretching myself to be the best I can be • Speed – exhilarated by taking risk and pushing boundaries • Continuous improvement – driven by the opportunity to get better and master difficult tasks	• Going beyond what I thought was possible
Completing big, complex financial deals	• Simplifying complexity – energized by taking multiple data points and creating order • Working collaboratively – thrive on working in a team environment building upon ideas • Solving problems – love coming up with answers and helping others	• Delivering massive value
Supporting my children to unlock their potential	• Helping others grow – passionate about unleashing curiosity and hunger for learning • Creating opportunity – driven by removing obstacles and making things happen • Opening possibility – committed to being a catalyst for new things	• Being a catalyst for change

Ben: How does that resonate with you as a sense of purpose?
Paul: It is like coming home to a truth which I already know but haven't clearly articulated.

I suggested that Paul use the following statement for his personal purpose:
To be a creator of opportunity
We used a 3C formula to test and validate the currency of Paul's purpose:

- **Consistency**. The world will change around you and the circumstances of your life will evolve, however your purpose stays constant. It is changeless in a changing world. Paul recognized that through all the major changes in his life, such as getting married, becoming a father, gaining promotions and navigating crises, the drive of creating opportunity endured and carried him forward.

- **Connection**. Your purpose is present with you on different levels of connectivity, including:
  o physical – you get energy from it
  o emotional – you feel strongly about it
  o mental – you derive intellectual stimulation from it
  o spiritual – you are inspired to follow it.

  Paul could see the connection between being a creator of opportunity and the impact it had on him and others. It was a source of inspiration and energy that lifted him up and provided grit to sustain him in difficult times, as well as challenging him to think differently and find solutions.

- **Clarity**. Your purpose acts as a North Star, giving you direction and focus. Paul applied his purpose to leadership and started to see the CEO role differently. Rather than relating to it as a role, position or title, by seeing it through the lens of opportunity he recognized that becoming a CEO allowed him to be a creator of opportunity on a bigger scale. He could provide opportunity for colleagues, customers, investors, suppliers and communities, which genuinely excited him.

Landing on his purpose gave Paul a different lens to look through on his journey to CEO. He developed a framework based on three key strategic priorities to shape what he wanted to stand for, which became the foundation of his compelling narrative to engage stakeholders (see Table 1.3).

TABLE 1.3 KEY STRATEGIC PRIORITIES FRAMEWORK

Purpose – to be a creator of opportunity	People	Growth	Sustainability
	1 Create an environment of psychological safety where everyone has a sense of belonging, speaks up and is able to be the best version of themselves. 2 Show true care through listening to understand others and going beyond expectations in response to meeting their needs. 3 Invest in talent to ensure people can thrive at work in dynamic ways and have a meaningful career pathway.	1 Drive a performance culture where all stakeholders benefit from growing the business. 2 Inspire a growth mindset where everyone has the opportunity to ignite their curiosity, learn and develop to deliver superior performance. 3 Maintain a balanced scorecard to ensure that business growth is balanced with people, profit and the planet.	1 Champion an environment, social and governance agenda in meaningful ways. 2 Improve education and opportunities for equality, diversity and inclusion across all stakeholders. 3 Develop organizational strategy, capability, talent and culture for the long term.

Alongside his personal purpose, Paul was able to turn his attention to the organizational purpose to make genuine linkages so that he could embrace it, not as a slogan but as the fundamental DNA within the company. Suffice to say the company purpose lacked authentic buy-in and traction. Its origins had been more of a corporate tick-box activity rather than an opportunity to engage colleagues in the creation and ownership of a meaningful understanding about why the organization exists. If Paul was successful in his application for CEO, he resolved to start by re-evaluating the purpose as he wanted to base his tenure on a truth.

Purpose has come of age. Research shared by McKinsey & Company in an article published in April 2021, entitled 'Help your employees find purpose – or watch them leave', cited: 'Nearly two-thirds of US-based employees we surveyed said that Covid-19 has caused them to reflect on their purpose in life. And nearly half said that they are reconsidering the kind of work they do because of the pandemic. Millennials were three times more likely than others to say that they were re-evaluating work.' A key message was: 'Employees expect their jobs to bring a significant sense of purpose to their lives. Employers need to help meet this need or be prepared to lose talent to companies that will.'

What is your purpose? Are you clear? How does it guide you? Are you able to articulate it in a way that inspires and engages others? Joel Burrows, CEO, Ghirardelli Chocolate Company, has championed being purpose-led over the last decade. First, he helped double the size of Lindt UK and Ireland, leading the business by continuously growing market share and brand equity through building a purpose-led organization. He transferred his knowledge and approach to Ghirardelli in January 2018. During our conversation, while enjoying the company's delicious caramel squares, Joel shared the following: 'I feel very fortunate to be working for the Ghirardelli Chocolate Company, a fantastic and fast-growing brand with over 160 years of history and more than 1,200 passionate employees. My purpose is to build real relationships and help others unlock their potential, which guides my every step and ensures that I help the organization and colleagues discover and lead with purpose.'

He went on to say, 'Early in my tenure with Ghirardelli, along with my management team and colleagues, we set out to define the company purpose through understanding the rich heritage and impact of the business. We reflected upon the magical journey of making great chocolate, starting with sourcing great cocoa beans, having the beans arrive in our San Leandro factory where the process of making our chocolate begins. Over many years we have become famous for our caramel squares, chocolate chips, intense dark range, peppermint bark and of course our hot fudge sundaes produced every day in our stores across the US. Our aim is to change the way the consumer experiences chocolate, contribute to the communities where we live and work, and have some fun along the way. With that in mind our purpose, "Make life a bite better", was born. This gives our company meaning and inspires everything we do. We have the strategic priority 'Be Purpose Led' baked into our strategic plan, positioned as one of our three strategic pillars. We have identified our four immediate stakeholder groups whom we impact, which we call our 4's – Consumer, Customer, Colleague and Community – and have a steering committee who help define what "Make life a bite better" means for each constituent group and how we measure it.'

The company's current focus is shown in Table 1.4.

TABLE 1.4 COMPANY FOCUS

	Consumer	Customer	Colleague	Community
Why we make life a bite better	Deliver premium chocolate and more with great taste and highest quality	Deliver category growth and excellent service level	Create a welcoming and vibrant culture through living our values	Make a difference in our local communities and operate sustainably
What success looks like	Market share Brand equity	Advantage survey Category growth	Great Place To Work Retention	Sustainable indicators Donated hours and dollars

In working with Joel and his extended leadership team, we reinforce personal, team and organizational purpose every month in management team and senior leadership team meetings, using them as a lens focused on areas like managing organizational change and transitions, building high-performing teams and collaboration, and inspiring and engaging different stakeholder groups, which results in a clear linkage between purpose, people and performance.

I appreciated the way Sam Barrell, Deputy CEO, The Francis Crick Institute, reflected upon being purpose-led: 'I've always had a very strong sense of purpose guiding me through my career. For me, this has been about patient care and scientific and technical advances that can really make a difference to people's lives. The advice I would give to those starting out on their careers is to really think about what your own key purpose is and to use this as a motivational and guiding force. It will help you stay resilient and positive through inevitable challenges and will ultimately ensure that your working life is enjoyable and rewarding.'

Helen Tupper, CEO, Amazing If, shared a strong view about the impact of purpose: 'Don't just pick the title. Pick your purpose. I wanted to lead an organization that made careers better for everyone and to drive a business forward that makes a tangible difference. Define why you want to be a CEO. It is such a pivotal role that you must care passionately about leading and creating meaningful value. By connecting the position and purpose it will make the role sustainable.'

Another purpose-led CEO is Jamie Bunce at Inspired Villages, focused on helping people live the best years of their lives. In Jamie's words: 'We make a positive and transformational difference in people's lives by providing villages which have vibrant communities where people who want to get the most out of life do it together. To be a purpose-led CEO means having the emotional intelligence to take people on the journey with you. Understand at what point you inspire people or confuse them. Keep people on the same path and enable them to take their own journey in the organization. As CEO your role is to create the conditions for people to connect passionately with the business. Help ignite the fire in people to go on their own journey for the good of the business.'

CEO NOTE

Use purpose as a way to provide meaning, energy and impact
for an organization.

PURPOSE MINDSET

Upon awakening, what is on your mind? What formative decisions
do you make? Having asked thousands of leaders these types of questions, the typical responses I get include:

Hit snooze
Tea or coffee?
Check inbox
How's the weather?
What meetings are in the calendar?
What to wear?
Get the kids up
Take the dog out
Any overnight crises?

It is a 'to do' list.
Urgent? Yes.
Energizing? Not particularly.
Meaningful? Not really.
Impactful? Marginal.

Neuroscientists estimate that on the unconscious level, the human
brain can process roughly 11 million pieces of information per second. Compare that to the estimate for conscious processing: about
40 pieces per second (DiSalvo, 2013). As a result, the brain creates
mental shortcuts to help us interpret information faster and save
energy in making decisions. We rely on our past experiences to do
this, and when faced with similar situations or people, we automati-
cally make associations. However, as you shift to being purpose-led,
operating on autopilot is insufficient.

In a fascinating McKinsey & Company article entitled 'Making a daily "to be" list: How a hospital system CEO is navigating the coronavirus crisis' (2020), Cincinnati Children's CEO Michael Fisher says he is communicating with purpose, leaning into tough choices and emphasizing trust as he leads through uncertainty. Asked about his personal operating model and what was serving him well, he said that he believes everyone has their unique approach to self-management, handling workloads, being accountable, and focusing on both short-term and long-term goals. Personally, he has always maintained discipline by jotting down daily "to-dos," ensuring he accomplishes tasks A, B, and C. Recently, he started incorporating a "to be" list as well, where he intentionally chooses how he wants to present himself each day. For instance, today, his goal is to be generous and genuine, especially during crucial meetings with his senior team. Another day this week, his focus was on being collaborative and catalytic. So, he selects two qualities each morning to guide his daily interactions and actions.

CEO NOTE

Every day put your 'to be' at the top of your 'to do' list.

Michael Fisher's example illustrates a fundamental mindset shift most people need to make from 'doing' to 'being'. The usual construct we have is shown in Figure 1.2.

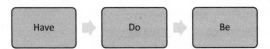

Figure 1.2 Mindset shift from 'doing' to 'being'

We tell ourselves when we have the things we want, we will do the things we want and be the type of person we want to be. A classic example is money: When I have enough money, I will do great things and be happy. In the meantime, we can postpone who we want to be. The invitation is to put our 'being' first – see Figure 1.3.

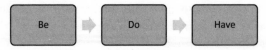

Figure 1.3 Putting our 'being' first

On the outside Susan had it all. She had climbed the dizzy heights to CEO of a global company, had a loving family and was admired in her profession. However, at the start of our coaching partnership she disclosed that was not happy and battled daily frustration. I asked Susan what was her best bet for happiness. 'Retirement. Just ten more years of angst and then watch me, I'm going to have a wonderful life.' I challenged her on this notion and the impact it could potentially have on all areas of her work and life. Having battled hard to reach CEO she was loath to change her approach. I introduced her to the concept of being purpose-led as a starting point to shift her experience of reality. She embraced the idea in her typical driven way and quickly reached a focal point: 'To be the best I can be.' We used this as a lens to define what it would look like every day, rather than waiting ten years.

Susan dug into exploring her criteria to being the best she can be:

- As a CEO, leading a company.
- As a Board member, collaborating with others.
- As a spokesperson, communicating with stakeholders.
- As a mum, parenting her children.
- As a partner, evolving her marriage.
- As a daughter, connecting with her parents.
- As a friend, nurturing others.
- As a member of society, helping the world be a better place.

I shared with her three different types of mindsets which could help her make this shift from 'doing' to 'being'.

1. **Autopilot**. Mentioned above, this is when we make unconscious, automatic decisions to help with certain routine tasks. It is an evolutionary mechanism that has developed to stop our brains from overloading. When we live on autopilot, it feels like someone else is driving, not us. As a CEO, tell-tale signs you are operating on autopilot include:

   - **You don't switch off**. You are permanently busy. You have no time or space to think or reflect. You get distracted and find it hard to be present with others.
   - **You are frustrated**. You feel that other people's expectations define your agenda and that you don't have sufficient opportunity to lead the company in the direction you want to go.
   - **Your work is predictable**. Your schedule has too many repetitive activities and you feel obligated to perform a role, rather than to shape your role as a challenging adventure.

2. **Choice**. This is the ability to choose our mindset in any given situation, which determines how we respond to events. Probably the most profound insight on the power of choice comes from the work of Viktor Frankl. Frankl was an Austrian psychologist and a Holocaust survivor. In his momentous book *Man's Search for Ultimate Meaning* (2004), Frankl shared the observation that in any situation, a person's freedom to choose their attitude and their own path remains inviolable, even when everything else may be taken away from them. As a CEO you recognize that there will be multiple events happening at any given time, but it will be the choices you make to respond which will determine the outcomes. For example:

   - **The business is underperforming**. You could choose to jump into a highly directive mode and start telling people what to do, diving into the detail and unnerving colleagues. Or you could step back, seek to understand the underlying factors causing the underperformance, and respond with a considered and constructive response.
   - **Employee engagement is down**. You could choose to respond by blaming others for poor leadership and failing to translate vision, set expectations, or help people learn and develop. Or

you could take ownership for the engagement results and set a powerful example by understanding the root-cause issues and changing your own leadership first.

- **Colleagues are reluctant to return to office**. You could choose to call remote work an 'aberration' and not conducive to productivity. Or you could choose to show high compassion and empathy in understanding the challenges colleagues are facing and respond with the right level of flexibility and encouragement.

3. **Intention**. Research shows that our brains are constantly being shaped by experience. Most of us have very different thoughts and behaviours than we did 20 years ago. This shift is known as neuroplasticity: changes in brain structure and organization as we experience, learn and adapt. Through neuroplasticity – the 'muscle build' part of the brain – we become what we think and do. Therefore, we can deliberately develop our mindset in conscious ways and become intentional about how we want to be. For instance:

- **Be purpose-led**. To be purpose-led starts by setting a clear intention every day. Just as Cincinnati Children's CEO Michael Fisher did, put your 'to be' at the top of your 'to do' list. I am a big advocate of adopting the principle of continuous improvement to being purpose-led. In his seminal book *Atomic Habits* (2018), author James Clear states a powerful case for nudging your 'to be': with a daily improvement of just one percent over the course of a year, your overall performance will grow significantly, reaching a remarkable thirty-seven times improvement by the end of that period.

- **Be a CEO**. No one says, 'I am going to do a CEO'. To be a CEO means developing the qualities and characteristics that are associated with leadership greatness, including being visionary, inspiring, strategic, bold, resourceful, thoughtful, collaborative, communicative, inclusive, trusting, compassionate, energetic, resilient and humble.

Susan clearly understood the concept of setting a strategic intent from a business perspective and therefore she loved the idea of setting a deliberate intent as CEO – starting with being purpose-led. She shared the idea about intent with her executive committee and together they agreed to reinvigorate the company purpose, which had taken a back seat. Before going out to the business with big purpose-led promises, they decided to test themselves by putting it on their weekly operational agenda and doing a deep dive at their monthly strategic meeting. They challenged themselves to identify genuine moments of being purpose-led in the business, lessons learned, challenges overcome and opportunities to progress going forward. For instance, a key priority was to develop a more sustainable business post Covid. They knew that just telling people to cut costs and be more efficient would deliver short-term requirements but could erode employee engagement in the longer term. They decided to take a different approach and set up listening groups, which they personally attended, to seek to understand colleagues' insight and ideas for addressing the priority. At the heart of the company purpose was the statement: 'Today, we are a purpose-driven company that's dedicated to empowering people through the value of opportunity.' Rather than simply paying lip service to the feedback, the executive committee held themselves accountable for putting plans in place.

Top of the list was to become carbon neutral. As a business they had committed to The Climate Pledge, which was to become net-zero carbon by 2040. However, given the impact of navigating coronavirus, the priority had taken a back seat. Susan asked for a steering group to be formed by enthused colleagues who wanted to own and drive the agenda. A diverse team was quickly established, which initially put in meaningful short-term targets such as regular reporting, carbon elimination and credible offsets. The team requested time at each monthly executive committee meeting to update on governance, progress and challenges to overcome. Susan developed a clear and compelling narrative about the significance of the business becoming carbon neutral and personalized it by calculating her own carbon footprint and sharing her most impactful reductions.

Another example was championing EDI. Susan had worked hard to ensure her executive committee had a fair representation of gender, ethnicity and thinking style. She consistently focused on and communicated about the need to build an environment where every individual can bring their whole self to work and to encourage them to draw upon their unique experiences, thoughts and perspectives to help deliver business goals and to build products and services that reflect the full markets the organization is trying to serve. One way to bring EDI to life was at the annual company conference. Susan made sure that every detail of the conference reflected the intent to belong, including the location, venue, food and beverages, and topics covered. One of the most meaningful sessions was a dialogue facilitated by her HR director with an external executive from the banking industry who had transitioned from a man to a woman, along with an internal colleague who had shared the same experience. It was an enlightening conversation which clearly indicated Susan's commitment to everyone having a sense of belonging within the organization.

In order to embed purpose, it's critical to be purpose-led. In my interview with Neil Jowsey, CEO of Cromwell, he shared: 'A primary requirement to be a highly effective CEO is to embody a strong sense of purpose. Be clear about why you are leading. I have discovered how powerful it is to inspire others and encourage them to follow me as a leader based on purpose. The way I have distilled my purpose is to lead growth. For instance, when I engage with new starters in the company, I share what is meaningful for me and how I thrive on helping people unlock their potential. With my executive committee I love figuring out how to make things better in order to unleash our growth. Every time I am intentional about being purpose-led, I see people wowed. I believe it sends the message – here is a leader who is super clear. I can get on board with it. I can see what's in it for me.'

Neil went on to say: 'Be intentional about the purpose of the organization by figuring out why the company exists and what role it plays in the world. For instance, at Cromwell our purpose is "To keep industry working". Many of our customers provide life-enhancing services, such as producing hip and knee joints or making insulin pens. I love the fact that we help them give people's lives back. I get excited by the impact of our purpose in the world, rather than focusing on putting products in boxes and shipping them around the world. Our purpose catches fire in the business and helps generate a sense of pride. The really special businesses and CEOs find ways to unlock purpose in multiple ways.'

CEO NOTE

Setting your intent to be purpose-led is a starting point for leading the business.

Take a Stand

I am reluctant to reference politicians in a business context, however the extraordinary events surrounding a recent high-profile figure are relevant when it comes to the impact of taking a stand. On 7 July 2022 Boris Johnson resigned as the UK's Prime Minister. It hadn't even been three years since he had led the Conservatives to their biggest election victory since 1987. The BBC recognized several elements that led to his downfall which are closely linked to personal reputation:

1. The Chris Pincher affair. On 29 June 2022, the then Conservative deputy chief whip MP Chris Pincher went to a private members' club in London. In his words, he 'drank far too much and embarrassed himself'. Mr Johnson claimed that he was not aware of 'specific allegations' about Mr Pincher before appointing him as deputy chief whip, which turned out to be inaccurate. Mr Johnson later admitted that he had been told and apologized for appointing Mr Pincher as deputy chief whip.

2. Partygate. In April 2022, the Prime Minister was fined for breaking lockdown rules when he attended a gathering on his birthday

in June 2020. He also apologized for going to a 'bring your own booze' party in the Downing Street garden during the first lockdown.

3. The Owen Paterson row. In October 2021 a House of Commons committee recommended a 30-day suspension for then-Conservative MP Owen Paterson. The committee said he broke lobbying rules, to try to benefit companies that paid him. But the Conservatives – led by the Prime Minister – voted to pause his suspension and set up a new committee to look at how investigations were carried out. After an outcry, Mr Paterson ended up resigning. Boris Johnson later admitted that he had 'crashed the car' in his handling of the case.

4. Lack of focus – and ideas. Boris Johnson's former advisor turned chief critic Dominic Cummings repeatedly accused him of being an out-of-control shopping trolley, veering from position to position. Others questioned Mr Johnson's philosophy – or indeed whether he had one.

In 'Strategy&', part of a 2018 PwC network article titled 'CEO success study', it was noted: 'Ethical lapses are on the rise. The overall rate of forced turnovers was in line with recent trends, at 20 per cent. But the reasons that CEOs were fired in 2018 were different. For the first time in the study's history, more CEOs were dismissed for ethical lapses than for financial performance or board struggles.' Some notable cases of the downfall of CEOs include:

- Kenneth Lay, who presided over the Enron accounting scandal, died before serving his prison sentence.
- Bernard Ebbers of WorldCom served half his prison term for fraud, dying shortly after his early release.
- After using corporate funds as his personal piggy bank, Dennis Kozlowski of Tyco went to prison.
- Conrad Black of Hollinger Inc served part of his prison term for wire fraud; after being released, he received a pardon from President Trump.

- Scott Thompson quickly departed from Tyco after false information was discovered on his resume. He has served as CEO of other companies since.

As a CEO people want to know what you stand for. Sneh Khemka, former CEO, Simplyhealth, gave his perspective: 'A CEO needs to understand that the reputation and brand of the organization are pinned on visible leadership, which they must take to heart. The rise of the superstar CEOs, such as Steve Jobs, Mark Zuckerberg and Elon Musk, has impacted smaller companies where new expectations have been thrust on CEOs. External personality defines the company success. This is amplified by the increased polarization of earnings between the CEO and colleagues, which needs to be justified and puts more demands on the CEO to represent the business in the right way.'

Sophie Moloney, CEO, Sky New Zealand, integrates her authentic self with the role: 'I never thought I would be a CEO, it wasn't even on my radar despite the fact that I grew up in an environment which nurtured leadership roles and self-motivation as my father was a headmaster. As a teenager I went through a dark time and came to realize that we are all unique and should all be able to be ourselves. I carry this with me as a CEO today.'

An essential part of what you stand for is to be clear and deliberate about living and breathing your values in a consistent way. Keith Barr, CEO, IHG, articulated the importance of being values based: 'Make sure your role fits with who you are. Ask yourself: Does my role align with my values and who I am? For instance, I am hardwired to care. During Covid-19 my commitment was to make sure that we could keep as many people employed for as long as possible based on what we could afford to do. I held monthly calls with 6,000 colleagues which were live and unscripted and faced into the tough questions to make sure people felt cared for.'

John Holland-Kaye, CEO, Heathrow, is a passionate advocate of values. One of his first actions when he took over the company was to refresh the existing values by engaging over 25 per cent of colleagues in the co-creation of redefining what matters most. 'As CEO you have the responsibility for the wellbeing of the organization and the stakeholders who use it. I don't worry about the day-to-day running of the business as it is in very capable hands. What keeps me awake at night is worrying about a plane crash, terrorist activity or an accident as a result of the organization. In a safety-critical business these are the type of incidents that matter most. When you look back at recent tragic incidents like the China Eastern Airlines Boeing 737-800 plane crash on 21 March 2022, or the Grenfell Tower fire on 14 June 2017, one of the most painful insights is when it looks like someone has put profit over safety. To do the right thing as a company comes back to leading with values and effective stakeholder management. It is vital to know what really matters in the business and to take a long-term view about what is right for the organization. At Heathrow we are responsible with money, but we will never compromise safety and security.'

The significance of values was reinforced by Stephen McCall, CEO, edyn: 'A CEO needs to live and breathe the company values. For instance, I didn't want values to become an operating statement in the business. I believe that values are a guide for people to find their own way. At edyn our values are "The courage to question, to evolve, to be human". For instance, putting your hand up in a meeting can be difficult. We encourage our people to be courageous and share their ideas without the fear of being ridiculed. This practice helps create an environment of psychological safety where everyone can have a voice without the fear of negative consequences. Where our values have probably become most valuable is as a guide when we are employing people. We ask potential colleagues about their work and life journey to understand what has shaped them and see their curiosity. We are wary of efficiency for its own sake as it often means doing repetitive tasks which are the end of human evolution. We use technology and the efficiency it creates to free people up and answer their own calling. We look for people who are curious enough to try new things, which is at the heart of creativity and innovation. We reward our people who demonstrate our values in the business by understanding who has acted with courage, shown insatiable curiosity, and evolved and shared their humanity.'

TABLE 1.5 LIFELINE: DEFINING YOUR VALUES

1 Event →	2 Impact →	3 Learning =	4 Value
Chronologically mark the key experiences and turning points that have shaped your life so far. These are sometimes called 'crucible' moments and are usually associated with adversity, setbacks and failures, e.g. family, education, relational, bereavement, life and career.	Against each event note the impact that it had on you, e.g. sense of loss, betrayal, injustice, failure, frustration, achievement.	Reflect upon the learning you gained and the conclusion formed from the experience, e.g. setbacks make you resilient, injustice can motivate, loss helps you appreciate life, achievement drives ambition.	Identify the specific value linked to the learning, e.g. honesty, optimism, fairness, respect, safety, opportunity.

Having coached thousands of leaders over the years, my experience shows that most people know what their values are. However, not everyone understands what has shaped them, which is an essential step to informing what you stand for. There are four steps to defining your values in a process known as a lifeline (Table 1.5). Table 1.6 is my personal example.

TABLE 1.6 MY PERSONAL LIFELINE

1 Event →	2 Impact →	3 Learning =	4 Value
Divorce of parents	Sense of reality shattered, feeling hurt, anger and betrayal	Importance of self-reliance, questioning the norm and not taking anything for granted	Honesty

(Continued)

49

TABLE 1.6 (CONTINUED)

1 Event →	2 Impact →	3 Learning =	4 Value
Quitting trajectory of becoming a classical violinist	Liberation of challenging expectations and standing up for my beliefs	Becoming a risk-taker, following gut instinct and backing own judgement	Freedom
Loss of a major work project	Sense of help-lessness at not being able to turn things around and make it happen	Importance of ser-endipity, timing and being in the right place at the right time	Trust
Working tirelessly to deliver a key project	Driven by work ethic, challenging self and overcom-ing roadblocks	Significance of playing to strengths and drawing energy from stretching goals	Achievement

Yvonne had succeeded in reaching the dizzy heights of CEO. She had worked tirelessly to attain her dream and was now faced with the prospect of giving her inaugural address to the top 100 leaders in the business. We sat down together to prepare. I asked what she wanted colleagues to take away: 'Inspiration and trust.' Yvonne worked in an organization run by metrics and data. She knew that people expected her to talk primarily about performance and her commitment to delivering the plan. This would not inspire or strengthen trust. She decided to take a risk, be vulnerable and use storytelling based on her lifeline to help people understand what she stood for through the lens of values.

Yvonne compiled a series of personal photos to bring her story to life. She started by showing herself as a child visiting her father's factory where he worked as an engineer and talked about her passion for understanding how things work and getting into the detail of technical issues. Next, she illustrated her love of winning by disclosing her medals for track and field while representing her university. Yvonne opened people's minds when she shared photos of her volunteering in animal sanctuaries in Asia and linked it to her determination to prevent cruelty, promote kindness and provide education. She shared a photo of her daughter with bright pink hair and talked about her passion for valuing diversity and unlocking potential. You could hear a pin drop in the conference room. Senior leaders were genuinely moved by her disclosure and the standing ovation confirmed that Yvonne's message and approach had hit the right chord.

What do you stand for in three words? The rule of three is one of the most powerful tools you can use as a leader. I was introduced to the concept while supporting David Woodward, former Executive Vice President, President and Chief Executive Officer at Heinz Europe. David lived and breathed the rule of three in his communications, delivering clear, concise and memorable messages that stuck. For instance, when I asked him about the role of a leader, he stated: 1) deliver the plan; 2) develop people; 3) plan the future. It makes sense and I have remembered it for the past 15 years. Research shows that the rule of three is a writing principle based on the idea that humans process information through pattern recognition. As the smallest number that allows us to recognize a pattern in a set, three can help us craft memorable phrases. For example, 'Friends, Romans, Countrymen' – Marc Antony in William Shakespeare's *Julius Caesar*. 'Blood, sweat and tears' – General Patton. 'Education, education, education' – Prime Minister Tony Blair.

I was coaching Sam on his quest to become CEO. As part of his preparation, I introduced him to the rule of three and we used it as a way to define what he stands for. We worked together to synthesize the essence of his purpose, values, strengths and achievements into three words (3Cs) that encapsulated what he was about:

1. Clarity. Sam had an amazing ability to take vast, complex ideas, concepts and data and distil them into bite-size chunks, providing clear direction for the way ahead.
2. Consistency. Sam was known for showing up in a calm, predictable and reassuring way whatever the circumstances. This instils an underlying trust which is essential for running an organization.

3. Courage. Sam took risks. He was constantly pushing the boundaries of what was possible with a restless drive to innovate and create better outcomes.

Sam evidenced each area with specific examples and created a 60-second high-impact elevator pitch, as well as a three-minute narrative giving a dynamic picture of what he stands for. Shortly after this preparation Sam met with one of the most experienced recruiters in the UK for a great CEO opportunity. In their initial meeting, Sam was able to deliver his 3Cs story in such a way that the recruiter understood who he was in a short amount of time, igniting the start of ultimately a successful selection.

> ## CEO NOTE
> Internalize what you are about so that others get you instantly.

Play to Strengths

The criticisms came thick and fast. 'Not sure of his real motives.' 'Will the real person stand up.' 'Doesn't always listen, already made up his mind.' 'When resistant wants to ram things through and gets frustrated.' 'Happy to put other people under the bus.' 'When there is push-back, he gets aggressive.' I was collecting 360 feedback on behalf of an organization for an internal CEO candidate. From many of the comments you wouldn't believe that this individual had the credibility to do the top job. Yet they had a track record second to none for delivering high performance, had great breadth of experience across the industry, covering strategic, commercial and operational roles in multiple regions, had created transformation within organizations, as well as driven continuous improvement, and were highly respected by analysts and industry decision makers.

When it came to debriefing the potential CEO, I was nervous. How would they react to the feedback? Were they aware of it? Would they own it? Would they question my approach? Would they throw me under the bus? Before sharing feedback findings, my approach is to ask the individual the same set of questions I asked contributors in order to assess the level of self-awareness. On this occasion the individual had high awareness. They were cognizant of the fact that they could come across as aloof, could be hard to read, would adopt a fixed position, and could be perceived as being on their own agenda. But they were quick to point out that the reason they were being considered as CEO was not for managing their weaknesses but for leveraging their strengths. At their best this person was visionary in generating futuristic scenarios which had already kept the business ahead of the competition. They had a track record of building high-performing teams who were able to collaborate across the organization and execute consistently. They had a depth of understanding about the business which allowed them to operate at high altitudes, or when needed to drop into forensic detail to ensure the right decisions were made about multiple areas such as prioritization, resource allocation and talent management.

As CEO, or potential CEO, it is vital to know what you can get fired for. Do you have a potentially fatal flaw that could derail you? Probably the biggest watch-outs for CEOs are:

- poor judgement – making decisions that are not in the organization's best interests
- failing to walk the talk – setting standards of behaviour or expectations of performance and then violating them; being perceived as lacking integrity
- resisting new ideas – rejecting suggestions from others; not implementing good ideas and the organization gets stuck
- lack of interpersonal skills – being abrasive and bullying or aloof and unavailable, causing a lack of followership.

Having worked in the field of leadership development for more than 25 years, I believe that the way to maximize your impact for the company is to play to strengths rather than mitigate weaknesses. The global strengths movement started six decades ago when Don Clifton, creator of CliftonStrengths, posed a simple question: 'What would happen if we studied what was right with people versus what's wrong with people?' He wrote: 'There is no more effective way to empower people than to see each person in terms of his or her strengths.'

My favourite definition of strengths comes from Marcus Buckingham, creator of the StandOut® Strengths Assessment: 'Strengths are not something that you're good at, just like weaknesses aren't something that you're bad at. A strength is an activity that strengthens you. That you look forward to doing. It's an activity that leaves you feeling energized rather than depleted.'

By focusing on your strengths you will become a better and stronger version of yourself, stay energized and operate at higher levels of performance. Keith Barr, CEO, IHG, shared his perspective on the importance of being strengths orientated: 'To succeed as a CEO it's vital to understand what gives you energy. I have found that what people often miss is having a better understanding of who they are, what gives them energy and what helps them to have a sense of purpose and accomplishment. Recognize that if you are taking the job of CEO for the title or for the money, it won't be sustainable in the long run.'

In developing others, taking a strengths-based approach is a game-changer. Emma Gilthorpe, COO, Heathrow, is focused on spotting strengths in others and the impact this can have on recruitment: 'My approach is to recruit will, train skill. If you get a motivated person who has the right attitude, work ethic and is a true collaborator then it's far more important than their skillset. I have found that collaborative, motivated and energetic people overcome most situations. In fact, sometimes having technical skills can be a hurdle because they can act as a blocker to collaboration or visualizing a shared outcome.'

Another big advocate of playing to strengths is Emma's colleague, Paula Stannett, Chief People Officer, Heathrow, who shared: 'When people play to strengths, they are doing what they are best at and what they enjoy. This combination builds confidence and enables them to be successful. When CEOs appreciate the strengths of people, they unlock high performance and collaboration. Colleagues can appreciate what others bring to the table, leading to good business outcomes as well as boosting wellbeing and confidence.'

The benefits of focusing on strengths are reinforced in recent research findings. The ADP Research Institute conducted research in 2019 drawing on over 19,000 workers across the globe to measure levels of engagement and identify optimal conditions at work. One of the most telling findings was: 'When a worker has the chance to use their strengths every day at work it builds trust with their team leader.' Hence, as CEO, it is essential to identify the strengths of your executive team members and learn to play to them. Communicate your intent to create an environment where everyone can play to their strengths every day. Set up dedicated conversations with each executive member to clarify their strengths and agree how they can use them every day. Offer to give them consistent feedback on where you see them playing to their strengths, the impact of those strengths and how they can leverage them more.

On one occasion when I was working as team coach for a CEO and his executive committee in a FMCG company, the CEO was a passionate advocate of adopting a strengths-based approach for performance. They had been doing some deep work on the company strategy and had shaped a three-year strategic plan focused on three core pillars: 1) sustainable growth; 2) great place to work; 3) continuous improvement. The question the CEO posed was: 'How could the executive committee play to strengths to deliver the plan?' I decided that the starting point was to personalize the agenda and use feedback to hold up a mirror for each team member to see their own strengths. I set up a 'speed dating' exercise where everyone had one-to-one time together. In their conversations they were asked to give and receive feedback using real examples based on the following prompts:

- I see you at your best when…
- I see you energized when…
- I see you at your worst when…
- I see you depleted when…

As is often the case with these types of exercises there was initial resistance and push-back about the value of spending time exploring behavioural aspects of performance. However, once the feedback got under way the team genuinely engaged and what should have been a one-hour process quickly became a full morning. The simple act of discussing strengths was thought provoking and highly energizing. In the debrief it was fascinating to see the fit between strengths and roles in the team (Table 1.7).

TABLE 1.7 TEAM ROLES AND STRENGTHS

Role	Insight	Strengths
Chief Executive Officer (CEO)	Energized by creating vision, being strategic, driving performance at pace and engaging multiple stakeholders De-energized by lack of ambition, ownership of plans, outcomes and accountability	Vision Drive Communication
Chief Commercial Officer (CCO)	Energized by thinking strategically, driving value, doing big deals, beating the competition and innovating new channels De-energized by failing to maximize opportunities, getting outpaced by the competition and losing in the marketplace	Futuristic Activation Influencer
Chief Financial Officer (CFO)	Energized by understanding the business, leveraging assets, driving efficiencies, being a trusted advisor De-energized by lack of tangibles, lack of accountability and personal agendas	Analytical Focus Connector
Chief Operating Officer (COO)	Energized by delivering projects, the challenge of being deadline driven and overcoming roadblocks De-energized by indecision, inefficiencies and lack of ownership	Execution Drive Focus
Chief People Officer (CPO)	Energized by being part of a team, creating joint solutions and developing talent De-energized by negativity, silo ways of working and personal agendas	Empathy Connector Relational
Chief Strategy Officer (CSO)	Energized by thinking ahead, conducting scenario planning and seeking causes/reasons De-energized by lack of sound theories, unclear patterns and outcomes	Analytical Planner Learner

Role	Insight	Strengths
Chief Technology Officer (CTO)	Energized by simplifying complexity, driving innovation and enabling performance De-energized by lack of knowledge, rigidity and process	Knowledge Learner Influencer
General Counsel (GC)	Energized by providing governance, ensuring fairness and driving sustainability De-energized by lack of process, big egos and personal agendas	Knowledge Judgement Communication

With 18 different strengths identified between them, it gave the team a new lens to look through when allocating resources to the key organizational priorities. Rather than just doing it on a task or capacity basis, they explored who was best suited to take the lead on cross-functional workstreams, giving the best opportunity for success. For instance, the CCO and CTO joined forces to own the strategic pillar entitled 'Sustainable growth', focusing on winning market share and accelerating the innovation pipeline. The CFO and COO teamed up, taking accountability for the strategic pillar focused on 'Continuous improvement', including cost, complexity, systems and the supply chain. The CPO and GC partnered to progress the strategic pillar 'Great place to work', covering agile leadership, high-performing teams, and equality, diversity and inclusion.

Sitting down with Mike Mathieson, Chairman, NED, advisor and founder and former CEO, Cake, in his funky West London office, he gave a concise view about playing to strengths: 'By the time you get to being a CEO you will know your strengths and weaknesses. Be comfortable indicating what is the best use of your time and value and what to stay away from. Make sure you have the right people around you who can fill in your gaps. In particular watch out for the arrogance of thinking you can do everything. There is no such thing as a perfect CEO. For instance, it is two different skills to be relational with high emotional intelligence and to be brilliant at the commercial agenda.'

Mike's perspective was reinforced by Amber Asher, CEO, Standard International, who explained: 'My strengths include coming up with a plan, getting everyone aligned, bringing the team together and delivering together. I am highly effective in a crisis and will always come up with answers. What inspires me to move the company forward is doing deals and stabilizing the business to drive performance.'

Amber went on to describe some of the main challenges that accompany the role: 'A CEO needs to lead the big picture, innovate, and decide where the business goes next. Some of the biggest challenges are making the time and having the mental space to come up with creative initiatives and the capacity to deliver on them. Although my tenure in role coincides with one of the toughest times in the history of hospitality, requiring me to be hands on, I need to learn how to pivot my focus so that I do have sufficient time to take a different view, think about what's next and engage with others to provoke my thinking. I once heard that you never have two good days in a row as CEO due to the fact that there are always some issues to manage. Using your strengths is a great way to strengthen your resilience and stay on top of your game.'

CEO NOTE

Being a strengths-orientated CEO will energize you
and those around you.

Be Skilled to be Yourself: Exec Summary

- 'Be skilled to be yourself' demands that you know the true self you are referencing.
- The most practical way of knowing yourself is through the lens of purpose, values and strengths. These are the building blocks upon which you can continuously learn, grow and become a better version of yourself.
- Every great CEO I have encountered is dedicated to their personal and leadership development. Richard Solomons, Chairman, Rentokil Initial plc, recounts his experience of

becoming CEO: 'In some ways nothing prepares you to be a CEO. It is a job like no other. You are the last point of call. If you are an executive committee member beforehand with a big function, you are mainly focused on your accountability rather than the breadth of the company. As CEO you are accountable for everything. Nothing prepares you for the step up. I remember on my first day in role staring out of my office window looking at the car park overflowing with cars and thinking, "This is it. The buck stops with me." Being a CEO is a job you grow into more than any other role.'

- Be purpose-led.
- Take a stand for what is most important.
- Use your strengths to be the best version of you every day.

CHAPTER 2

Be Inspired to Inspire Others

• • •

Clear Vision

Vision is the lifeblood of a CEO. It is the super-fuel to sustain you, both on a personal and an organizational level. On a personal level it is critical to ask yourself, 'What is my vision as CEO and how will I know if I realize it?' I have been heavily influenced by the research and insight of Richard Boyatzis, a distinguished professor at Case Western Reserve University and an adjunct professor at the international ESADE Business School.

In *Helping People Change*, co-authors Melvin Smith and Ellen Van Oosten put forward the power of a personal vision: 'Put simply, a personal vision is an expression of an individual's ideal self and ideal future. It encompasses dreams, values, passions, purpose, sense of calling and core identity. It represents not just what a person desires to do but also who she wishes to be.' They ask the reader to consider the following question: 'If your life were ideal (you could substitute incredible, amazing, awesome, etc. here), 10 to 15 years from now, what would it be like?'

Joel Burrows, CEO of Ghirardelli, the iconic chocolate brand in San Francisco, has invested considerable time in developing his personal vision, which also shapes how he leads. 'To thrive as CEO requires you to have clarity about your bigger picture because if you are too hell bent on achieving one thing, you might land up disappointed or miss vital signs along the way.' His number-one priority is being a husband and father, and while he has always been competitive and wanted to succeed as CEO, it has not been at any cost:

'I know that being sucked into a business that takes everything and leaves me too tired to put my kids to bed is not for me.'

Joel leads the company in a highly personalized way. He shows up with a level of humanity and compassion that can be disarming for colleagues as they tend not to be used to having such a human CEO at the helm. He prioritizes having open and honest conversations to ensure that everyone has a voice, contributes ideas and feels valued. He is relentless about being a purpose-led company and starts management and leadership team meetings with important conversations linked to purpose. He loves to win and sets ambitious targets for the company. Together with his leadership team he has worked tirelessly to define and drive their game plan to make it happen.

As CEO, keep your personal vision simple but memorable. I suggest having a clear statement to articulate the essence of your vision, with three key points to bring it to life. Building upon the methodology of Richard Boyatzis, ask yourself, 'If my role as CEO were ideal (you could substitute incredible, amazing, great, etc. here), 10 to 15 years from now, what would it be like?'

One CEO I coached developed the following articulation: 'My vision is to unlock the potential of people and the organization to achieve greatness.' The CEO came up with his 3Bs to evidence how they would know:

- **Benchstrength**. Champion the next generation of leaders for the business.
- **Belonging**. Ensure we have a genuinely inclusive place to work that drives high performance.
- **Brand**. Drive sustainable growth and outperform the competition.

Once you have clarity about your personal vision, you need to address the organizational one. When asked about his definition of leadership, Jeff Weiner, Executive Chairman at LinkedIn, shared: 'Simply put, it's the ability to inspire others to achieve shared objectives, and I think the most important word there by far is "inspire". I think that's the difference between leading and managing. Managers will tell people what to do, whereas leaders will inspire them to do it, and there are a few things that go into the ability to inspire. It starts with vision, and the clarity of vision that the leader has, and the ability to think about where they ultimately want to take the business, take the company, take the team, take a particular product.'

In all my conversations with CEOs, one of the recurring themes is the challenge of where to spend their time and how to prioritize what is most important. Richard Solomons, Chairman, Rentokil Initial plc, illustrated the relationship between vision and time: 'You have to decide what you do and where to spend your time. There is a job description, but it is sterile. Every day there is a different situation to handle. What needs to inform your decision making and where you spend your time is your vision for the business. Be clear about what success looks like from a cultural, operational and competitive perspective. One way of summing up where to spend your time is to only do what you can do within the context of what you are trying to achieve.'

Your ability to align your personal vision with the vision of the business is a winning formula for driving a relentless focus that sustains and inspires you along the way. Richard went on to say: 'In defining your vision about the business it doesn't have to be about transformation. It could be a plan for continuous improvement focused on what is needed for the business to succeed coupled with the ability to execute it. As part of my preparation for becoming CEO at IHG, I did an exercise where I sat in a room with the strategic plans from the last 10 years. I recognized that within the plans the same issues had been identified, however they had never been resolved. I vowed that if I became CEO, I would get them fixed for the good of the company.'

John Holland-Kaye, CEO, Heathrow, stated: 'Probably the two most important characteristics a CEO needs to embody are humility as evidenced through low ego, and boldness as shown through clear vision. When leading in a dynamic environment where change is top of the agenda, you need the ability to quieten your ego so that you can listen to people, and have a curious mindset to learn from different scenarios, while providing a clear vision about where the business is going and how you are going to navigate the forces being faced.'

John's point of view was reinforced by his Chief People Officer, Paula Stannett, who stated: 'Everybody needs to understand where an organization is going and what it is trying to achieve. A vital role of CEOs is to establish a compelling vision of what the organization looks like to help people understand the part they play and how they contribute to transforming the business for a better future.'

In the July 2022 *Harvard Business Review* article 'Does Elon Musk have a strategy?', Andy Wu and Goran Calic look across Tesla, The Boring Company, SpaceX, and Elon Musk's other companies to reveal a consistent vision. They write that the most successful approaches typically share a common element: they stem from a visionary and ambitious outlook for the future, which provides the business with its current purpose. Back in 1980, Bill Gates famously expressed a bold and clear vision of "a computer on every desk and in every home". Similarly, each company associated with Elon Musk possesses its unique sense of boldness and clarity. Tesla's purpose is "to accelerate the world's transition to sustainable energy", while SpaceX aims "to make humanity interplanetary".

There is no one or right way to define your vision of the business. However, it must be a priority to ensure you have an aspirational picture of future success which you then engage your immediate leadership team with to refine and generate shared ownership. At this point you are in a position to set up a process with colleagues in the business to contribute, challenge and iterate. To evolve your vision here is a proven formula:

Combine core ideology and envisioned future: Core ideology defines what a company stands for and why it exists. The envisioned future is what the company aspires to become and that sets the direction going forward.

As a CEO it is essential to immerse yourself in the existing core ideology, or to shape one if there is a gap. IHG Hotels & Resorts grounds itself in its purpose, values and culture. The purpose is brought to life by 325,000 talented and passionate colleagues delivering 'True Hospitality for Good, every day'. The values – 'Do the right thing', 'Show we care', 'Aim higher', 'Celebrate difference' and 'Work better together' – guide everything the company does, including supporting and recognizing colleagues, growing the business and working with owners and partners. IHG's envisioned future is reflected in its ambition: 'To deliver industry-leading net rooms growth'. When I asked Keith Barr, the CEO, for his perspective about vision, he shared: 'To set a clear vision, know what you want to achieve, map out the future and be on message. Ensure there are no surprises. Make the vision easily communicated and sustainable, so people know what to expect.'

If there is a need to discover the core ideology, look inside the company. Ideology has to be real; you cannot fake it. If the company purpose is not defined, you could use the tested formula of the *five whys*. Start with the descriptive statement, 'We provide X services, or we make X products, or we create X solutions, why?' Five times. Keep digging until you get down to the core purpose of the organization. Examples include:

> Blackrock: We help more and more people experience financial well-being.
> Nestlé: Unlocking the power of food to enhance quality of life for everyone, today and for generations to come.
> Unilever: To make sustainable living commonplace.

To understand the organizational values, see the behaviours that are already in existence and being demonstrated, rather than trying to impose values that you think should be adopted. It's better to start where you are and evolve, rather than impose. For instance, if a company is in the manufacturing sector and 'keeping everyone safe' is a core value but it is not fully embedded, then make sure you acknowledge it and engage colleagues with the fact that you must work hard to develop a genuine safety culture.

The role of a core ideology is to guide and inspire, not to differentiate the company from others. Many companies can have similar purpose and values, however what matters is how you make them meaningful for where you are. The core ideology is also a powerful way of discerning whether people are the right fit for the company. If people don't resonate with it, then trying to force fit won't work, so let them go elsewhere. Focus on those who are inspired by it; attract and retain them.

Creating an envisioned future consists of two parts – articulating a big goal that stretches the business along with vivid descriptions to bring it to life. This is somewhat of a paradox because you need to combine the aspiration of something not yet achieved with a tangible narrative to make it real. The simpler the better. I find that CEOs and organizations have good intent in describing an envisioned future, but it is usually too long and complicated and results in people finding it hard to remember. Not inspiring! Some powerful examples include:

Amazon: Amazon strives to be Earth's most customer-centric company, Earth's best employer and Earth's safest place and is guided by four principles: customer obsession rather than competitor focus, passion for invention, commitment to operational excellence, and long-term thinking.

Cisco: Cisco helps seize the opportunities of tomorrow by proving that amazing things can happen when you connect the unconnected. An integral part of our DNA is creating long-lasting customer partnerships, working together to identify our customers' needs and provide solutions that fuel their success.

Sainsbury's: Driven by our passion for food, together we serve and help every customer. Offering delicious, great quality food at competitive prices has been at the heart of what we do since our first store opened in 1869. Today, inspiring and delighting our customers with tasty food remains our priority.

In our data- and metric-driven world, it can be challenging to allow yourself to create an envisioned future without feeling that you have to evidence every word. It is difficult to analyse your way into the future. It requires a different type of mindset. When John Holland-Kaye, CEO, Heathrow, took over the organization in July 2014, the identity of the company was shaped by the massive infrastructure programmes it delivered, led by engineers. Although this was a fundamental part of the business to build the best terminals and baggage systems possible, John recognized that the future of the business lay in the quality of its service to passengers.

At its peak in 2018, the company served 80 million passengers. Together with his executive committee, John redefined the vision: *To give passengers the best airport service in the world.* This was hugely ambitious given that Heathrow operates as a private business within a regulated environment and competes against airports such as Doha Hamad and Singapore Changi, which enjoy the benefit of being owned by their respective governments. As John says in Heathrow's strategic brief: 'Over the past few years, the airport and airlines have made great progress towards our vision of "giving passengers the best airport service in the world". Passengers regularly now rate Heathrow as the best major airport in Europe. We have set our sights on enhancing our reputation as a world-class hub. This has been underpinned, not just by the investment our investors have made in rebuilding the airport, but also by the highest levels of punctuality and baggage connections ever, improved security and resilience, and a real focus on developing a service culture. At the same time, we have been steadily reducing our costs and building a strong global investor base. We have also become a better neighbour by working hard to make Heathrow cleaner and quieter, while providing career opportunities for local people.'

In meeting Jamie Bunce, CEO, Inspired Villages, at one of his newest sites I put on a pair of protective boots and hat. As we walked around, I learned that as of August 2021, and after four years of phenomenal growth and numerous awards, the company had secured considerable investment from a joint venture partnership between Legal & General and NatWest Group Pension Fund. The Inspired Villages vision is to significantly transform the later-life experience in the UK, with a commitment to expand its portfolio to 34 retirement villages, which equates to around 5,000 age-appropriate homes for older people. In Jamie's words: 'Inspired Villages is a rapidly growing company aiming to become a world-leading operator of retirement villages. We want residents to enjoy the best years of their lives with us, employees to develop fulfilling careers with us, and for the local communities around our villages to benefit from being neighbours with us.'

Another inspirational company is ClearScore, a business dedicated to helping its users improve their financial wellbeing. Justin Basini, CEO and co-founder, has spent his career thinking about data, privacy and finance. ClearScore's vision is to help everyone, no matter what their circumstances, achieve greater financial wellbeing. As Justin shares: 'We've started this journey by giving everybody access to their credit score and report for free, for ever. By combining a brand which people trust, a product which is beautiful to use, amazing technology and deep analytics, we deliver a unique experience that helps people take control of their financial future.'

I had the good fortune to support Stephen McCall, CEO, edyn, along with his executive committee, in the creation of the company vision. As a former CFO Stephen has been on a transformational journey, from operating in the depths of internal audit to developing one of the most exciting hospitality companies in the world. Stephen blocked out a couple of days in a rural retreat to dream up the future. In preparation he had sought some of the most passionate advocates in the company to conduct focus groups ahead of our session and, through creative processes like storytelling, drawing and painting, had brought together ideas about the company purpose, values and vision. When it came to the vision element, I provoked the team's thinking with examples including Starbucks – to inspire and nurture the human spirit – one person, one cup and one neighbourhood at a time; and Coca-Cola – to refresh the world in mind, body and spirit. To inspire moments of optimism and happiness through our brands and actions.

We played videos from the focus groups of colleagues sharing their stories about what inspires them to work with the company. I then conducted a thinking circle which gave each executive committee member equal time to share their vision for the organization. What emerged was a collection of themes:

- Be a major presence in every European gateway city.
- Bring inspiration to every major European gateway city.
- Inspire the urban soul.
- Deliver hospitality with soul.

Upon reflection, the team aligned on the following vision statement: 'Creating sanctuaries where free thinkers belong.' The longer narrative is: 'Our vision is to create sanctuaries across European cities which provide a sense of belonging to the free-thinking urbanite in all of us. Our hotels are gateways to their neighbourhoods, and we work with the most interesting and vibrant partners to reflect that excitement and diversity in all our spaces.'

In some ways the creation of the vision is the straightforward part. Much of its power lies in nurturing the core, driving progress and getting everyone aligned. In his TED2016 talk, neuroscientist Uri Hasson researches the basis of human communication. Experiments from his lab reveal that even across different languages, our brains show similar activity, or become 'aligned', when we hear the same idea or story. This amazing neural mechanism allows us to transmit brain patterns, sharing memories and knowledge. As Hasson shares: 'We can communicate because we have a common code that presents meaning.' This shows that the starting point is to share the same story to create common understanding.

Stephen McCall and his team set up a two-day immersive experience, SoulFest, to help align the organization with the core ideology along with the envisioned future. Each executive committee member shared their personalized version of what it meant for them, their function and the company. Stephen was typically direct in his style, informing colleagues that if they didn't resonate with the direction of the business, they were welcome to make other choices. At least two colleagues went up to Stephen to thank him for his directness and share that the new vision was not what they had signed up for when they joined the company. Following numerous break-out sessions, Q&A time and a big party in the spirit of free thinkers, the top 100 in the business had come a long way together.

The new vision became the context for moving the company forward, which has endured and gathered momentum even through the setbacks caused by the global pandemic. The narrative shared with guests states: 'At edyn we believe travel should be a rich journey of discovery. We want to put the soul back into hospitality, creating sanctuaries rooted in the local neighbourhood where free thinkers feel at home. Our vision is to rediscover the emotion and joy of travel, which at the moment has never felt more relevant. Yet that vision has felt distant in recent times. Though this brief pause in our day-to-day has allowed us a moment to reflect on ourselves, our story and our future aspirations. It has been a challenging time, but we have adapted, evolved, and come out the other side ready to help our guests discover new destinations and experiences.'

Francesca Lanza Tans, CEO, The Alexander Partnership, reinforced the significance of creating vision. In her pragmatic style she linked it to three primary components in the CEO role:

1. 'Paint a picture of where you are heading. On its own, an organization could go in any direction. It is the responsibility of the CEO to steer it, by setting and articulating a vision. Even if you may not yet know, step by step, exactly how you are going to get there.

2. Once you've set the vision, inspire and energize those around you so that they buy into it. People are likely to have different reactions about the direction of travel – some may love it, others might have preferred to do it differently. Your role is to create alignment, not consensus, by inviting people to endorse the vision, even if they don't agree with it.

3. Create an environment where people feel proud, energized and connected. This involves people having a strong sense of belonging, being in the right roles, having the right skills and resources to be effective in their roles, and having the autonomy to make mistakes, learn, grow, challenge and find their flow.'

Make vision a signature of your CEO tenure. More importantly, be relentless in creating organizational alignment by enabling colleagues to understand and buy into the vision. Ensure everyone can make a tangible linkage between their objectives and the overarching vision. Start with yourself by being very clear about how your role aligns with the vision. Jamie Bunce, CEO, Inspired Villages, communicates relentlessly about transforming the later-life experience. He has made 'championing the company vision' his number one priority and holds himself accountable to his OpCo Board, JV Board, executive committee and colleagues. In a recent 360-feedback process, he scored 4.7 out of 5 for his CEO effectiveness in championing the company vision. Comments included: 'He understands the broad societal problem of later living. He has found a way to solve it. He is totally focused on finding solutions. He is a great ambassador for the company.' 'Jamie is visionary. He sees and knows where he wants the business to be.'

As CEO it is vital to carve out the precious time to stay connected with vision. Amber Asher, CEO, Standard International, shared: 'I have found one of the biggest challenges is making the time and mental space to come up with creative initiatives as I am still in a position to be hands on. This impacts my ability to have sufficient time to take a different view, think about what's next and engage with others to provoke my thinking. You have so many people, including shareholders, board members and colleagues, that need you and naturally you want to do everything right for everyone.'

Helen Tupper, CEO, Amazing If, echoed one of the conflicts facing CEOs: 'One of the biggest challenges as CEO is to manage the ongoing tension between the needs of the business and time. As CEO of a small and fast-growing business, my time is split between daily operational issues and strategic aspects about how the business needs to evolve to be fit for the future.'

Vision is a primary lens for CEOs to look through and needs to be invested in accordingly. Find ways to consistently put vision at the forefront of your mindset and communication:

- Put vision at the top of your 'to do' list. When Justin King, former CEO, Sainsbury's, came into the role, part of his vision was to put the customer back at the heart of the business. In his first 100 days he was hardly seen at HQ. He was on the road, visiting stores with a clear message – 'stores are our castles, and store managers are our heroes'. Later Justin institutionalized 'meeting-free Fridays', where all colleagues were encouraged to get back to stores and work on the front line serving customers.

- Use vision as a lens for decision making. In the words of John Holland-Kaye, CEO, Heathrow: 'The best management framework I have found which applies for any leadership role is the iconic work of Stephen Covey, *The 7 Habits of Highly Effective People*. It is a very powerful system. For instance, when we were going through the Covid crisis I used Habit 2: Begin with the End in Mind to guide my decision making. When in a crisis it is tempting to only deal with the immediate stuff in front of you, like cutting costs. However, it is critical to think about how to come out of a crisis. For instance, beginning with the end in mind meant that we didn't cut recruitment and training as we knew that they would be essential areas to ramp up once the heat of the crisis had passed.'

- Start meetings with a 'vision moment'. Ask team members to share stories of vision in action, or where improvements can be made. One hospitality company I worked with set up an empty chair in meetings to represent the voice of the owner. This acted as a conscience when decisions were made to ensure the voice of the customer was recognized.

- Ensure vision is on the agenda in individual meetings with team members. Often one-to-ones are devoted to task. Getting stuff done is important, but don't let it eclipse the significance of vision. Asking, 'What are your highest leveraged priorities this week, and how can I help you?' sends a powerful message that vision comes first.

CEO NOTE

Vision sets the organizational context, defines success and inspires people to act.

Big Strategy

According to McKinsey research, five bold strategic moves best correlate with success: resource reallocation, programmatic mergers, acquisitions and divestitures, capital expenditure, productivity improvements, and differentiation improvements (the latter three measured relative to a company's industry). To move 'boldly' is to shift at least 30 per cent more than the industry median. Making one or two bold moves more than doubles the likelihood of rising from the middle quintiles of economic profit to the top quintile, and making three or more bold moves makes such a rise six times more likely. Furthermore, CEOs who make these moves earlier in their tenure outperform those who move later, and those who do so multiple times in their tenure avoid an otherwise common decline in performance. Not surprisingly, data also shows that externally hired CEOs are more likely to move with boldness and speed than those promoted from within an organization. CEOs who are promoted from internal roles should explicitly ask and answer the question: 'What would an outsider do?' as they determine their strategic moves.

Creating and delivering strategy are two of the most important roles a CEO plays. Richard Solomons, Chairman, Rentokil Initial plc, stated: 'CEOs need an innate belief in their own judgement. As CEO you need a point of view like cutting cost, renaming a brand or completing an acquisition. You need to form a strategy bolstered by facts and science and then the ability to take people with you. As CEO you are making a call and most people don't want to make the big calls. It requires a large element of gut and self-belief; however, confidence grows with experience. When you get calls right, it will reinforce your judgement. When I was CEO at IHG I had 350,000 colleagues reliant on the business. It was a lot of people to be impacted by the wrong decision. I developed sufficient self-belief combined with an ability to work through plans and execute, such as going asset light as a business, selling our entire portfolio of hotels, relaunching the loyalty programme and reworking the organizational structure. There are no right answers to a lot of business issues. There are problems to solve with multiple answers and as CEO you need to pick one and go after it.'

Amber Asher, CEO, Standard International, gave a valuable insight about how to approach strategy: 'Being curious is a vital ingredient as CEO. I have always wanted to understand more and have cultivated a learning mindset. I bring that curiosity to some of my most pressing strategic issues, including the ability to scale the business across the world at the same time; finding and developing great colleagues, especially at the hotel level, which has been severely impacted by Covid-19; and balancing the needs of the Board with the team so that you meet stakeholder expectations.'

Will Stratton-Morris, CEO, Caffè Nero UK, shared his perspective about the importance of strategy: 'Whichever company you are running, the CEO role starts by constructing a strategy and plan for the business. This requires you to understand your market, customer segments, your people and what differentiates you. There is a whole lot of digging and research to be done in order to get under the skin of the business. As you engage in your discovery, the key question to keep in mind is "What do we do that is different and better than others in our space?". You have to get to the heart of your competitive differentiation. You can then build your purpose and strategy rooted in something that is different and better. At Caffè Nero we never aspired to be a big company; in fact, even today we see ourselves as a start-up. We have grown one coffee, one customer and one store at a time – always trying to be the best at what we do. We have reinvested in the business to stay true to our founder's original vision with resilience and determination.'

Each organization has a slightly different way of developing and executing strategy, so it is essential to develop your own definition and approach. One definition of strategy I resonate with comes from Michael D. Watkins, a professor at IMD Business School and the author of *The First 90 Days*: 'A business strategy is a set of guiding principles that, when communicated and adopted in the organization, generates a desired pattern of decision making. A strategy is, therefore, about how people throughout the organization should make decisions and allocate resources in order to accomplish key objectives. A good strategy provides a clear roadmap, consisting of a set of guiding principles or rules, that defines the actions people in the business should take (and not take) and the things they should prioritize (and not prioritize) to achieve desired goals.'

Before starting as CEO, part of your due diligence is to understand the business and to get to know the existing strategy. By the time you have been through multiple rounds of interviews with Board members and others involved in the selection process, you will have formulated an initial view about the opportunities and threats to the organization and what you think could be the big moves to make early. Every situation is different, however the ideal is to get immersed in seeing what the business is about, what is working, what is not, and what is missing across all areas. This can be simplified into three areas:

1. Who the company is – purpose, value, culture.
2. How the company operates – structure, decision making, talent.
3. How the company grows – ecosystem, tech platforms, learning.

The following is a simple checklist to support your thinking:

- Purpose: is there a clear and compelling purpose that has meaning, energizes the business and has the necessary impact on the big decisions in the business?

- Value: is it clear how the company creates value, what sets it apart from the competition and how it will achieve greater value to accelerate success?

- Culture: is it clear how the company runs things as a strong backbone of its organizational health and that it will sustain performance?

- Structure: is the organization set up for success through having the right structure that makes it fit for purpose?

- Decision making: is the organization able to make fast, high-quality decisions?

- Talent: what is the talent required to help the company succeed, how can the organization attract and develop it?

- Ecosystem: is the organization networked to succeed where the supply chain, partners and communities of businesses leverage value together?

- Tech platforms: does the company have an evolved relationship with data so it continually empowers decisions and the value agenda?

- Learning: does the company prioritize and accelerate learning to fuel its talent pipeline and create high performance?

To inform the above it is useful to study market and competitor analysis, as well as customer and employee feedback.

Joel Burrows, CEO, Ghirardelli, immerses his management team in strategy. Together they have developed a clear and compelling company five-year game plan which gives a high-level direction of the business, capturing the key priorities and projects to double the size of the business. They have translated it into a one-year plan which they drive with their extended leadership team. Joel and his management team work diligently, taking one day a month to deep dive on areas such as:

- Purpose: the company purpose is to 'Make life a bite better'. Joel and his team start each monthly meeting with a one-hour slot to discuss purpose-led opportunities, which I have the good fortunate to facilitate, like creating a Great Place To Work, working collaboratively and building high-performing teams. We recently placed attention on helping all leaders discover and lead with their own sense of personal purpose to make an authentic linkage with the company purpose.

- Big bets: the company has three strategic pillars: 1) sustainable growth; 2) be purpose-led; 3) continuous improvement. The team consistently explore where will be the biggest opportunities to innovate and leverage the business assets, such as its amazing dark chocolate, famous Ghirardelli squares, simplifying complexity and improving systems.

- Resource allocation: Joel challenges the team to think about where and how they can improve their resource allocation to ensure they are investing in the right stuff, creating a transparent environment for having challenging conversations about the necessary trade-offs to drive the business forward.

- Talent: one of the most important conversations to have in the business is about people. Sometimes this can get overlooked, either due to apparently more urgent operational issues, or because leaders can be uncomfortable talking about people when they don't appear to have sufficient visibility about their potential and performance. However, Joel puts people first in the business and sticks relentlessly to substantive conversations about talent for succession and future proofing the company.

- Engagement: Ghirardelli participates in an annual Great Place To Work certification in order to get an external benchmark about building a high-trust, high-performance company culture. The team debriefs the data and agrees a meaningful plan to improve employee engagement, which is reinforced during the year.

- Personal development: Joel recognizes that in order for a company to grow, the leaders need to grow. Therefore, he prioritizes the personal, leadership and career development of his team in multiple ways, including:
  o Putting family first. Joel not only believes in family first but insists that his team do whatever they need to do and take whatever time they need to care for family.
  o Seeking meaningful feedback. The team engages in ongoing feedback to ensure a regular pulse check on what people appreciate about each other's performance and behaviour, and make suggestions for improvements.
  o Developing leaders. Joel brings together his top 30 leaders as a leadership team for monthly meetings to support ownership and challenge of the company game plan. The team aligns on a couple of key themes to collectively develop each year, such as collaboration and high-performing teams. He schedules two leadership team offsites each year to strengthen the identity of the group and address the big topics which unlock the potential of the team and support collective performance.

Joel recognizes that everyone works approximately 2,000 hours a year. He is passionate about making the best use of time and constantly challenges people to think about how they are using their time. Beginning with the end in mind, Joel thinks strategically about each year. He paints a compelling picture of what he will focus on and how he will spend his time, including his family, prioritizing activities and new experiences. His commitment to his friends is second to none and ensures that precious time is allocated to enjoy great times together. He then clarifies his company commitments, which tend to focus on people, purpose and performance. He shares his personal strategic picture with his direct management team and extended leadership team to inspire others, and to hold himself accountable to his word.

How do you approach strategy? When and where in your schedule do you think ahead, immerse yourself in future trends, challenge yourself to explore opportunities, understand risks and create scenario plans accordingly? Who are your trusted advisors that support and challenge you to strategize effectively? How do you use time with your leadership team to lift up out of the day-to-day and plan ahead?

Walking past Number 10 Downing Street took me to the UK Cabinet Office building, where I sat down for a fascinating conversation with Simon Baugh, Chief Executive of the Government Communication Service. Operating within a political environment is not straightforward at the best of times, however Simon took over at an unprecedented time of multiple issues, including Build Back Better: the UK coronavirus recovery campaign, Levelling Up the UK, and the transition to two new prime ministers in quick succession. When setting the strategy for the Government Communication Service, Simon used a campaign framework called OASIS, which is a series of steps to bring order and clarity to planning. The five steps are:

- Objectives
- Audience/Insight
- Strategy/Ideas
- Implementation
- Scoring/Evaluation.

Simon's starting point was to define the outcomes he wanted to drive in five years. He asked questions like:

- What are the big-ticket items we are going to drive?
- How can we do things differently?
- How can we work with others to deliver the plan?
- How can we invest in our capability to be ready for the future?

The audience and insight focused on understanding the context in how the world is changing and defining the most important things that government communications would need to do differently. The strategy and ideas elements involved making the right choices and prioritizing of resource to be fit for delivery. Implementation required creating the plan for delivery, including the ability to translate it into something that all 7,000 colleagues in the organization could understand.

Simon named the strategy *Performance with Purpose*. He broke the strategy down into three big pillars: 1) Collaboration; 2) Innovation and Improvement; 3) Great People. He then provided the support for colleagues to translate what it meant into individual roles so that everyone could understand what was being asked of them. Simon went on to say: 'As well as driving incremental improvement I believe that strategy should consist of having what I call some "moon shot" aspirations, which challenges everyone to think beyond what they believe is possible. I wanted to have the best professional accredited learning and development programme for communication in the UK, which is also a critical ingredient of the outcomes we wanted to achieve and could be broken down into bite-size chunks. The scoring element is about how to measure success to ensure delivery against outcomes. Getting the timing right is important. I found developing a three-year strategy allowed us to be far reaching enough to deliver difficult areas at pace. If it was five years, it would take too long. However, my aim is to deliver 80 per cent within two years so that we can turn the handle again.'

Jonathan Mills, CEO, EMEA, Choice Hotels, shared his perspective on the strategic aspect of the role: 'To be strategic starts by taking a fact-based approach to ensure you have a holistic lens about the business, enabling you to understand the opportunities and challenges. Take a 360-degree approach so that you are able to bring together all the pieces of the jigsaw.'

Jonathan went on to say: 'Involve others from inside and outside the business. Take views and perspectives from formal and informal sources. Glean others' opinions to formulate your own picture to build and/or reinforce your strategy. Ultimately, decide what you are going to do and not going to do with your immediate leadership team and invest the necessary time to create clarity and alignment in the business. Make sure you get the right pace to do the things you need to do quickly, while investing sufficient time in the significant requirements to make sure you don't make unnecessary mistakes.'

Sneh Khemka, former CEO, Simplyhealth, brought me into his world: 'I was tasked to transform a 150-year-old business. The first step was to establish the trust of the Board to understand my agenda and to help me deliver it. It was critical to get the right governance and infrastructure in place to sweep away any barriers. I needed to bring my personal intellect and imagination to idea generation about how we could diversify the business. Some of the best ideas were generated by being networked with multiple ways of thinking, which were then filtered from an external environment and would surface in quiet moments. I would take these ideas to my executive team to progress to the next stage. We would then share with the Board for approval, at which point we could execute. These ideas have included building a new leadership team, implementing a new IT system, and launching new ventures. As a result, we have grown as a business in revenue, membership and profitability to get transformation in place.'

John Murray, CEO, Sonesta International Hotels Corporation, shared his approach: 'One of the first things I did when I took over as CEO was to provide a North Star for the business. In this age of permanent busyness, it is essential to set aside time to focus on the big picture. We schedule quarterly events to talk about strategy and make it a recurring process to revisit our strategic goals.'

John's emphasis on the importance of big strategy was shared by Paula Stannett, Chief People Officer, Heathrow: 'The role of the CEO is to translate the company vision into a clear strategy. They need to have a broad understanding of the business to ensure that all parts of the organization come together to make the necessary trade-offs and deliver the strategy.'

To understand in more depth about the role of the CEO in setting strategy I turned to Paula's colleague Chris Annetts, Chief Strategy Officer, Heathrow. Chris explained: 'To set strategy it is essential to devote the right amount of time. A strategy won't get anywhere unless the right parts of the business are involved in its creation and accountability for the delivery. From the CEO perspective, start by clarifying the questions you need to answer. Define the problems you are trying to solve, for instance delivering sustainable growth, attracting and developing top talent, improving data and systems. While you do this, take a step back from the day-to-day. Let your executive committee run the business so that you have the time to scan the horizon, identify the big issues to be solved, seek the big opportunities and risks in order to understand what they mean. Once defined, the CEO needs to go to their strategy director and team to work together to put forward an initial plan. It's down to the strategy team to assimilate the data, get the issues structured in order to set out the right questions and recommendations for discussion. One important watch-out is that the strategy work needs to be grounded in data, facts and evidence, not just instinct. Watch out for people talking about strategy versus sharing an opinion.'

Chris went on to say: 'Once this initial work has been done, the next step is to engage the hearts and minds of the executive committee. Schedule sufficient time together to come up with the right hypotheses, options and recommendations to evolve the strategy and create ownership and alignment. Use the executive meetings focused on strategy to drive clarity and alignment about the problems to solve. It will be critical for the team to make clear and unequivocable decisions. If clarity is not possible, the CEO needs to call it out and agree what the team will do about it so that there is no ambiguity. The draft strategy must be taken to the Board for robust evaluation. It is the role of the Board to review the strategic options, advocate those to be pursued and support the means to implement them. A Board does this best by bringing external perspectives to challenge the executive committee's thinking to make sure that all considerations have been made, and ensuring that delivery will meet expectations for all shareholders and stakeholders.'

Chris said: 'Once agreed, it is the role of the CEO to lead the direction of the organization. Subject to the outcome of the strategy work, if there is a change in direction, or a continuation of the existing plan, the CEO must provide the necessary clarity to mobilize the organization. The CEO needs to launch and communicate the strategy in a way that inspires, provides clarity and enables people to see how their role fits to help execute it. The CEO then needs to hold the business accountable to delivery. There is always a risk to get blown off course and it is the responsibility of the CEO to keep the business focused and on track.'

As Chief Strategy Officer, Chris said he doesn't believe there is a magic formula, framework or model for looking at things. 'It is not a case that one size fits all. What a good formula does is to simplify the complex and distil important material into bite-size chunks for key questions and hypotheses to answer. It is vital to generate options informed by analysis with a set of recommendations to enable people to make informed decisions. It saves a lot of time if the set-up work is done well. I believe that CEOs and any executive member can become better at strategy and learn new ways to think strategically.'

CEO NOTE

Strategy is the roadmap for the company to deliver brilliance. The clearer the strategy, the better the chance of achieving superior performance.

Energize the Organization

According to Steve Jobs, the storyteller holds the greatest influence in the world. They shape the vision, values, and direction of future generations. Mastering the art of storytelling is one of the most important skills as a CEO. Neuroscientist Paul J. Zak has shown how stories change our attitudes, beliefs and behaviours: In his *Harvard Business Review* article 'Why your brain loves good story-telling' (2014), he writes that, as social creatures, humans depend on others for survival and happiness. A decade ago, his lab made a significant discovery that identified oxytocin as a key neurochemical responsible for the "it's safe to approach others" signal in the brain. Oxytocin is produced when he is trusted or shown kindness, motivating cooperation with others by enhancing his sense of empathy, allowing him to understand and connect with others' emotions. Empathy is crucial for social creatures, enabling them to anticipate how others will react to various situations, including those with whom they work.

Zak's research on the neurobiology of storytelling is relevant to business settings, where his experiments show that character-driven stories with emotional content result in a better understanding of the key points a speaker wishes to make, and help with better recall down the road. He has also shown that sharing stories about the organization's purpose, vision and strategy improves lives – for example, by bringing to life the impact the company has made on named customers and how their problems were solved.

Every company I work with has a compelling story. It is the role of the CEO to bring it to life and share it across all stakeholder groups, including colleagues, consumers, customers and community. Stephen McCall, CEO, edyn, described how from a branding lens the company story is 'to create sanctuaries which nourish and enliven the soul. We design hotels, firmly rooted in their local neighbourhood, and offer vibrant experiences and connections for guests, colleagues and local communities. We want guests to leave our hotels with stories to tell, with enduring memories and new friendships. Our purpose, values and culture – what we call the edyn ideology – are aligned with the intent of our brands. It is impossible to create vibrant, distinctive brands unless you have a vibrant, distinctive culture supporting them.'

Effective storytelling fulfils a deep human need to understand the why, what and how of scenarios, so that they can be translated into personal and emotional experiences. However, I have witnessed numerous examples of companies, on behalf of CEOs, sending out important messaging to colleagues from the organization vision, purpose and value statements to strategic plans and priorities, in glossy presentations only for them to have no currency, no impact and, at their worst, switching people off from the content they are trying to convey.

A fundamental role of a CEO is to energize colleagues to deliver great performance. A key enabler is to engage emotions, and the key to connect hearts is a compelling story. However, most executives are trained in conventional communication, which prioritizes an intellectual process, giving statistics, facts and quotes from authorities. The challenge with this approach is that while sharing your script, others are arguing with you in their heads with their own version of reality. If you do succeed in persuading them on a cognitive level, it is not enough because people are not inspired to act by reason alone.

The art and skill of connecting with others is to link ideas and information with energy and emotion. It requires vivid insight and a clear narrative to make a memorable story, but through right practice a CEO can become known as a memorable storyteller. Some of the important elements to include are:

- **Why**. The global pandemic provided a burning platform for CEOs to have to make tough and swift decisions such as cutting costs, making structural changes and simplifying systems. Given the significance and implications of what was going on, employee acceptance levels were high as everyone could clearly understand the rationale for change. It showed that when there is a strong why, no matter how hard the decision or change, people can get on board swiftly. CEOs need to apply this principle when communicating to help colleagues understand the why in any situation, for instance bringing the company vision and purpose to life, highlighting a critical business priority such as sales or customer service, or making the company a great place to work.

- **What**. As a storyteller, you want to position the problems to solve in the foreground. The more personal you make the scenario, the easier it will be for colleagues to relate to it, thereby creating a sense of ownership. Sharing your own vulnerability is an essential part of storytelling as it humanizes the experience. It is also essential to be as candid as possible because simply painting a positive picture doesn't ring true. Everyone knows business is not easy and involves challenging trade-offs. One CEO I was supporting during Covid had to make hard calls between reducing operating costs and delivering quality customer service. It was literally a case of survive or die. The CEO scheduled daily briefings with senior leaders speaking openly about the current state of conflicting priorities, the need to manage multiple stakeholder expectations, and the pros and cons of each decision. This approach strengthened a foundation of trust so that when difficult decisions needed to be executed, the leaders were ready and could authentically engage with their own people. Facing into fear with truth helps us adapt to the brutal facts and roots out the shadows of denial and avoidance.

- **How**. A powerful story mobilizes people for action. Some of the best CEOs I have seen in action set out BHAGs (Big Hairy

Audacious Goals), which force a company to think big, create a plan for success and get everyone working together achieving it. On one occasion a CEO set a target to double the size of a company within five years. This was met with disbelief. However, the CEO had done it in his previous company and therefore brought a conviction that was infectious. The CEO shared stories about the mindset, skills and behaviours required to grow the company and, together with a broad leadership team, worked relentlessly on the formation of a plan to deliver. The logic of the plan was combined with an emotional element, allowing people to share their fears and disbeliefs in an environment of high psychological safety. The CEO personalized the experience, sharing stories about how setting stretching targets forced them to think differently, manage senior stakeholder expectations and drive their personal development.

Use questions to discover a story. Begin with the end in mind. Ask, what does success look like? Paint a compelling picture to bring success to life for key stakeholders such as colleagues, customers, consumers and community. Next ask, what are the challenges to overcome? Be direct about the problems to solve, including internal blocks like lack of clarity, alignment and doubt, and external barriers such as resource, time, structure, capability and market conditions. Then ask, what will it take to succeed? Go on a journey to decide the choices to make and actions to progress.

To become a great storyteller takes high self-awareness. Your ability to know yourself well means that you can anticipate the needs of your audience due to your own humanity and can adapt your story accordingly while staying true to your beliefs. The good news is that you can develop your self-insight and skills through your willingness to keep learning, growing and staying humble.

CEO NOTE

A great storyteller sees the humanity in others and takes them on a journey blending compassion with realism.

Are you the type of person who lights up a room when you walk in or when you walk out? As CEO you set the temperature for the organization. Your mood is infectious, as shown in a 2002 study from Yale University entitled 'The ripple effect: Emotional contagion and its influence on group behaviour'. The study compared the moods and emotions between work groups and showed that members of groups with positive emotional contagion experienced improved cooperation, decreased conflict and stronger perceived task performance.

I have witnessed the impact of mood contagion in multiple organizations, through a range of CEOs, and the effect of their mood on thousands of colleagues. Some CEOs are highly sensitized to the effect of their mood and use it to their advantage, while others undermine the very efforts they are trying to achieve through lack of awareness. At the root of mood contagion is emotional intelligence, popularized in the pioneering work of Daniel Goleman, who showed how emotions and moods play an important role in performance.

In one organization I worked with it was folklore to avoid the CEO on a Friday afternoon. Everyone knew that this individual would be in a bad mood, spreading fear and negativity to whomever they encountered. However, the CEO's emotion was not grounded in facts or figures. It had become an unconscious habit driven by tiredness and a build-up of frustrations during the week. On one occasion I got a call from one of the CEO's direct reports on a Friday evening, ready to hand in their notice. They had attended a Board meeting in the morning and were under the impression that they had performed well, delivering a value-adding presentation, as evidenced by seemingly positive feedback from the Board. However, after lunch they happened to walk past the CEO office and the CEO called them in for a quick chat. The CEO questioned the effectiveness of their presentation. This pushed a hot button for the recipient, who welcomed robust feedback but given in a timely and constructive way. Before resigning, I suggested that they go back to the CEO to enquire in more depth about what had happened. First thing Monday morning the executive member stopped by the CEO's office and asked if they could qualify their comments from Friday. The CEO couldn't even remember what they had said and shrugged it off with an apology as they had been tired and it had been a long week. Not clever.

Contrast this with another CEO who was renowned for the inspiration, optimism and energy they imparted to their immediate leadership team, as well as through the company. A powerful example was the way they conducted annual performance reviews with their executive committee. I have heard the good, the bad and the ugly when it comes to performance reviews. At their best they energize people to deliver outstanding performance, own their personal development and accelerate their career progression. At their worst they can demotivate colleagues, causing them to quickly find an exit from the organization. This CEO invested a full half-day preparation for each performance review. They were diligent in the way they recognized the achievements of each team member, providing evidence-based feedback to build upon strengths and address key development areas to drive performance. They explored career aspirations and together set stretching targets. They prioritized personal development to ensure each executive member had an inspiring plan. They also sought to understand how they could help each person better and adapted their approach accordingly. The result was that executive committee members came away clear, aligned and energized for the year ahead. The mood spread through the company as each executive felt inspired to conduct memorable performance reviews with their own team members and the pattern continued throughout the organization.

Being CEO is comparable to living and leading on a reality TV show. Every move is watched. Every statement interpreted. Andy Cosslett, CBE, Chair, ITV plc and Kingfisher plc, is highly sensitized to how the CEO sets the climate. When CEO at IHG, Andy was the architect of virtually every interaction he took to deliberately make a point. On one of Andy's first visits to China when IHG was focused on accelerating growth in the country, he was not seen on his phone in 48 hours, which sent a powerful message that he was present, available and cared about being there. He spent precious time engaging with front-line colleagues learning about their roles, hopes and fears.

On another occasion, in America, he delivered a personalized talk with some of the most important hotel owners who partnered with the company. Andy spoke about his past, recounting stories to strengthen their emotional connection: 'I was born in Manchester, in Whalley Range, next to the infamous Moss Side. My father was an accountant and a great rugby player. My dad was an interesting fellow. He had a shop in Manchester, so we had always been in the commercial and mercantile way. My mother worked for Bupa. I went to Manchester University, where I studied economics and then European politics. I thought I was going to be part of the European system of government as a political scientist, but in my year they weren't taking quotas, so I had the prospect of sitting the course out for 18 months or doing something else. In the end it was the something else that won.

'In 1979 I joined Unilever's graduate management programme, which was one of a number of breaks I got. I was persuaded to go to university by my next-door neighbour, which was the first piece of luck, because I wasn't going. Then I was lucky to get into Unilever: out of thousands of applicants they only took 20 in my year. I guess whatever they were looking for, I had it. My first job was selling ice-cream in Liverpool in winter, so that taught me a lot about life and I've never forgotten it. I know what it means to get these nonsensical memos from the centre when you're out on the front line. Money is tight for most people and you can't lose sight of that. You have to remember the basics of how hard people work. You need to spend time out there living, knowing and seeing that.'

The impact of these behaviours and stories spread around the world within the company.

At the time I was fortunate to be running the senior leadership programme for IHG called 'Leading with Purpose'. The first question we asked leaders attending was, 'Who is your most admired leader, and why?' Over a ten-year period with over 1,000 participants, Andy was consistently cited as one of the most popular leaders as a consequence of his ability to inspire, energize, relate and get the best out of people. Andy talked about the 'leader's walk'. Every time you walk the office floors, or while in the hotels, walk slowly, say hello, make eye contact, engage people in conversation. Find out about their work, their hopes and concerns. Contrast this to another CEO I encountered who was renowned for walking quickly through offices with their eyes glued to their phone. In fact, colleagues made a deliberate point to avoid this CEO. The company was based in a high-rise office block. If anyone found themselves standing in line for the elevator with the CEO present, they would find any excuse to get away: the prospect of an awkward few minutes in the same elevator was not worth enduring.

The key to mood contagion is to be deliberate about it. Don't just let external circumstances dictate the temperature you set. Research cited by the Proceedings of the National Academy of Sciences (PNAS) captured 27 distinct categories of emotion bridged by continuous gradients (2017). The findings show that emotional experiences are so much richer and more nuanced than previously thought. I supported a CEO and their global leadership team recently. Driving accelerated growth in the business, the task was to double revenue from $5 billion to $10 billion in five years. The initial primary emotional response was concern as the team was already stretched in numerous ways, such as capacity, resource, capability, knowledge and systems. However, the CEO had a way of building high psychological safety within the team, creating the environment where everyone could speak up without the fear of negative consequences. As a result, the team spoke freely about their various feelings and agreed that a fundamental requirement to succeed was to bring together emotion and performance. They set a principle that everyone is encouraged to speak up about how they feel in order to help unlock the potential to perform. Leaders will ask team members how they are feeling in performance conversations to ensure everyone feels safe to share what is going on and get the help they need to succeed.

The biggest risk to setting the right climate is narcissistic behaviour. Narcissistic individuals have a strong sense of entitlement and often have difficulty handling criticism. They can overreact and get defensive, failing to recognize that they have problems. It is vital to be aware if you have this tendency and counteract it by asking for feedback about the mood you are setting. Demonstrating humility is the best way to offset narcissistic tendencies. Justin King, former CEO, Sainsbury's, was a master at getting feedback. He had numerous ways of eliciting direct and indirect feedback so that he could have an accurate pulse about the organizational temperature. He set up an informal dialogue known as 'Tell Justin'. All colleagues were able to write notes to Justin about what was on their mind. He was habitual in his responses, investing time each day to share handwritten notes sharing his view. He prioritized leadership development in the business within the organizational goal of *Making Sainsbury's Great Again* using feedback as one of the main ways to assess behaviour, and included himself in the process. He led by example. On one occasion I had the opportunity to coach him in front of his top 100 leaders, focused on how to change for the better. His curiosity and hunger for learning and development were infectious and helped turn the business around.

Jonathan Akeroyd, CEO, Burberry, is very conscious about how the mood of a CEO impacts an organization: 'Self-awareness is super important as a CEO. Be dynamic and approachable. Stay positive. If you're not in a good mood, people notice and it spreads.'

CEO NOTE

A CEO is the weather. The way they show up sets the climate.

The schedule is relentless. An annual cycle of executive and Board meetings, conferences, presentations, announcements to the markets, shareholders and media demands one-to-one conversations, plus precious time to horizon scan, think, plan and prepare. As Stephen McCall, CEO, edyn, shared in our conversation: 'One of the biggest challenges as a CEO is endurance. I was tasked with transforming the company. The impact has been staggering. Initially it was easier to execute change as we were smaller. As a result of our growth, executing strategic priorities at pace becomes harder. I can get tired and lose the spring in my step because I am dealing with problems all day rather than possibilities. When this happens, I remove myself from some of the noise to stay focused on leading the vision. I have learned how to pace the business based on what we need to deliver now and what can come later.'

One of the leading researchers on advance scientific insights that help people thrive is Angela Duckworth, a professor of psychology at the University of Pennsylvania and author of *Grit: The Power of Passion and Perseverance.* Angela's work demonstrates that the secret to outstanding achievement is not talent but a special blend of passion and persistence, what she calls 'grit'. As Duckworth defines it, grit entails a combination of passion and unwavering perseverance directed towards long-term accomplishments, with little focus on immediate rewards or acknowledgment. It brings together resilience, ambition, and self-discipline in the pursuit of goals that span long periods.

John Holland-Kaye, CEO, Heathrow, gave his perspective: 'A CEO needs to be able to compartmentalize multiple priorities and the pull on their time to survive. It is essential to have a great team in place, develop a shared strategy with the right processes and systems to deliver the business. You then need to think about what's next and dedicate yourself to strategic thinking in order to create the next iteration of the business.' John went on to say: 'Learn how to invest in your own stamina and pace yourself. It is easy to burn out by stretching yourself too thin. In the early years as CEO I accepted most invitations to front the business, however it meant that I was out most evenings. I now delegate to my team to give me precious breathing space, but also to give them development opportunities to represent the company. It's important to cut yourself slack sometimes as you will be working all hours. Have the tools to keep yourself in harmony, such as the "wheel of life", which is a simple way to recognize and assess the various elements of your work, life and relationships so that you are managing them deliberately rather than finding yourself negatively impacted by the role.'

John's view was echoed by Paula Stannett, Chief People Officer, Heathrow: 'A great CEO creates energy and enthusiasm about the future through their credibility and confidence. People get energized when a CEO is trusted and believed. They need to help people generate excitement and enthusiasm by translating the vision to multiple stakeholders, helping understand what's in it for them. This means having sufficient emotional intelligence to make the business a win/win environment and a great place to work.'

To add to this insight Will Stratton-Morris, CEO, Caffè Nero, shared: 'The likelihood as CEO is that you will have long days followed by dinners, travel and executive lounges. You will need to find your own discipline to nourish your wellbeing. If you are going to be indulgent on food and drink, you will need a counterbalance, such as your sleep and exercise. You need to know where your peace comes from. It might be from faith or different techniques; however, recognize that these are important dimensions of our lives. Be intentional about how you are going to keep yourself fit, healthy and spiritually strong. Don't be guilt ridden. If you slip, you have to accept it will be difficult at times. The key is to have a plan for your personal resilience so that you can get back on it when needed.'

A fundamental premise for a CEO to thrive under pressure is to use a simple eight-step framework to sustain and nourish energy, which we have touched upon (see Table 2.1).

When Jan Smits was CEO of AMEA IHG, he devoted one day a month to ensuring he was in the best possible place to thrive under the pressure of helping lead a global organization, which included looking after the group's most geographically diverse business unit, comprising 300 hotels and resorts operating in 47 countries under six internationally renowned brands. During his tenure, Jan led a 60,000-strong workforce, launched several new brands and created new business models to grow the region into a $4 billion business.

TABLE 2.1 FRAMEWORK TO SUSTAIN AND NOURISH ENERGY

Purpose	Be intentional about energy, meaning and impact
Values	Live your beliefs about what is most important
Strengths	Engage in activities that energize and strengthen you
Vision	Be inspired by a compelling picture about what success looks like
Strategy	Drive a clear plan about how to achieve success
Narrative	Share a compelling story to set direction and instil belief
Approach	Provide visible and authentic leadership
Development	Commit to continuous learning and improvement to stay on top of your game

He set aside sacred time for his personal development, which could involve some of the following:

- Thinking: Jan would file different articles, ideas and observations from the month and take time to ruminate on what they meant for the business and the culture.

- Learning: subject to the demands on his leadership and changes in the marketplace, Jan would immerse himself in the latest learnings to ensure he stayed ahead of the game.

- Relationship: Jan developed through the connections he built and invested heavily in cultivating meaningful partnerships with multiple stakeholders.

- Exercise: Jan had a disciplined routine which set him up for success under pressure. A combination of pilates, jogging and gym balanced out his demanding travel schedule.

Jan set the example for his team. He ensured that they all took their personalized version of 10 per cent of their work time dedicated to their personal and professional development. As a result, his direct reports progressed in their careers to CEOs, MDs and other top senior roles either within IHG or in other organizations. However, his passion for personal development didn't stop with his executive committee. Through his own experience and years in the trade, Jan is fully aware that hospitality is an industry where you can work your way up to the top, regardless of where you started. As such, he is committed to giving everyone a chance to rise to the top.

'One of the main items on my agenda for IHG in AMEA was the acceleration of our talent into general managers. In the hospitality industry, it typically takes an individual anywhere between 17 and 20 years to become a GM of a full-service hotel. With more tools and resources available to them these days, people are getting smarter, and they are less willing to wait two decades to become a GM,' he explained in an interview with *Travel Weekly Asia*. 'Working with people with great potential, we see a huge opportunity to fast-track some of our hotel managers to become GMs within a shorter period of time. And Holiday Inn Express, our select service brand, gives us the perfect setting to do this.'

As a coach I am obviously biased about the value of CEO coaching when thriving under pressure. I will leave it to CEOs to share their view. Jonathan Mills, CEO, EMEA, Choice Hotels, said: 'Having a coach plays a very important role in supporting a CEO. You are limited to who you can talk with and what about. Using a coach for a sounding board, and to challenge your thinking, agility and approach in a changing marketplace, is essential. You can then extend the partnership with the coach to help build a high-performing organization, working together to develop capability through the business. By owning your personal development, you set the tone with your leadership team to take responsibility for their own development, which will permeate through the business.'

Joel Burrows, CEO, Ghirardelli, echoed the importance of having the right support in place: 'As CEO it's important to know where you can go for advice and support to challenge your thinking, strategy and plans.' Joel brings that support to his own team: 'I have weekly one-to-ones with my direct reports where I combine a mix of leading, managing and coaching. Be conscious about what you're doing. I like to see how people have evolved, as well as managing the checklist. However, my drive is to only do the things I can do in order to have conversations focused on what's important, not urgent. If there isn't a burning platform, then I ensure we are able to have the conversations about the critical success factors for the long term and make sure we are setting up the conditions to deliver. Sometimes you are required to seek more clarity in the short term, otherwise I find people appreciate having meaningful conversations about the future and developing a shared understanding about how to get there.'

I appreciate the view of Richard Solomons, Chairman, Rentokil Initial plc, about the value of CEOs and how to help them thrive under pressure: 'I believe CEOs get the big bucks because they have to make the big calls and see them through. You do get arrogant CEOs who just assume they are the cleverest in the room. However, thankfully the majority of CEOs I have encountered make calls with humility. There is a fine line between confidence and arrogance. CEOs need people who ground them. When I was CEO, my family and friends kept my feet on the ground. It is also the responsibility of

Boards to make sure the CEO appointed has the relevant experience and personality to be right for the role.'

CEO NOTE

Energize the organization to help deliver the plan.

Be Inspired to Inspire Others: Exec Summary

- The number one trait people look for in a CEO is inspiration. Inspiring others starts by being inspired. This does not mean that you need a personality transplant to become charismatic and extrovert. It does mean that you need to define your vision, set the strategy and energize the organization.
- Start by shaping your personal vision. Where do you want to take the business, take the company, take the team, take particular products or services?
- Next, develop the company vision by combining core ideology with an envisioned future. Core ideology defines what a company stands for and why it exists. The envisioned future is what the company aspires to become and that sets the direction going forward.
- Setting big strategy requires you to understand in depth:
  - What the company is – purpose, value, culture.
  - How the company operates – structure, decision making, talent.
  - How the company grows – ecosystem, tech platforms, learning.
- Invest precious time with your executive committee and senior leaders to co-create a clear roadmap that guides the company on key priorities and projects to define the actions people in the business should take (and not take) to deliver the plan.

- Drive performance by having a compelling story which links ideas and information with energy and impact. Provide vivid insight and a clear narrative to make a memorable story.
- Pay attention to your mood as it is contagious. Be deliberate about it. Don't let external circumstances dictate the temperature you set. Choose your mood to lift the business up, or to create a calm environment, or to install sufficient edge to deliver results.
- Thrive under pressure by establishing a personal operating rhythm that sustains you every day.

CHAPTER 3

Be Equipped to Succeed

● ● ●

Preparation is Everything

Listen, learn and lead. This was the positioning used by Ranjay Radhakrishnan when he became Chief Human Resources Officer at IHG. Ranjay set out a very clear 100-day plan which included interviewing 100 leaders across the business, setting up listening groups with colleagues, and visiting strategic locations to send important messages about his care for the front line, passion for customers and creating a great place to work. He agreed with the CEO and Board that he would take his first 100 days to understand the business and prepare his recommendations for a future meeting. This is the best positioning I have witnessed for a leader, either coming into an organization or gaining a promotion. Listening shows a genuine commitment to understand, to empathize with others, combined with humility. Learning demonstrates a thirst for knowledge, an inquisitive mindset and a commitment to making things better. Putting leadership as the final step promotes a sense of equality and inclusion. It says that we are all in this together and that acts of leadership will result from a commitment to listening and learning.

I was fortunate to coach Justin Reese, President and CEO, Lindt & Sprüngli Canada, as he transitioned into his first CEO role. As part of his preparation Justin spent time in the business having one-to-one meetings with his soon-to-be direct reports. Justin started on a personal note seeking to understand them as people, enquiring about what they were proud about in terms of both the business and life, which helped him learn about their motivation and drivers. He asked about the challenges they were facing and what they believed would be best to help improve the business. He finished his conversations by asking how he could help, thereby setting the tone for his leadership. This led to a series of meaningful conversations and rich insight, which were extremely valuable before even starting in role. He immersed himself in the history of the business, learning about the original entrepreneurial spirit which helped Lindt & Sprüngli Canada become recognized as a leader in the market for premium-quality chocolate.

As part of Justin's in-depth preparation, he formulated his personal vision for being CEO, which he captured in the following way, 'Build a sustainable future', underpinned by the work we had done together:

1. Purpose – help everyone unlock their potential.

2. People – create a great place to work.

3. Performance – celebrate amazing results.

Justin developed a one-page document that crafted the detail of what these statements meant at a high level, which he used to connect with others and help them understand his direction and what was important to him. Justin adopted the approach of 'Listen, learn and lead' for his first 100-day plan, which included setting up listening groups across the organization to understand others' views about the business, what was working, what needed improving and how he could help. He set up a schedule to visit as many stores as he could during this time to engage with colleagues and the consumer experience.

Justin developed an initial narrative which he could adapt for different audiences, however the key points included:

- acknowledging the impact of a new CEO coming into a business and how people will want to put their best foot forward, which is only human

- recognizing that as a new CEO starting in a new role, different company and new city, he would also want to put his best foot forward

- understanding that showing up as the best version of ourselves includes being transparent and open about the strengths of the business and opportunities for improvement

- using his first 100 days to set up listening sessions across the business to help him deeply understand the enablers that drive great performance, as well as any interference that needs to be managed

- in order to understand the business, he would continue to strengthen an environment of psychological safety where everyone can speak up and share ideas without the fear of negative consequences

- ensuring his approach fits with his personal sense of purpose to help others unlock their potential and thrive at work

- being proud to have the opportunity to lead a company which delivers amazing results

- together, aligning on the biggest opportunities to deliver sustainable growth for Lindt Canada and continue its success story.

Justin was fortunate in having highly supportive leaders in the business to give valuable guidance. His previous CEO, Joel Burrows at Ghirardelli, had championed him into role and helped pave the way with global stakeholders to ensure senior executives understood Justin's strengths and value to the business. His predecessor provided a thoughtful handover, helping Justin understand the critical success factors for the business and opportunities for improvement. His HR business partner had unique experience, having been in the business from the start-up phase, and could give a rounded picture. Justin used a simple framework during his first 30, 60 and 100 days, focused on what was working in the business, challenges to overcome and potential solutions.

It's vital for a new CEO to not underestimate the significance of their initial time in the business as they will never have the luxury again. As Richard Solomons, Chairman, Rentokil Initial plc, recounts: 'Subject to your understanding and grounding in the organization, within your first 90 days buy yourself time to get your head around the business. Even though I was well versed in the company I initially worried too much about what other people would think. Your role is to make the tough calls. It is not about pleasing everyone. When I look back at some of the early mistakes I made, they were caused by not having the right clarity and facts, as well as failing to ask the right questions.'

Jonathan Akeroyd, CEO, Burberry, reinforced the importance of getting off to a strong start: 'It is valuable coming into role to be in a position to do a quick assessment about the business. When I started with both Versace and Burberry, I gave clear updates with an external lens based on the information I had, giving a snapshot about the business and immediate areas to focus on. In both cases it was well received. I started with my leadership team, shared my priorities, and together we got aligned about what was most important. The Board loved the clarity we brought and the way it was delivered in a short and clear way. We then rolled out the priorities to all employees, within a month, about what we were going to focus on in the short term. It got me off to a good start on both occasions.'

I resonated with the insight from Sophie Moloney, CEO, Sky New Zealand: 'It's important to "shift gears" when you become a CEO. I was fortunate to have an experienced mentor who helped me to do this. It is critical to understand your key stakeholders, the state of the strategy and core operational metrics. Make sure you are fully prepped for your first Board meeting to be on top of your game. If you are stepping up from within the organization, make sure you jettison your previous role as quickly as possible. Develop a game plan which gives you the confidence to articulate how you will no longer be the person in your previous role, and prioritize the relationship with your chair. They are your boss, but it's quite different from a day-to-day boss. They are non-executive, so they don't get into the operational detail and instead will rely on you to get it right. Their reputation is on the line to select the right CEO.'

Sophie continued: 'As you step up, enjoy the moment. It's a phenomenal privilege to be a CEO. Having the level of responsibility and opportunity to shape an organization is awesome. Continuing to be yourself in role with more skill enables others to relax and perform. Have a growth mindset, be open and prepared to adjust. You learn the most when things don't go right. It is exciting to try new things and have the ability to do things differently, but make sure you have the right team around you to move swiftly.'

Francesca Lanza Tans, CEO, The Alexander Partnership, shared her words of wisdom in preparation for becoming a CEO: 'Being a CEO can be all-consuming, and there may be times when you feel like you don't have enough hours in the day to be on top of it all. Resist the urge to cross off every item on your 'to do' list and recognize the difference between what appears to be urgent versus what is truly important. As CEO, your role changes. Your time goes into setting direction, creating alignment and fostering the right environment for high performance. Don't be tempted to spend time getting everyone to agree or to make everyone "like" you. As democratic and empowering as you aim to be, recognize that the organization wants (and needs) to be led. Have the courage to express clear views and help people understand what you truly think.'

Francesca pointed out some other key learnings: 'Be comfortable with the discomfort of the unknown: at times you will be faced with uncertainty and you won't have all the data in advance to make your next decision. Be prepared to trust your gut, not just your head. Think like a parent. Being a CEO is similar to the role of a mother or a father. Your job is never done, and it may not always be fun. Yet it can be transformational: for people, for the organization and for yourself. Embrace it with energy and generosity. Be clear on the legacy you want to leave.'

These points were reinforced by Dr Sam Barrell CBE, Deputy CEO, The Francis Crick Institute, about navigating your first 90 days: 'Gather as much information as you possibly can. Observe, fact find, use data, listen to colleagues and key stakeholders. You will start to get a feel for where the biggest strategic focus is needed and what you need to prioritize. Make sure you progress the priorities that you have identified and avoid becoming distracted by reacting constantly to the demands of others. You will see things very clearly in your first few months as you are not yet influenced by organizational group think. If radical change, or indeed any change, is needed, be brave and make this happen. Be tactical about the timing of change – consider whether it could be done incrementally or whether a bigger, bolder approach is needed.'

Sam went on to say: 'Make sure you have the right team with the right skills for the job ahead. Take time to get to know key people and to understand their whole self, not just their work self. If it's obvious that you need to make changes to your team, it's often better to do this sooner rather than later. Be careful about your leadership style; a dominant, authoritarian style may achieve quick initial results but it can be damaging in the long term. I prefer a compassionate, approachable leadership style but one with clear focus and objectives so that everyone understands the direction in which they're heading.'

Paula Stannett, Chief People Officer, Heathrow, shared her perspective about the right preparation: 'A CEO needs a plan focused on the short- to mid- and long-term needs of the business. In the short term the plan must focus on the current state of the business from an operational and customer lens. It needs to reflect what teams are saying about the working environment, the culture of the business, the strengths of the leadership team and opportunities for improvement. Dependent on whether the business is a public limited company or within the private sector, the plan also needs to capture what the Board and/or investors are saying.'

Paula went on to say: 'The CEO needs to use the plan to build trust with their leadership team and employees, and to build relationships with customers and shareholders. They need to be laser like about the top relationships to build. Once they have socialized the plan, they can then move on to what needs to change and to articulate where they want the business to go and how to get there. They will need to develop clear propositions enabling the required decisions to be made in the short to medium and longer term.'

Viviane Paxinos, CEO, AllBright, gave a concise view about what it takes to be prepared: 'When I was offered the opportunity to be a CEO it came quicker than I had expected. Remove yourself from what happened in the past so that you can influence everything going forward. Be ambitious, pragmatic and stay focused. Focus drives results.'

Once settled in the business a CEO needs to have ongoing time and space for preparation. I see most mistakes result from CEOs failing to give sufficient time to preparation, whether it be for thinking, planning, meetings, communications, decisions or actions. Amber

Asher, CEO, Standard International, shared her experience: 'I have found one of the biggest challenges is making the time and mental space to come up with creative initiatives and deliver on them, as I am still in a position where I need to be hands-on. This impacts my ability to have sufficient time to take a different view, think about what's next and engage with others to provoke my thinking. You have so many people, including shareholders, Board members and colleagues, that need you and naturally you want to do everything right for everyone.'

Dr Sam Barrell CBE, Deputy CEO, The Francis Crick Institute, shared her experience: 'Coming from a background in healthcare, it was a steep learning curve when I started in my current role. There was a great deal of information to assimilate very quickly about the life sciences and biomedical research. But although the environment was quite different, in many ways the thread of patient care which has run through my career has continued here too. I've always believed that medicine is multifaceted, and that disruptive technologies and scientific advances lead to pioneering medicines which can really make a difference to people's lives. The Crick's mission, to understand how life works in order to drive benefits for human health, is what attracted me to the institute in the first place. As the largest single-site biomedical research institute in Europe, the Crick is at the forefront of world-class discovery research, and I am lucky enough to work on a daily basis with the brilliant scientists who are making these discoveries.'

Sneh Khemka, former CEO, Simplyhealth, draws upon his past to be ready today: 'My skills as a doctor stand me in good stead for being in a quickly changing environment because, as a CEO, you need the ability to think rapidly and make quick decisions. For instance, my work schedule is filled with 30-minute interviews. I use my medical background to conduct the following procedure:

- Assimilate information.
- Synthesize data into a diagnosis.
- Make a treatment plan.
- Communicate the treatment plan in plain language.

It is essential, as a CEO, to have the ability to assimilate random information into one place, to simplify complexity and to articulate the outcome well.'

A big insight was made by Sophie Devonshire, CEO, The Marketing Society, to be equipped to succeed: 'Communicate, communicate, communicate. It's vital to share what's going on so that people are in the know. Understand the channels you will use to communicate. Make it human and make it regular.'

Sophie also highlighted a watch-out as CEO: 'Sometimes people see the title before you. As the title has power in it, recognize the privilege of the position.'

Figure out your preparation regime and stick to it. One study from *Harvard Business Review* entitled 'How CEOs manage time' (July 2018) analysed how CEOs spend their time. They found that 72 per cent of CEOs' time was spent in meetings versus 28 per cent alone. Moreover, 25 per cent was spent on relationships, 25 per cent on business unit review and functional reviews, 21 per cent on strategy, and 16 per cent on culture and organization. Given the fact that the schedule gets booked up one year ahead with the rhythm of strategy, organization and culture planning and reviews, and time with key constituencies including the Board, direct reports, senior managers, consultants, customers, investors, bankers, suppliers, industry groups, media, government, regulators and community organizations, scheduling the right preparation time to be fit for purpose across such a plethora of activity is a lifeline.

A vital relationship to support preparation is the executive assistant (EA). The EA can shield CEOs from distractions and unnecessary activities as they do their best to ensure that the CEO maximizes time. However, EAs can often get caught in seemingly conflicting priorities as there are so many demands placed on a CEO and, sometimes, an EA believes that a full calendar signals that they are being efficient in role. They tend to book back-to-back meetings, limiting time for spontaneous communications or solitary time to think. To help improve the efficiency and effectiveness of working with an EA, invest in the following:

- Clarify priorities. CEOs need to have a written agenda specifying what's most important and where they need to spend their time which is updated on a quarterly basis. It's helpful if this agenda is shared with the executive committee so direct reports have transparency about what the CEO is focused on. This agenda needs to be internalized by the EA so that they are able to use it as a lens to look through when each request is made.

- Delegate brilliantly. A great CEO delegates well, and to do so they need their direct reports and affected managers to be available. An effective EA will work with the relevant executive committee EAs to ensure that people can step in for the CEO, providing clarity and consistency in the business.

- Schedule space. Preparation requires time and space. Most CEOs are overbooked. They need more time to prepare, whether that is time alone, time walking the office to initiate unplanned connections, time with customers to get real-time feedback, or time with other CEOs to compare notes. Making space sacred prevents having to cancel or reschedule appointments, which can cause frustration or disappointment.

- Protect personal time. A CEO needs to sustain their life, which is ideally built into their preparation. This could include time with family and friends, as well as other activities like exercise, meditation, reading and opportunities to recharge on a regular basis. An EA will anticipate what the CEO needs and do everything in their power to ensure the CEO sticks to the plan.

I tend not to draw upon sporting comparisons in business as the context is so different, however one relevant observation is that in sports, the majority of time spent by peak performers is in practice and recovery. If we look at Novak Djokovic, the world's number one tennis player, he starts his day with around 20 minutes of yoga. Post this, he eats breakfast. He then takes to the court with a training partner for an hour and a half. Novak also does some stretching to cool down. After that he has lunch and does a one-hour workout using weights or resistance bands. He takes a protein drink immediately afterwards to aid recovery. He then goes for another 90-minute hitting session and once again stretches to cool down.

Imagine as CEO spending that amount of time preparing to be the best CEO you can be. The reality is that you need to apply a methodology of continuous improvement for your preparation. Simply focusing on one thing every day to become better prepared will multiply over time, helping you to excel in how you prepare for success.

> **CEO NOTE**
>
> The quality of your preparation equals the quality of your performance.

Build Capability

As of 12 December 2022, the top 10 most valuable companies in the world by market cap included Apple, Microsoft, Alphabet, Amazon and Tesla. One of the areas that distinguishes these giants from other companies is how they've created a platform, a system that entails ongoing business rather than simply selling a single widget. This system is part of their capability, which is anything an organization does well that drives meaningful business performance. As CEO it is vital to understand the capability required to enable your business to outperform and to be as efficient and effective as possible.

Keith Barr, CEO, IHG, clearly stated the importance of fine-tuning company capability: 'Understand what creates competitive advantage and what makes or breaks your business. For instance, data, technology, procurement and systems. Define the value chain and the capability required to execute the strategy. This requires you to look at your business model and understand the direct and indirect benefits of investing in different capabilities. Given our business model as a franchise operation, I could have convinced myself not to invest in procurement as it was not a direct benefit for the business, but it provides an important service for our owners which then becomes a competitive advantage for the company. Similarly, with HR we don't hire the vast majority of people directly for our hotels. However, we decided to invest in putting hotels on our system for recruitment because it provides a better system for the whole.'

Sneh Khemka, former CEO, Simplyhealth, gave his viewpoint about the significance of having the right capability in place for an organization to thrive. He highlighted three key areas:

1. 'Be purpose driven. Companies need to operate delivery to provide a return on shareholder value through money, but in today's world a significant return comes from conducting responsible and sustainable practice in your environment. It is vital to set up your business so that it relates to government, society and communities in ethical and responsible ways. For instance, we were the first health insurer to get B Corp certification, which demonstrates our tangible commitments.

2. Implement the right structure. Decide what the business needs and put the necessary infrastructure in place. At Simplyhealth we needed an agile, product-led structure and based our organizational design on this requirement.

3. Hire rock stars. Find the Freddie Mercurys of this world who can write hit songs which won't be forgotten. Having top talent in the business stimulates cultural change and means that your culture follows the structure. For Simplyhealth this translated as being a digital innovator in health galvanized around a clear need due to the lack of service in the NHS.'

Justin Basini, CEO and co-founder, ClearScore, shared his perspective: 'There are three buckets required to develop organizational capability:

1. People. The number one area is getting the right people into the right roles. The processes which support this are critical: recruitment, onboarding, ensuring high productivity and managing performance. One of my biggest learnings as CEO is that putting in effective people systems early becomes a real driver for the company as it sets up the scaffolding to grow them.

2. Product. The second priority for me is about building a great product and the engineering you need as a foundation for a great product. For instance, if you are a product-led organization it is vital to make sure there is a fast cycle of generating consumer

insight, understanding what's going on with the product, turning it into short-, medium- and long-term roadmaps and then turning it into user experiences and code. I have learned that determining the right customer experience must be built from the right insight.

3. Process. The third bucket is to develop operational processes. This area is less important when you are small. For example, in the early days at ClearScore, if we had an operational urgency everyone would join in, from me to our developers, we'd order some pizza and do whatever it took to get stuff done. In a new business you can't put in too much complexity too early because you don't know what the right processes should be. You need to solve the first problems first and learn fast. As you scale it's important to have robust operational processes, however you need front-line experience to understand how to manage them as the business scales.'

Jan Smits, CEO and Deputy Chair, APAC, Pro-invest Group, advocated the importance of beginning with the end in mind: 'To develop the right organizational capability, start with what you want to do and then work out how you are going to do it. You need to be innovative and take complexity out of the business. As human beings we tend to make things more complicated than they need to be. Simplifying complexity gives people time to think, which enables performance. Constantly challenge yourself if you are being the most efficient you can be. Set key measures to assess the business, e.g. to double the size of the business with the same amount of people. These types of boundaries drive innovation and test the organization to be as capable as possible. You want to create the environment where everyone is thinking about continuous improvement and measuring progress as you go.'

The significance of building capability was reinforced by Sophie Devonshire, CEO, The Marketing Society: 'Fixing the organizational foundations and making sure that you are set up to structure speed and success are critical factors. You must put in place the right strategic partners and experts to deliver the basics and accelerate progress. If the foundations aren't right, you need to be close enough to the organizational detail to understand and make sure the business works as it is the oxygen that runs the business.'

Another CEO obsessed with ensuring the company has the right capability is Sophie Moloney, CEO, Sky New Zealand: 'As of 2022, Sky NZ has served our customers in Aotearoa (New Zealand) for 32 years. Some of our technology has been around for a couple of decades. Legacy is important, but it can't hold you back. We nurture two different approaches: we celebrate our core business which has to be always on and needs to work, alongside our digital transformation focused on customer centricity, which needs to be agile and able to move to sprint.'

Sophie continued: 'I am obsessed with the idea about how to get flow into the business. For this to happen it requires having real clarity and alignment on your core priorities and capabilities. Get rid of the busyness that detracts from what is most important. Develop a climate of accountability which means everyone has clear responsibilities. I believe one of the roles of the CEO is to "edit things out of the way" for people so that you can get to a place of real flow in the organization. If your organization has built up silos over time and it's hard to get things done, re-orient the focus. Move away from being centralized and insist on being a business that is focused on your customers.'

Paula Stannett, Chief People Officer, Heathrow, highlighted the role CEOs play in building organizational capability: 'CEOs need to be open to the current mega-trends impacting business. They need to show up with intense curiosity to think about the marketplace disrupters and what the business needs to be doing to grow. CEOs don't need to be technical experts in areas like automation. However, they do need to establish a high external presence about leading the art of the possible.'

As Paula inferred, some of the most challenging organizational capability requirements to develop are digital and automation. I have witnessed the evolution of multiple companies investing massive time, resource and commitment into transforming their technology for competitive advantage. On one occasion I was asked by a CEO to partner the CIO in support of a transformation programme essential for company success. The CIO was new to role and at the point of taking over, the failed technology platform was costing the company several hundred million in lost revenue each year. The previous CIO developed innovative ideas but lacked the ability to drive execution. Together with the new CIO we created a 'good to great' three-year journey from 'fix the basics' through to 'accelerate growth'. The CEO provided visible sponsorship of work throughout the organization to ensure it had the right profile and opportunity to succeed. The CIO's immediate priority was to get the right people in role. They recruited two heavy-hitting technologists to head up the critical functions and gave them the autonomy to make necessary changes. Once the new senior leadership team was in place, we brought them together to focus on the alignment of the plan, the barriers to overcome and the way they would work together to succeed.

The initial focus was to reinstall trust in technology as it was broken across the business. The CIO was a captivating storyteller and spent the first 90 days in role engaging with customers from all functions to understand their needs and to learn how the new technology team could help. This was played back to the team in real time so that immediate adjustments could be made. Over the next few months, the plan was developed, covering most needs, including data management, analytics, supply chain, people platform, customer experience and e-commerce solutions. The CEO played a highly enabling role, continuing to give the CIO sufficient air cover to get stuff done, including managing the Board as they were understandably nervous about the potential risks to the company should the plan not work. It was a great example of the CEO giving sufficient weight to the priority without disempowering the CIO. In fact, they acted as an effective tag team, which drove momentum.

Jonathan Akeroyd, CEO, Burberry, captured the right sentiment for how a CEO should approach building capability: 'My background is based in commerce, therefore I have to make sure my team are better than me at the back end of the business. I trust them implicitly to have the right processes and systems in place. As a CEO it is your responsibility to make sure you have the right specialists in the team with the necessary knowledge to run the business.'

Dr Sam Barrell CBE, Deputy CEO, The Francis Crick Institute, reinforced the importance of being set up for success: 'Digital tools have a critical part to play in developing organizational capacity. Moving away from manual processes and towards enabling technology allows an organization to become more efficient and productive. Of course, it requires up-front investment to install the digital tools and platforms, but if you invest wisely, it will pay dividends.'

Another CEO who reinforced the role of technology was John Murray, CEO, Sonesta International Hotels Corporation: 'In today's world there is almost nothing that does not touch technology. As CEO it is important to understand the aspects of technology that run the business. For instance, we are using artificial intelligence to understand what guests have done, and their interests, so that we can create a personalized experience.'

Given the critical role technology plays in building organizational capability, I turned to Laura Miller, CIO, Macy's, for an in-depth perspective: 'In technology we are constantly delivering new features and functions, therefore it's essential to have the right talent in place to execute the strategy. You need leaders who have the vision but also the ability to execute at pace. This means having an agile mindset and the skill to take risks, fail fast and course correct. We are in a new era in the economy where consumers and customers are changing all the time. Things that were predictable in the past are not happening now, therefore a CEO needs to ensure that an organization has the basics in place, including fiscal responsibility, driving value and delivering new products or services on a consistent basis.'

Laura continued: 'Every business is different; however, the CEO is at the helm at the ship. Subject to the way they ultimately define the vision and strategy of the company, the role of support functions like technology is to help them figure out what it will take to achieve the plan. For instance, in our world the CEO thinks about how to delight and inspire customers to win market share and be the retailer of choice. They then pick the bets that are going to help us win, such as making sure we have a frictionless, omni-channel customer experience where our digital capabilities elevate us above the competition.'

Laura recognized the significance of data: 'It is super important for CEOs today to make sure they are getting the value out of data. Companies have countless pieces of internal data, as well as the ability to purchase more data. The CEO needs to monetize this data and leverage it for the business. From an internal position they need to ensure the company is doing everything possible to drive value, such as maximizing sales. From an external perspective they need to make sure that the business uses data wisely with suppliers and vendors. For instance, to help decide if the organization sells it to them, or if it gets betters result by sharing to inform the insight about customer demographics, products, research and recommendations. CEOs also need to leverage data to future proof organizations through enablers like machine learning and artificial intelligence. A company will not be able to build a sustainable future without necessarily being at the forefront of these capabilities.'

Laura gave an example referencing GM's CEO, Mary Barra, as the first woman to lead one of the big automakers in the US. 'Mary has invested billions in electric vehicles, self-driving cars and a ride-share service called Maven. These big bets are driven by technology.'

Laura also highlighted the value of the CEO and CIO partnership: 'In order for CEOs to optimize the role of technology and digital capability, it's important to partner with the CIO so that they can be educated on what is out there and together determine how the capability fits into the strategy. A CEO can't know everything about technology. They need a CIO who they trust implicitly and can empower to drive the technology roadmap. I also believe that the relationship between the CEO and CIO is critical from what I call an "air traffic standpoint". As CIO you have the opportunity to work with all business partners and to see what everyone is doing from a unique perspective. I believe that an effective CIO can help a CEO understand where the business is working well together and where are the opportunities for improvement. On a personal note, I have conversations with my CEO about how we can work better as an organization to get more out of our investments by implementing an agile product model. To be at the forefront of technology, a CEO needs to stay current, understand the trends, know the buzz words and use the CIO as a wall of defence.'

Subject to the preference and strengths of a CEO, prioritizing organizational capability is not always top of mind; however, neglect at your peril.

> ### CEO NOTE
> Enable the organization to build and run a highly effective machine, setting the business up for success.

Unlock Potential

As a new CEO taking over a company Janet thought she had inherited a high-performing organization. Prior to starting, the numbers seemed rosy and everyone shared good news stories about the great work being done by colleagues to deliver the customer experience. However, during her first 90-day immersion in the business, a different picture started to form. Once Janet had dug behind the glossy PowerPoint presentations, she realized a different reality. What emerged was a business with poorly defined success metrics, broken systems, lack of transparency and accountability, and silo ways of working which resulted in failed decision making and execution. We sat down to assess the situation. It seemed a daunting task given the scale of the business and the expectation to succeed at pace.

Janet had a track record of delivery in turnaround situations. She had to pivot quickly away from the false reality she had been led to believe and to confront the brutal facts. The first step was to bring her executive committee together for an honest airing of what was going on. As preparation she wrote a one-page memo about the state of the business, with some initial options to consider, and shared it with her team. Janet asked everyone to bring fact-based assessments of their part of the business to an offsite. She deliberately chose an understated venue to send a message that 'looking good' was off the table and that it was time to address the real issues causing the business to underperform.

My role was to facilitate the conversation and ensure that everyone genuinely disclosed what was going on without finger pointing.

Prior to the offsite I had conducted individual conversations with each team member to provoke thinking and lay the foundations for transparency. It's always challenging to know if people are being straight with me, however I assume positive intent until proven otherwise. The overall picture I gained did correlate with Janet's reality, albeit most team members started their conversation with an inflated version of how well everything was working. I distilled the insight into three major obstacles to address:

1. Be fit for delivery – clarify what success looks like and have an aligned approach to deliver the plan.
2. Fix the basics – upgrade systems and processes to enable delivery.
3. Create a great place to work – provide the right leadership and environment for everyone to thrive.

I asked the longest serving member of the Exec to share their view first. This individual had the reputation of being a survivor, having endured numerous organizational restructures. They had learned how to play the corporate game and to make themselves appear indispensable. However, they were at a point in their career where there was no need to duck and dive and they were prepared to speak candidly. As COO they were in the best possible position to lift the lid on what was going on. They shared an emotive picture about the unresolved business drivers which resulted in the current chaos. The previous CEO had done a great job boosting investor confidence and winning over shareholders. However, they had neglected the business and had only wanted to hear a 'positive spin'. The COO spoke about their regret at colluding with this approach as they cared passionately about the health of the business. It was a relief when they received Janet's memo, although it spiked their conscience. Their belief was that the main interference to progress was the Exec's lack of candour, which resulted in an unclear plan and implications for the business.

As we went around the team, similar views were expressed. Once everyone had been heard I used a simple and effective tool (Figure 3.1) to address the obstacles based on a hypothesis:

Performance equals potential less interference.

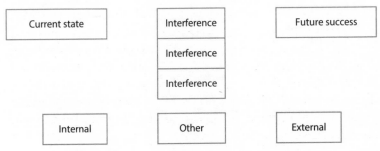

Figure 3.1 Structure of a problem tool

I challenge people to evaluate whether the business has the potential to perform. If the answer is yes (which it usually is), then by identifying and reducing interference you achieve a closer relationship between potential and performance.

The steps are:

1. Identify the current state of the business. Understand what is working, what is not working and what is missing. Bring together an accurate view about the strengths, opportunities, weaknesses and threats to the business.

2. Clarify what future success looks like. Align on the specific outcomes across the business so that everyone is clear about the tangible metrics to achieve.

3. Uncover the interference, blocks, barriers and limitations that will prevent the business from delivering success.

4. Recognize where the interference resides.
   - Internal – obstacles that are within the control of the CEO and/or executive committee to resolve.
   - Others – obstacles that sit in other areas such as the chairman, Board, investors, suppliers, customers, community, government, or systems which the CEO and/or executive committee can influence.
   - External – blockers that are external to the business, for instance globalization, war, pandemics, environmental disasters, recession.

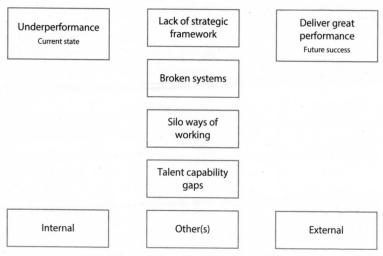

Figure 3.2 Problems identified by Janet's team

Continuing the coaching with the team, we applied the tool to their situation and they articulated what is shown in Figure 3.2.

What transpired was that the major interferences were primarily internal obstacles for Janet and the executive committee to remove. This insight mobilized the team into action. They agreed to invest sufficient time in co-creating a crystal-clear strategic framework so that everyone in the business could know what success looks like and how their role fits. This shifted behaviours away from 'looking good' to providing transparent ways of working as clarity was sought every step of the way. They operated with a simple dashboard highlighting the top 10 company metrics and showed progress using a red, amber and green coding system on a weekly basis to galvanize the organization. They fronted proposals to the chairman and the Board requesting the sufficient investment required to fix systems, with the priorities being the information management system controlling security and data, the operations management system delivering and managing the company creation of customer value, products and services quality, and the management systems organizing and monitoring business performance improvement.

The team agreed to champion collaboration as a behavioural priority for the business. They decided to model the way by having shared ownership of metrics outside their immediate areas. They set up cross-functional steering committees, resulting in colleagues from across the business working together to drive value-adding projects. This action impacted the talent capability gaps as it gave greater exposure to what development needs were required to help lead, manage and deliver the strategic plan. As a consequence, Janet prioritized learning and development throughout the business, ensuring that everyone formulated a meaningful personal development plan to accelerate their progress.

One of the main responsibilities of a CEO is to remove interference. This was expressed in different ways by CEOs in my interviews. Richard Solomons, Chairman, Rentokil Initial plc, reflected: 'As CEO it is ironic that you have less direct ability to make stuff happen than in a functional role. There are only a few times you can bang the table to make things happen. The role is about creating a vision and then influencing people to come with you. In a big organization, if you try to control others it will limit your breadth of influence. If you are a bad delegator and a control freak, you will be the bottle neck to getting stuff done. The best CEOs have the ability to let go of control, enable others, and are the most open to new ideas and ways of delivering the business.'

Wim Dejonghe, Senior Partner, Allen & Overy LLP, framed it this way: 'As CEO your role is to understand the voice of your customers, people, the business, and the markets around the world. Be versed in what your competitors are doing. Get as many inputs as possible from different stakeholders. You need the ability to cut through the detail, see the big trends in the data, spot the opportunities to go after, and with your leadership team define what it means for the overall direction of travel. Set the strategy together so that everyone feels ownership of it. In the short term it might look inefficient as it takes more time to make decisions; however, in the longer term you have gained the buy-in required for delivery. There is a big gap between having an idea, forming a plan and delivering on it. Your role is to close the gap.'

John Holland-Kaye, CEO, Heathrow, is clear about his role to remove interference: 'My leadership approach is to choose great people, set the strategy together and let them get on with delivery.

I aim to lean in when particular help is needed, or where I can add specific value. My focus is to do the things that only I can do. Having a great team and trusting them to deliver is also an effective way to attract and retain top talent.'

Dr Sam Barrell CBE, Deputy CEO, The Francis Crick Institute, called out a couple of key factors to manage: 'Never get complacent. It's important to remain clear about the value you're adding. This isn't a "one-off" hit. You need to consistently add value and demonstrate that you are doing so. Maintain your energy and drive as this will transmit to others.'

Sam also shared: 'All organizations are political. Do not be naïve about this. Remember to listen carefully, engage with colleagues and key stakeholders, and create allies. Learn to trust people and, when you do, allow them the freedom to flourish whilst always keeping close enough to provide support if and when it is needed.'

As CEO, probably some of the most difficult interference to manage comes in the form of the chairman, and less frequently Board members. On one occasion I was coaching a CEO who had to navigate a well-intentioned but meddling chairman. Although they had set up agreed ways of working together, the chairman ignored them and would go directly to executive committee members with points of view about their role and area and with offers of guidance. This put the executive members in a compromised position because it is hard to not act upon points of view from the chairman. As a result they felt divided loyalties when the chairman had a different perspective from that of the CEO. Eventually I mediated a three-way conversation with the CEO and chairman to reinforce what was going on and to lock in solutions. It transpired that the chairman was genuinely unaware about the ripple effect of their actions, which is often the case. We agreed that the CEO could inform the executive committee that if the chairman reached out directly in the future, they had the licence to remind them that although they welcomed the chairman's perspective, they were not in a position to act upon ideas unless those ideas were shared with the CEO. This removed the discomfort executive members felt at being in a potential loyalty conflict. It took into account that with the best will in the world, the chairman would probably drop into detail at some point in the future, and it enabled the CEO to have control over the flow of ideas.

A valuable exercise is to anticipate interference by setting aside time to think ahead. Joel Burrows, CEO, Ghirardelli, shared his experience: 'As CEO you need to have an inbuilt curiosity about what's going on and why. It is essential to look at a mix of data from the marketplace to understand the context, competition, consumer, customer and community requirements so that you can define your problems and put the resource against them. Learn from what you have done well with all aspects of the business. Constantly look at what is being delivered, what is working well, what can be improved and how to build a better business. Make sure you apply the same rigour about people development and succession as you do about financial metrics, or any other metrics of success.'

Employing this level of discipline to understanding what's going on means that, to the best of your knowledge, you take owner-ship for protecting the business from unnecessary interference, and when major obstacles do arise, you are set up to overcome them in agile and effective ways.

I wanted to conclude this section about unlocking your potential on a personal level as there are multiple interferences to manage as CEO.

In our conversation, Sophie Moloney, CEO, Sky New Zealand, highlighted some of the areas to watch: 'I was told that being a CEO is lonely. At the outset I rejected the concept because there are so many opportunities that come with the role. However, what I have realized is that it is quite isolating. Having sat at the executive table previously, stepping up into the CEO role meant that I needed to make some people changes. I am empathetic but not to the detri-ment of the company, and these decisions caused me to feel isolated. I learned that it is not straightforward to take the temperature of the organization as CEO. You need to be intentional about get-ting feedback across the business so that you can be connected with what's going on in a way that doesn't disrupt the flow of leadership. For instance, I love hearing what people are doing. I show natural enthusiasm. However, I have to be careful about the "office of the CEO" because people can have time with me which then quickly translates to "Sophie wants …". You need to be conscious about how you frame meetings. I now clearly signal when I am there to listen and learn rather than to make decisions, otherwise you can end up with unintended consequences and people acting upon your good intentions.

'I have also come to recognize that little moments can matter more than the big set pieces. People are always looking at you, therefore it's important to be present. I describe being present as a "superpower". The way you look and listen makes a huge difference through being present in meetings and demonstrating conscious leadership. The simple fact is, you are "always on" as a CEO. It is not acceptable to bring your baggage to work. It's your responsibility to be aware of your shadow.'

CEO NOTE

Remove interference to enable the organization to perform and maximize its potential.

Be Equipped to Succeed: Exec Summary

- Being equipped for success requires you to plan what you need to succeed.
- Make preparation a priority. This starts with your first 90 days and never stops. Apply the approach to listen, learn and lead. Stay curious to strengthen your understanding and awareness about the business.
- The better your preparation, the better the performance in the business.
- Set the cultural mix. You are the cultural architect of the organization. Your shadow sets the tone, whether you like it or not. Be clear about how you want things to be done around here and apply symbolic leadership to model the way. If you want

equality, treat people equally. If you want diversity, seek different views. If you want inclusion, include people. If you want accountability, own stuff. Employ a say/do one-to-one ratio, meaning you do everything you say you will do.

- Unlock potential. Be passionate and relentless about unearthing the blocks, barriers and obstacles that limit the organization from maximizing its potential to perform. Most importantly, make sure you are not part of the interference. Seek continuous feedback to ensure that you are operating at the right level, not diving into unnecessary detail that irritates and disengages capable people.

STAGE II

People

So far during *How to Be a CEO* we have covered the Purpose stage of the 3P Model, focusing on the insight and approach required to set the organization up for success:

- Our **first step** (Chapter 1) looked at putting purpose first from a personal perspective to ensure you are clear about your 'why' and defining it for the business.

- Our **second step** (Chapter 2) challenged you to recognize the role of inspiration and how you bring it to life through defining vision, setting strategy and energizing the organization.

- Our **third step** (Chapter 3) nudged you to be equipped for success through right preparation, setting the culture and unlocking potential.

We now move on to Stage 2: People, which puts forward a fundamental proposition. The quality of your people determines the quality of the business. You can have a shining strategic framework, a well-manicured organizational structure and flawless systems, but without great people working together, you will fail. This stage challenges you to move from the sentiment of putting people first to genuinely putting people first.

CHAPTER 4

Be Human

• • •

Psychological Safety

In the words of Amy Edmondson, Novartis Professor of Leadership and Management, Harvard Business School, and originator of psychological safety: 'I don't think a CEO is going to wake up in the morning and think about psychological safety. However, I do think they will wake up and think about the potential impact of failing to innovate and create the new products and services required for the company to thrive in the future. A CEO is responsible for innovation and delivering excellent performance. In order to prevent failure, you need people to speak up in a timely way, and to catch and correct problems before they might turn into headline news. You must be interested in creating the type of culture where you can deploy the three steps for building psychological safety:

1. Setting the stage – clarify expectations to encourage taking risk-taking, failure, uncertainty and the need for voice.
2. Inviting participation – create forums for input, asking great questions, listening intently and acknowledging gaps.
3. Responding appropriately – expressing appreciation of contributions, looking forward, offering help and championing continuous learning.'

Paula Stannett, Chief People Officer, Heathrow, is a passionate advocate of psychological safety. In our conversations she shared: 'It is mission critical for a CEO to champion psychological safety for people to thrive. Unless people are encouraged to have healthy debates and challenge in a safe space then the organization is at risk of failing to innovate and grow. The CEO needs to set expectations at the top and create an environment where everyone is encouraged to have voice, challenge with respect and learn from mistakes. When a CEO takes a stand about the ways of working in a company, it creates safety.'

I witnessed the creation of psychological safety early on in the tenure of a new CEO. Eric asked me to interview his leadership team to get an accurate picture about the current state of the business, operating conditions and culture. Before starting the conversations, I spoke with the CPO to align on what areas to cover and the best way of conducting the interviews. I was surprised to receive the advice to not take my laptop into the meetings and to make no notes. The CPO informed me that trust levels were so low and fear levels were so high that an external coach linked to the new CEO asking questions would be perceived with concern.

I am glad I followed the advice. Team members were suspicious about my agenda, asking how the feedback would be used. I was very clear that this round of conversations was not a substitute for their direct engagement with the CEO. It was an opportunity for the team to clarify what was working and what in their opinion needed to be addressed. The more conversations I had, the more I realized that there was an undercurrent of fear permeating the business as a consequence of previous leadership. There were stories about people getting fired for no particular reason, accountabilities being moved without clear explanation, and favourites being 'in the know', leaving others to feel excluded. At the root of the issue was a lack of trust, which presented itself as silo ways of working, protectionism of ideas and failing to share talent across the business.

I initially shared the insight with the CEO and the CPO in a non-attributable way to maintain the strictest of confidentiality. We agreed to set up a workshop to address the presenting issues and to reach alignment about a way forward. The priority was to accelerate the journey of restoring trust, hence our starting point was to introduce the concept of psychological safety. We referenced the pioneering work of Amy Edmondson, who first developed her research into psychological safety in the hospital sector. There she saw how 'the best teams have a culture where workers feel able to speak up about medical errors, to learn from them and prevent harm to patients' while 'in less effective teams nurses remained silent about the errors they saw'. Amy concluded: 'In the past two decades, hundreds of academic studies about psychological safety have been conducted that measure the positive correlation between psychological safety and desired outcomes, such as error reporting, quality improvement and high performance.'

Eric's approach as CEO was to create a high-trust environment as the foundation for performance. He was familiar with the research on trust developed by Paul J. Zak. Research cited in his *Harvard Business Review* article, 'The Neuroscience of Trust' (2017), showing how the brain chemical oxytocin facilitates collaboration and teamwork. Zak identified eight management behaviours that stimulate oxytocin production and generate trust, including recognizing excellence, inducing 'challenge stress', giving people discretion in how they do their work, and showing vulnerability. Eric wanted to start the workshop with a process to accelerate the formation of trust. However, it was a risk because there were high levels of scepticism in the team. We used a process known as a 'lifeline' where participants are asked to reflect upon crucible moments, which are transformative experiences through which people have come to a new or an altered sense of identity. Sharing these experiences helps to build trust as it enables intentional relationship building and the showing of vulnerability.

We allocated ten minutes for each person to share their story of key crucible moments, which should have taken 90 minutes. Four hours later we were still locked in a riveting disclosure of life experiences. Eric set the tone by sharing both personal and business moments which had defined his leadership approach. For instance, his primary leadership style was to be a collaborator, seeking people's views, asking probing questions and looking at how to drive alignment. Prior to the session team members couldn't figure him out. Eric's predecessor had a highly directive style, telling people what to do and dropping into detail on multiple decisions and actions. The Exec found it unnerving with Eric to be asked questions and given the autonomy to get on, make decisions and deliver stuff. Eric explained that at the birth of his first child there were complications. The child's heart was back to front and therefore needed open heart surgery. It was one of the first times in his life where Eric was out of control, had no solutions and needed to place his trust in the hands of the surgeons.

Thankfully the operation was successful. The impact on Eric was a profound shift in trusting others' expertise and letting them get on with it. He had adopted this in his leadership approach and found that the majority of people welcomed the freedom to operate within a framework. The team found both the content and his sharing of vulnerability disarming. As the researcher and storyteller Brené Brown explains in her popular TED Talk, 'The power of vulnerability', vulnerability is central to meaningful human experiences. By the time the entire exec had shared their stories you could sense a tangible shift in the team dynamic. Genuine compassion, openness, humour and appreciation were shared. Eric made it very clear that this was the foundation he wanted for the team working together and leading the business.

Research by the global organizational consulting firm Korn Ferry entitled 'Future of work trends in 2022' positions this age as 'the new era of humanity'. The report states: 'The last 24 months have changed everything. For businesses. For leaders. For employees. Now, as the dust settles, one fact becomes clear: power has shifted. From organizations to people. From profit to mutual prosperity. From "me" to "we". Employees are now starting to ask human questions about the work they perform. Why am I doing this? What is it for? How can we do it better? Many are choosing to leave their jobs. The competition to attract new talent is growing fiercer than ever. This poses an existential threat to businesses everywhere. An organization is only as good as the people it employs; those organizations that want to survive and thrive in 2022 will need to respond to the new power dynamic in kind. Look beyond financial goals to consider the needs of all their people. Treat employees as human beings, not parts of a machine. Break down silos and overcome remote working challenges to ensure people feel connected to the company purpose and vision and each other. Embrace the possibilities of the future and make work, work for everyone.'

The basic ingredient in leading with humanity is psychological safety. In 2012 Google researchers set out 'to discover the secrets of effective teams at Google'. Code-named Project Aristotle – a tribute to Aristotle's quote, 'the whole is greater than the sum of its parts' (as the Google researchers believed employees could do more working together than alone) – the goal was to answer the question: 'What makes a team effective at Google?' Using over 35 different statistical models on hundreds of variables, they sought to identify factors that:

- impacted multiple outcome metrics, both qualitative and quantitative
- surfaced for different kinds of teams across the organization
- showed consistent, robust statistical significance.

The researchers found the most important ingredient for a high-performing team was psychological safety, which they referred to as an 'individual's perception of the consequences of taking an inter-personal risk, or a belief that a team is safe for risk-taking in the face of being seen as ignorant, incompetent, negative or disruptive. In a team with high psychological safety, teammates feel safe to take risks around their team members. They feel confident that no one on the team will embarrass or punish anyone else for admitting a mistake, asking a question or offering a new idea.'

I appreciate the view of Emily Chang, CEO, Wunderman Thompson West, on psychological safety: 'Simply put, it's about creating a safe work environment, where people feel comfortable enough to be vulnerable, and to be themselves. It's letting people know you have their back, so that they can take interpersonal risk without fear of retaliation. It's about creating the space for people to speak up with ideas, questions and concerns. And as a result, psychological safety enables colleagues to trust each other and feel free, even responsible, for being candid.'

Emily went on to share the impact when organizations lack psychological safety:

- 'People hold back. They worry that their comments may be perceived as sensitive, threatening, political or wrong. They fear being criticized, mocked or degraded.

- People exhaust themselves doing mental math. They're constantly calculating the downside of sharing versus the upside of speaking up. They weigh the positive of improving our business with the negative of being humiliated or even blamed.

- People are unusually, unnecessarily anxious. The stress of constantly watching how they are being perceived adds a layer of wearisome stress on top of the daily pressures we all face.'

As CEO you need to be deliberate about building psychological safety by creating the right climate, mindsets and behaviours within your immediate leadership team, which sets the tone for the organization. A starting point is to ensure that everyone on the leadership team values others' contributions, cares about others' wellbeing, and has input into how the team carries out its work. You need to demonstrate this through your own actions.

John Holland-Kaye, CEO, Heathrow, prioritized the need to invest in his team: 'I have learned that you need a diverse team who are able to work together in an inclusive way, where the whole is greater than the sum of the parts. As a team you need to reach a point where you have common values and can leverage different thinking styles. I have discovered that having common values has high importance, such as respect and collaboration, as in situations where there are different values, conflict can swiftly rise and interfere with the teams' ability to lead the business. You definitely need high trust around the table, particularly in a matrix environment where people play different roles. The leadership team also has to demonstrate flexibility to navigate challenging times. For instance, at Heathrow when I took over the business, we were in a stage of continuous improvement with a particular focus on improving employee engagement and passenger service. We then moved to a period of investing in growth, delivering a campaign to expand the airport. This was swiftly followed by the impact of Covid and needing to manage severe cost cutting. The current phase is organic growth as the skies reopen. Each stage has required different leadership approaches and our success has been determined by the quality and flexibility of the team.'

I have been fortunate to support John and his leadership team during the different phases of the business. What has stayed consistent over the years is their commitment to leading with shared values, and embracing diversity and inclusion, which has built psychological safety, enabling them to navigate turbulent times in an effective way.

Stephen McCall, CEO, edyn, is another leader who places high significance on creating psychological safety: 'As a human business we try to assume good intent in dealing with others. If something goes wrong, our assumption is that a genuine mistake was made, rather than thinking that it was a deliberate act. We bring people together in various forums to build empathy, which prevents them from assuming the worst in others.'

An effective way of putting psychological safety into action is to orchestrate meetings so that each person present has voice and can be open and transparent in sharing their viewpoints. Use a tool known as a 'thinking circle' to create a safe environment and equal share of voice. The way it works is to take a topic, such as a strategic focus, a problem to solve, or an opportunity to go after, and formulate a specific question for everyone to answer. Allocate some time to think and then go around the team giving a set amount of time. As CEO, go last, summarize what you heard, reinforcing any points and/or making any builds. Give people another set time to reflect upon what they heard and conduct a second round to progress the conversation. Upon completion of round two there tend to be some clear themes to take forward, which you can then take into open dialogue. This can be particularly effective working in a virtual or hybrid way to maximize your time.

The principles for a 'thinking circle' are:

- Speak in turn.
- Have no interruptions.
- Listen to understand.
- Build on ideas.
- Be present.

In many meetings people listen to reply rather than listen to respond; they interrupt rather than wait for an appropriate moment to contribute; they want to be 'right' about their point of view rather than capitalize on ideas; and they are distracted rather than being fully present. Given that we are wired to connect, these types of behaviours are interpreted unconsciously, causing a 'fight or flight' reaction in others, which is the opposite of psychological safety. Being deliberate about developing the right working conditions for everyone to have a sense of belonging and care can become a powerful signature of your CEO tenure.

Another way of embedding psychological safety is through creating a safe environment which enables people to take risk, make mistakes and move forward. Mike Mathieson, Chairman, NED, advisor and former founder and CEO, Cake, shared his view: 'When things go wrong in the company, make sure you help everyone learn from the mistakes. Have the ability to take the pain by analysing what happened, understanding where you went wrong, look at processes and systems, unpick the detail to make sure it doesn't happen again. Taking this approach turns out to be a bonding experience and enables you to come out recognizing that you weren't at your best, but you have come out stronger as a team.'

He also highlighted the need to protect your employees, which creates a sense of safety. 'Operating in the service industry meant every now and again we would have a very difficult client. On one occasion we had a client who acted as a bully and treated suppliers as second-class citizens. This caused real issues with employees to the point of bringing them to tears. As soon as I got wind of this, I went to the client CEO and complained. It sent a clear message to my team that I had their back and I am not afraid to challenge the way we are treated by others.'

CEO NOTE

Champion psychological safety by creating the conditions where everyone feels safe to speak up without the fear of negative consequences.

Belonging

As a new CEO coming in to lead an organization in the transportation section, Lorna was passionate about the equity, diversity and inclusion agenda. Her history with EDI was deeply rooted in her upbringing. Lorna's father had been an engineer and had wanted a boy as the first born. Unfortunately, Lorna's parents were not able to have more children so the father's preference for a son was transferred onto her. It turned out to be a mixed blessing. On the upside, Lorna got a lot of attention from her father, who introduced her to the world of engineering from an early age. They made a wide range of gadgets together, including transistor radios, walkie talkies and train sets, and once computers came along he introduced her to coding. Some of her happiest moments were spent ensconced in her father's shed surrounded by an engineer's treasure trove. The downside was that Lorna felt excluded at school and within a wider social context. Growing up as a woman in the 1970s in southern Georgia, the STEM topics (science, technology, engineering and mathematics) were not top of the agenda. However, she developed a steely determination to address this imbalance. Little did she know that three decades later she would be heading up a company where she had the opportunity to make EDI a reality.

Thankfully, over the years EDI has become one of the most important priorities for CEOs and companies in general. Research by McKinsey & Company in a report entitled 'Diversity wins: How inclusion matters' (2020) covering 15 countries and more than 1,000 large companies shows not only that the business case remains robust, but also that the relationship between diversity on executive teams and the likelihood of financial outperformance has strengthened over time. The report highlights: 'Companies need a systematic, business-led approach to inclusion and diversity, as well as bolder action on inclusion.'

The authors recommend two key steps:

1. A systematic, business-led approach to inclusion and diversity (I&D).
   a. Increase diverse representation, particularly in leadership and critical roles.
   b. Strengthen leadership and accountability for delivering on I&D goals.

2. Bold steps to strengthen inclusion.
   a. Enable equality of opportunity through fairness and transparency.
   b. Promote openness, tackling bias and discrimination.
   c. Foster belonging through support for multivariate diversity.

Lorna championed both. She developed an effective EDI strategy to support the company objectives which articulated the rationale for action and outlined steps to implement, from communication and training to addressing workplace behaviour and evaluating progress. She was diligent about adopting a one-to-one say/do ratio, meaning she did everything that she said she would do. It started by weaving EDI into most aspects of the company plan. She set clear metrics about basic EDI factors, including age, disability, race, religion, gender and sexual orientation. Lorna started at the top to address the inequality of her executive committee. She devised a one-year plan which would ensure the necessary changes on the team to build a diverse and inclusive team.

Lorna ensured EDI featured in all her company communications so that she was visible, vocal and transparent about why she was championing the agenda, combining her personal experience along with the moral and business case for building fairer and more inclusive workplaces. Her primary message was that regardless of our identity, background or circumstances, we all deserve the opportunity to develop our skills and talents to fulfil our potential, work in a safe, supportive and inclusive environment, be fairly rewarded and recognized for our work, and have a meaningful voice on matters that we care about and that affect us. Lorna also articulated the benefits for the sustainability of businesses and economies when we embrace and value diverse thinking and ways of working that people from different backgrounds, experiences and identities bring to an organization.

Lorna's number one priority was people, which she translated as a great place to work where everyone has a sense of belonging and can thrive. She recognized that to truly enable EDI, everyone needed learning and development to ensure the common understanding about inclusion, diversity, bias (conscious and unconscious), workplace behaviour and communication. Along with her executive committee she modelled the way in putting their learning and development into action, including:

- Collect and analyse high-quality diversity data, e.g. ensuring employees' consent when collecting data, making sure that workforce data is representative, protecting collected data in line with legal requirements.

- Root out bias in job specifications and selection, e.g. stress-test job descriptions for EDI to remove bias, ensure that hiring managers are aware of any limiting assumptions they may have that could result in bias.

- Be ambitious in taking positive action on diversity, e.g. ensure company and function objectives are aligned with diversity targets, allocate sufficient resources and effort into delivering the outcomes of any positive action, guide managers on what to do if they perceive a tension between EDI and other targets.

Learning boost sessions were set up for all employees to get buy-in and alignment for EDI. Lorna and her executive committee ensured they had representation at every session, sending a clear message that this was an organizational priority. She had observed the impact on companies when they had to respond to allegations about racial discrimination, such as when Starbucks closed more than 8,000 US cafes in May 2018 for racial bias training. The company put 175,000 colleagues through a training which the company said 'isn't a solution, it's a first step' as it sought to rebuild its damaged reputation.

Lorna was also inspired by CEOs like David Joseph, UK CEO, Universal Music, who publicly stood up for difference by leading a quiet revolution in the business, changing the culture so 'neurodiverse' thinkers could flourish. He explained the case for why atypical minds, from popstars to activists, are key to the future. It was a timely initiative. High-profile public figures talked about their conditions, including Greta Thunberg, the climate change activist who has been open about her Asperger's and OCD. Musicians who volunteered conditions included Billie Eilish, who has Tourette's, Justin Timberlake, Solange Knowles, Adam Levine and will.i.am, who all have ADHD. Florence Welch has dyspraxia. Of course, the relationship between creativity and quirkiness has always been there. John Lennon and David Bowie were frequently called 'hyperactive'. One of David Joseph's primary messages was: 'We want artists to flourish and that means introducing new styles of working where people can discuss difference.'

Every leader I interviewed was passionate about taking a stand for EDI in their own unique way. The importance of the area was reinforced by Amy Edmondson, Novartis Professor of Leadership and Management, Harvard Business School: 'In your role as CEO, be explicit about the genuine need for diverse talent, ideas and perspectives to accomplish what the business is trying to achieve. Being explicit in your messaging and actions sends a powerful message that everyone belongs. Be intentional to override any bias to signal that even if you are not part of the dominant group in the organization, you belong, and the company welcomes as many different voices as needed.'

Sophie Devonshire, CEO, The Marketing Society, shared her strong views: 'It is a scandal that there aren't more female CEOs. Part of the reason I took this job is to support women in leadership. We need to expand the talent pool available for great roles. As we have not done a great job with equity, diversity and inclusion over the years, we have limited our talent pool. Now if you are in a majority, you can help others by being deliberate about closing the gap.'

Sophie reinforced the importance of creating environments where everyone has a sense of belonging: 'Working in advertising and marketing clearly shows the power of diverse thinking required for our future. I champion conversations about belonging in business. As CEO, one of my KPIs is about team happiness, which we partly measure through having voice and psychological safety. We ask our team every quarter if they feel comfortable to express their opinion in the team. Measuring voice is an important step to encourage a sense of belonging.'

Another powerful voice championing female CEOs is Viviane Paxinos, CEO, AllBright, who shared: 'I focus on supporting diversity in the workplace and championing more female leaders. Having more diversity in the workplace drives better business outcomes. Equity, diversity and inclusion is a leadership issue where all leaders need to step up and create more inclusive workplaces.'

Sophie Moloney, CEO, Sky New Zealand, gave her view: 'In the New Zealand political sphere, we have outperformed as women. However, in the business world, women CEOs are few and far between. My own experience being female and growing up in a male-dominated legal environment meant that I kept quiet to be accepted by the machine. Now that I have a big seat at the table I no longer need to put up with any form of prejudice. I bring a different lens to the table. Sometimes I use humour to unlock negotiations. Other times being a woman can help put people at ease. I still come up against a perception that success as a female is linked to a male as if I am in role due to a male connection. Overall, though, it hasn't been a hindrance and I relish the opportunity it presents me to help other women succeed.'

Wim Dejonghe, Senior Partner, Allen & Overy LLP, translates equity, diversity and inclusion through decision making: 'In a global law firm, the heart of our culture is to have a sense of ownership spread across all partners. As senior partner, I adopt a collegiate style of decision making. At the executive level, we make collective decisions. While it might save time for me to make the decisions on behalf of the firm, it is not our culture to do so.'

Wim went on to say: 'Leverage cognitive diversity. Bring people together, define a common goal, create conditions for people to feel empowered and express views. Encourage different perspectives to improve the quality of decision making. A good CEO thrives on hearing different points of view. Be deliberate about how you lead equality, diversity and inclusion. I am fortunate to be able to select people for many committees within the firm and therefore can be deliberate about our selection process to cover all aspects of diversity, including different ways of thinking, involving the next generation, as well as ensuring equality of gender, age, ethnicity and other aspects of diversity. I'm a big believer in operating with a relatively large decision-making body. Have the next generation involved so that they can participate, take a role and learn from more experienced people.'

Wim's passion and commitment to EDI run right through the firm: 'You have to be deliberate about being inclusive and developing capability to succeed. Commission formal leadership training to develop capability based on an assessment of skills and individualized personal development plans. Combine academic rigour alongside learning on the job.'

Will Stratton-Morris, CEO, Caffè Nero UK, encourages a learning mindset to support EDI: 'Highly effective people tend to be intellectually curious. This can range from engaging with how someone is going to spend their weekends to deeply understanding their roles and impact in the business. Be interested and interesting. Learn what others are passionate about and be open to multiple perspectives. As CEO, people will constantly bring you ideas and therefore you need to be able to look at them in different ways.'

Amber Asher, CEO, Standard International, is cognisant of gender bias: 'I was chosen for this role regardless of my gender. My Board and the industry have always been supportive of me. My track record speaks for itself, but I am mindful of needing to prove myself again and again. In certain situations, I could have been compromised in dealing with certain stakeholders but I know my stuff and so I have always navigated the terrain in front of me. I think people underestimate a female in role and we need to change people's preconceived ideas. I believe that I have the opportunity to set an example for the future generations of women in business as well as continuing to create equality between genders. Getting here was the hard part. Being here is not as hard.'

Another woman who shared her perspective on being a female CEO was Helen Tupper at Amazing If: 'I only see advantages to being a female CEO. I bring different perspectives to the position, including high empathy, understanding others and the ability to create psychological safety. As a mother it helps me understand the priorities and choices people have to make. My breadth of understanding can support and inspire people to seek the right guidance and support from others.'

Keith Barr has championed the EDI agenda as CEO, IHG, and explained some of the behavioural characteristics required: 'The next generation of colleagues expect authenticity and transparency. In the past people got respect through a position of authority. Now, rightly so, you need to earn the right to be respected. People judge you on doing the right things in the right way.'

One of the most significant aspects of EDI is about helping everyone have a sense of belonging. Paula Stannett, Chief People Officer,

Heathrow, went one step further in her view, stating: 'Belonging is the most important aspect of the equity, diversity and inclusion agenda. The CEO needs to set the tone. They need a good people team to implement a robust EDI plan, but the CEO needs to champion a sense of belonging to ensure everyone can be themselves and do their best work.'

In our conversation, Emily Chang, CEO, Wunderman Thompson West, highlighted three practical ways to create a culture of belonging:

1. 'Embrace with language. Resist the impulse to "separately include" others by extending exclusive invitations like "join us". Instead, consider how we might embrace each other by cultivating a language of belonging, like "let's go!".

2. Mind the optics. Plan ahead to ensure no one is accidently called out or left out. For instance, make sure there are enough seats, space and consideration for new hires joining the company so they feel a sense of belonging and care.

3. Acknowledge contribution. A great way to help people feel a sense of belonging is to highlight their contributions to the company. Identify the unsung heroes, or those trying to find their place, and give them a shout-out.'

Emma Gilthorpe, COO, Heathrow, advocates the importance of understanding others: 'Listening is one of the most important skills to demonstrate as a CEO. I mean properly listening to what people are saying. It's hard to do when things are busy, however people tell you a lot in what they say. They will give you valuable indicators to pick up on. For instance, I was chatting with a team member recently about the opportunity to go for a new role. They appeared hesitant in their response. I took the opportunity to ask them what was on their mind. What transpired was that there were family matters which they needed to prioritize. It would have been easy to have interpreted their hesitancy as a lack of ambition or drive, however taking the time to let the conversation evolve meant that we got to the heart of the issue. It is vital to learn how to switch on your active listening capability. My commitment is to ask one more probing question rather than rushing on to the next task.'

139

The importance of listening and giving people voice was reinforced by Mike Mathieson, Chairman, NED, advisor and former founder and CEO, Cake: 'It's very easy as CEO to jump into conversations, talk over people, or be a poor listener. It's important to give people voice. Take the time to listen to what people have to say. It might be appropriate to give your perspective; however, make sure you have listened first. For instance, if someone wrote a presentation and my initial thought was that it was a disaster, I disciplined myself to sit down with them and work collaboratively to help them learn. This would send a powerful message to the team about continuous learning, valuing people and everyone having a sense of belonging.'

Graham Alexander, founder, The Alexander Partnership, applies it to a team make-up: 'Ensure there is diversity around the team. Don't recruit people in your own image. Have different people who will do things differently to you.'

Javier Echave, CFO, Heathrow, makes the linkage between EDI, engagement and performance: 'Most companies are service organizations providing a service for people by people. We are in a service game, therefore employee engagement has a direct impact on performance. The best way to unlock value is to make sure people are engaged.'

Jonathan Akeroyd, CEO, Burberry, laid out a simple proposition: 'It is clear that EDI is a central part of an organizational plan. As CEO you need to lead from the front and make sure all initiatives are done from a company and cultural point of view. At Burberry we have always had a strong reputation to be a people-first organization, which fits with my own philosophy for creating environments where everyone belongs.'

As CEO, be educated and articulate about EDI. Formulate your authentic position, then be visible and vocal about it to champion the agenda and ensure you create an environment where everyone belongs and thrives.

CEO NOTE

Make equity, diversity and inclusion personal. Don't make it a corporate initiative. One of the biggest contributions you can make as a CEO is to help everyone feel valued and add value.

Thrive

I got a call asking for help from the HR director of a high-profile digital company. The business was experiencing hyper growth; however, it was haemorrhaging talent. Although it attracted some of the brightest and best people from top consultancies, the average tenure was 18 months, and some employees were literally collapsing at work from exhaustion and burn-out. The message from the CEO was clear. 'Shape up or ship out.' I had worked with the HR director in a previous company and they had hit a wall in their existing role. The CEO didn't listen, didn't care and believed that people were a dispensable commodity.

I listened to the scenario and gave my honest assessment. Unless the CEO changed their tone, trying to address the toxicity and impact on people would at best be a superficial short-term remedy, but more likely a waste of time. There was one ray of hope. One of the C-suite leaders on the executive committee understood the people agenda and was prepared to put their head above the parapet to try to influence the CEO. When it came to the business agenda the CEO was a data geek, making the majority of decisions heavily based by an informed point of view. However, when it came to people it was a different story, driven by an obsession for fast, short-term growth at whatever cost.

I suggested that we meet with the C-suite leader to put together a business case to present to the CEO about the value of attracting, retaining and developing top talent and the cost of losing great people. Before we even had a chance to map out the presentation, the C-suite leader was fired. The CEO got wind of the fact that the C-suite leader was bringing together the necessary people data and got spooked. Suffice to say, I also never stepped over their office threshold again.

This was an extreme case of a CEO taking zero accountability for the health and wellbeing of their 'greatest asset' – people. But the truth is that until the impact of Covid, many CEOs and organizations paid lip service to wellbeing. I frequently heard supportive comments like 'part-timer', 'it's alright for some', 'another half-day' if people worked from home. Mental health was under the radar and in most environments, success was measured by permanent busyness, working fast, being scheduled back to back, and hyperactivity was considered smart. However, some progressive CEOs had started to embrace health and wellbeing and make it part of their leadership ethos.

After taking over as CEO in 2009, Jeff Weiner, now Executive Chairman at LinkedIn, saw the membership base grow from 33 million to more than 430 million and revenue from $78 million to over $3 billion by 2017. On September 28, 2017, Jeff Weiner sent out a simple tweet to help put things in perspective: 'One of the benefits of my getting older: far greater appreciation for three things that are too often taken for granted: health, love and time.'

Weiner's leadership philosophy is based on compassion and was influenced by a book called *The Art of Happiness*, which is about the teachings of the Dalai Lama. Weiner describes compassion as 'empathy plus action' and references an explanation by the Dalai Lama: 'Picture yourself walking along a mountainous trail. You come across a person being crushed by a boulder on their chest. The empathetic response would be to feel the same sense of crushing suffocation, thus rendering you helpless. The compassionate response would be to recognize that the person is in pain and do everything within your power to remove the boulder and alleviate their suffering.'

Jeff Weiner is a great example of a CEO who invested in his own leadership development and became an exemplary leader, achieving a 97 per cent approval rating on Glassdoor in 2019, which was a far cry from a journalist once describing his management style at Yahoo as 'wielding his fierce intelligence as a blunt instrument'.

While the notion of health can take on many forms, Weiner has always encouraged the use of meditation in the business world. He uses the Headspace app to meditate daily and talks about the impact of meditation to stay positive and focus better. Drawing upon the influence of the Dalai Lama and his mentor Ray Chambers, Weiner has described five keys to happiness:

1. Embrace mindfulness and live in the present.
2. Prioritize love over being right.

3. Observe your thoughts, especially during emotional moments, to foster compassion.

4. Cultivate gratitude by writing down and revisiting one thing you're thankful for each day.

5. Actively seek opportunities to serve and help others whenever possible.

We are in a new era of health and wellbeing. Covid has continued to have an extensive impact on ways of working and patterns of behaviour, with widespread implications including hybrid working, working from home, flexible working, mental health, absenteeism, presenteeism (working when ill), leaveism (using holiday entitlement to work), digital technologies, financial wellbeing, bereavement and trauma. As CEO, you cannot be expected to be an expert in health and wellbeing, however it is essential to have an informed point of view and to take a genuine and meaningful approach to ensuring people can thrive at work.

In my conversation with Keith Barr, CEO, IHG, he shared: 'Probably the important thing to be known for is that you care. As CEO you are responsible for many people's lives and livelihoods.'

Javier Echave, CFO, Heathrow, highlighted the importance of supporting people: 'Wellbeing is the fastest way to unlock productivity for an organization.' He went on to suggest: 'Create an environment where people feel safe with uncertainty. Have a workforce where people feel confident and resourceful to find solutions. Help people feel empowered to make decisions, fail fast, share learning and move on.' He also acknowledged the need to manage your own health and wellbeing: 'On a personal level, catch your mood quickly and have the tools to bounce back. Ensure that you have the mechanisms to be at your best on a consistent basis.'

This was echoed by Javier's colleague, Paula Stannett, Chief People Officer, Heathrow: 'People will thrive when the CEO creates the conditions for basic needs to be met in terms of reward and remuneration, ensures they operate in an environment of psychological safety, can play to their strengths, and have access to wellbeing resources. It is also important for a CEO to sponsor learning and career development opportunities so that people can keep their skills current. An organization needs to invest in all generations and make sure everyone has access to varied learning opportunities to build long-term careers.'

Sneh Khemka, former CEO, Simplyhealth, reinforced the need to sustain your own wellbeing: 'Being a CEO is the most stressful and enjoyable job I've had. I find myself waking up at 4am every day with lots of thoughts swirling. I use the first part of the morning as an important meditative time to process my thinking and to put ideas into the right categories. As CEO you get threats from all directions and therefore the more slings and arrows you get, the thicker your skin needs to be. You cannot slack off. You are constantly watched and your performance is constantly monitored. In truth, being a CEO is a lifestyle, not a job.'

As a mother and leading the global career network for women, Viviane Paxinos, CEO, AllBright, knows the important of setting yourself up to thrive: 'Put wellbeing first. Taking care of your health is very important. Running a company is a big responsibility and learning how to manage your wellbeing is key. You have to look after yourself. Find ways to integrate work and life that work for you. Set boundaries which your team understand.'

In my coaching of CEOs, I encourage them to look at four different capacities to help them thrive – see Figure 4.1.

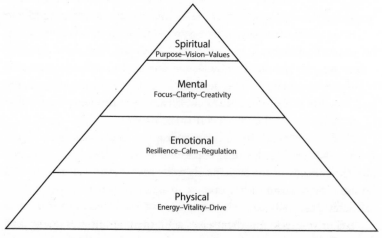

Figure 4.1 Capacities required to thrive

1. **Physical**. What energizes you? What de-energizes you? What nourishes your physical health? What gets in the way? Physical health and wellbeing are the foundation for sustaining high performance. What I tend to find is that people know what they need to do in terms of managing the basics like nutrition, hydration, sleep, exercise and recovery, but they don't have a consistent approach unless they have experienced some form of wake-up call which jolts them into a supportive routine. On a personal note, in 2012 I hit a wall. Supporting my young family of three children, travelling the world with global clients, running my business and writing books, I was exhausted. I had turned into what nutritionist Patrick Holford calls 'a knackered ape'. I set a personal intent to be energized. I didn't know what it would look like, but I started an inquiry to understand what I needed in place to replenish and sustain my energy. The starting place was no surprise. Exercise. However, I came up with every excuse for why I couldn't do it – too tired, too busy, it's too hot, cold, wet. Yet I noticed on the days I did exercise I had more energy. I decided to make it a non-negotiable and exercise every day. I decided it was better to do at least 30 minutes' exercise than nothing. It became a habit and I have done it ever since. From a nutritional perspective, having tried a macrobiotic diet, vegan, vegetarian and eat whatever I want, I have found what works best for me is to be gluten free. I have an intolerance to gluten and going gluten free sustains my energy and alleviates other symptoms like bloating and headaches. I find sleep the most challenging to master after years of overcoming jetlag and having young children. I keep a notebook by my bed and jot down my thoughts in a random fashion before going to sleep. If I wake in the night I reach over for the notebook and, without turning on the light, scribble down thoughts to clear my mind.

What works for you? I resonate with the idea of the corporate athlete made popular in the seminal *Harvard Business Review* article 'The making of a corporate athlete' by Jim Loehr and Tony Schwartz (2001). The authors say: 'If there is one quality that executives seek for themselves and their employees, it is high performance in the face of ever-increasing pressure and rapid change.' They go on to say that physical wellbeing is the foundation for peak performance in business. I resonated with the view from Phil Bayliss, CEO, Infinium, about the role energy plays: 'When I reflect for myself if I have been successful, the answer is no. I don't believe the mindset of a CEO should be to measure success whilst still on the journey. I think you should direct your unlimited energy to try to achieve something beyond your own expectations and those that you work with. For instance, I achieve less than I think I can in a year, but far more over a five-year period. The art of the possible keeps growing at a rate of knots. We use a balanced scorecard to measure success, but the real primary motivation as CEO is to come up with new things and remarkable outcomes to achieve.' I love the ideas from Sophie Devonshire, CEO, The Marketing Society: 'Consciously manage your energy and the energy of the organization. For example, if you are in change mode, the pace can be relentless. See yourself as the chief energy officer, or the chief encourager officer. Make sure you have moments to reflect on progress and when times are tough, strengthen your connection with people as they need to see you are part of the solution.'

2. **Emotional**. What sustains your emotional health? What derails you? What helps you feel great? Emotional wellbeing has gained awareness through the advances made in understanding and developing emotional intelligence. Keith Barr, CEO, IHG, recognized the importance of emotional health: 'To be a successful CEO requires resilience. You are at the top of the pyramid, and you have to carry the organization. During Covid, the crazier things got, the calmer I needed to be. Every day you will have something coming at you. As well as the global pandemic, in recent times we have had to navigate a war, energy crisis and an unauthorised intrusion into our systems.' Emma Gilthorpe, COO, Heathrow, puts significant effort into improving emotional intelligence: 'I recognize that there may be limits to the extent that you can develop EQ. For instance, some personality profiles are not wired to project emotion. I have one brilliant team member who has had to learn how to smile more and show others how he feels. However, whatever

your genetic predisposition for EQ, you can improve on it, and that starts with self-awareness. Be straight with yourself. Conduct a simple self-audit asking yourself, "How do I really feel?" Learn how to clearly articulate your emotional state to help others understand you. When you wake up in the morning, ask yourself, "How do I want to be today?" Practise interpreting and managing your emotions so that you can be the leader you want to be and, in the process, help others develop their own self-awareness.'

A large extent of my CEO coaching focuses on resolving emotional interference that could prevent CEOs from demonstrating their value, in particular focused on relationship issues. On one occasion I coached a CEO who had a major trust issue with one of their executive committee members. The CEO had got wind that the executive was going behind their back and trying to undermine their decision making and credibility. It was hard to evidence as the executive had a loyal following. It came to a head when the chairman became involved as they had heard rumours about the executive behaviour. I introduced the CEO to a simple communication tool known as *Every Fish Needs Batter and Chips*:

- Explanation – present the facts.
- Feelings – share the emotional impact.
- Needs – state what's required to move forward.
- Benefits – offer the win/win outcome.
- Consequences – outline what will happen if a solution is not reached. Do not share consequences unless you are going to act.

The CEO used the tool to process their thinking, set up a meeting with the executive member, and communicated in a clear and rational way to seek a solution. Thankfully they were able to reach a robust agreement for the way forward which included a series of regular one-to-one meetings aimed at rebuilding the broken trust and moving the business agenda forward. Take ownership of your emotional wellbeing. I have seen CEOs derailed by emotions such as anxiety, anger and frustration, which they take out in unintentional ways on loved ones or colleagues. This is not clever and will damage a reputation if left unchecked.

3. **Mental**. A CEO is paid to think. The quality of thinking determines the quality of value added to the business. Therefore, making mental health and wellbeing a priority is vital to fulfil the function. Yet even though a CEO is theoretically in charge of their schedule, quality think-time is usually the first thing squeezed. Bill Gates is known for taking a self-proclaimed 'think week'. Twice a year he spends seven days of solitude in a forest cabin where he reads paper after paper, for up to 18 hours a day, of innovation and investment ideas from Microsoft employees, relentlessly scribbling notes. Emma Gilthorpe, COO, Heathrow, is clear about the importance of having time to think: 'As CEO, make sure you have a clear focus and narrative for the business so that people can follow. Schedule precious time to think, to plan and to harness your team to make sure you are going in the right direction. Carve out quality time with your executive committee to align on the direction and narrative. Time well spent early on aligning the leadership team will save you months of effort later as colleagues will see and hear consistent messages from their leaders.' Richard Solomons, Chairman, Rentokil Initial plc, emphasized the need for mental agility: 'As CEO you need to develop the ability to synthesize everything. At IHG I needed to engage with the owners of our hotels, deeply understand our colleague and customer needs, be across the competition and partner with our suppliers. It is vital to be able to synthesize multiple data points to make the tough calls. Initially I got accused of doing too much analysis, but after navigating several global crises I learned to utilize an 80/20 approach. In other words, be prepared to make decisions based on 80 per cent readiness and get on with it.'

Wim Dejonghe, Senior Partner, Allen & Overy LLP, showed the importance of mental acuity: 'One of my biggest learnings as senior partner is that things are often categorized as "false dilemmas" – for instance, issues are made right or wrong, black or white. The challenge is to look for the right balance whilst accepting that you will never find it, such as trading off short- and long-term choices.' Phil Bayliss, CEO, Infinium, also highlights the need for mental fitness: 'The moments that can make the biggest difference as a CEO are driven by the agility to flex your approach or direction of travel and drive change. In order to make this happen you need to respond to data and people. I have a bias for data; however, I have learned that having a check-in call with the most experienced person in the business is as valuable as digesting all the data.' It is helpful to understand how our brains have the ability to adapt (known as neuroplasticity), as explained by the neuropsychologist Celeste Campbell (February 2009): 'Neuroplasticity refers to the physiological changes in the brain that happen as the result of our interactions with our environment. From the time the brain begins to develop in utero until the day we die, the connections among the cells in our brains reorganize in response to our changing needs. This dynamic process allows us to learn from and adapt to different experiences.' Make sure you understand when and where you do your best thinking so that you optimize your mental faculty.

4. **Spiritual**. On 15 September 2022, as I was writing this chapter, Yvon Chouinard, founder of the outdoor fashion brand Patagonia, gave his company to a charitable trust. He said any profit not reinvested in running the business would go to fight climate change. The brand's website now states: 'Earth is now our only shareholder.' Thankfully there are multiple CEOs driven by a bigger mission than profit. John Mackey, co-founder and CEO of Whole Foods Market, has led the natural and organic grocer to a $13 billion Fortune 500 company. With more than 370 stores and 80,000 team members in three countries, the company has been named by *Fortune* magazine as a 'Best Company to Work For' for 16 consecutive years and the 'Number One Most Admired Food and Drug Store Company in the World' in 2012. John was the visionary for the Whole Planet Foundation to help end poverty in developing nations, the Local Producer Loan Program to help local food producers expand their businesses, the Global Animal Partnership's rating scale for humane farm animal treatment, and the Health Starts Here initiative to promote health and wellness. He co-founded the Conscious Capitalism Movement and co-authored a *New York Times* and *Wall Street Journal* bestselling book, entitled *Conscious Capitalism: Liberating the heroic spirit of*

business, to boldly defend and reimagine capitalism and encourage a way of doing business that is grounded in ethical consciousness. At a 'Conscious Capitalism' conference attended by 220 CEOs in 2016, one of the primary messages was 'CEOs need to become more aware, more conscious, of the moral and economic virtues that capitalism advances spontaneously'. It also advocated the need to recognize the purpose of business and the contribution of capitalism to human flourishing. A report from Globescan, a research firm that specializes in corporate reputation, defined purpose as the process by which a company 'marries business value with societal value'.

CEOs like Yvon Chouinard and John Mackey demonstrate what management thought leader, physicist, philosopher and author Danah Zohar describes as Spiritual Intelligence (SQ). Zohar has identified 12 principles of SQ:

- Self-awareness – knowing what you believe in, what you value and what deeply motivates you.

- Vision and value led – acting from principles and deep beliefs, and living accordingly.

- Positive use of adversity – learning and growing from mistakes, setbacks and suffering.

- Holistic – seeing larger patterns, relationships and connections: having a sense of belonging.

- Compassion – having the quality of 'feeling with' and deep empathy.

- Celebration of diversity – regarding other people for their differences, not despite them.

- Field-independent – standing against the crowd and having one's own convictions.

- Ask fundamental 'why' questions – needing to understand things and get to the bottom of them.

- Ability to reframe – standing back from a situation/problem and seeing the bigger picture; seeing problems in a wider context.

- Spontaneity – living in and being responsive to the moment.
- Sense of vocation – feeling called upon to serve, to give something back.
- Humility – having the sense of being a player in a larger drama, of one's true place in the world.

It is important as a CEO to find your place on the spiritual dimension of health and wellbeing. It is not enough today to be a brilliant strategist and to run organizations. You need to extend your curiosity to questions about purpose, meaning and value which go beyond traditional forms of shareholder return. Amber Asher, CEO, Standard International, shared what is most meaningful for her in role: 'I love being with the team. We recently had a big retreat and seeing everyone working on a shared mission, with a brand they believe in, and driving global growth together is a joy.'

Javier Echave, CFO, Heathrow, put his perspective on spiritual intelligence: 'Be the ambassador of the company. Role model the company purpose, values and inspire people to feel part of the company. The CEO is the steward of the organization. Accept that you are the temporary custodian of the brand, and your goal is to make the company better.'

Keith Barr, CEO, IHG, tapped into the heart of spiritual health: 'The rewarding part of being a CEO is knowing you have made a difference. Have the vision and drive to make the company better and unlock its potential. There will be a lot of bumps along the way. It's easy to think that being a CEO is a fun job without seeing all the challenges behind it.'

Given the size and breadth of the health and wellbeing agenda it is advisable to chunk it down to make it manageable to progress in a sustainable way. As with all strategic focus areas there needs to be a combination of awareness, alignment and application to help everyone understand what is going on, what is required to make things work and how to embed the plan into the business using an approach of continuous improvement.

CEO NOTE

Role model health and wellbeing for the good of everyone and the business. For the business to thrive, people need to thrive.

Be Human: Exec Summary

- Psychological safety is not a soft option. It takes courage and strength to create an environment where everyone has voice. Set clear expectations to encourage risk-taking, failure, uncertainty and the need for voice. Invite participation through forums for input, questions, listening to understand and acknowledging gaps. Respond appropriately by expressing appreciation for contributions, looking forward, offering help and championing continuous improvement.
- Make equity, diversity and inclusion personal. Understand what it means for you so that you can drive the agenda in meaningful ways, rather than it being a tick-box activity to hit some targets. Ensuring the conditions are in place for everyone to belong will drive engagement and translate into performance.
- It is difficult to sustain performance over time if people are exhausted. Prioritizing wellbeing on physical, mental, emotional and spiritual levels is an investment in your most precious commodity – people.

CHAPTER 5

Be a Connoisseur of Talent

● ● ●

Teaming

On day one as a new CEO, Paul brought the executive committee together for a half-day meeting. Paul had been successful as an internal promotion and was familiar with the previous executive committee led by his predecessor. The outgoing CEO had no interest in the executive committee operating as a team. They had deliberately recruited technical experts in role and managed them in silos. It was an effective way to execute a short-term plan, however it had serious limitations in terms of creating the necessary shared vision, strategy, capability and culture to accelerate the sustainable growth of the business.

Therefore, Paul inherited an executive committee which had no team identity. It was an environment of low trust, where people protected their own agenda and resources and collaborated only when forced. There were some individual relationships on the executive, however people didn't know each other and visibly winced at the prospect of spending time together. I had coached Paul with his previous functional team, so he invited me to become the executive committee coach. My initial approach to coaching a team is to conduct a set of diagnostic interviews to understand what is working, gaps to address and to formulate shared outcomes. Given the time pressure in the business, we had agreed for the first meeting that I would be an observer and follow up with the team to gather early views. As we commenced the meeting, seeing people's body language was revealing. Folded arms, crossed legs and little eye contact demonstrated the type of environment we were dealing with. The most disengaged member actually sat away from the table and, on occasion, stood up when making their point to create even more tension and discomfort.

Despite the backdrop Paul wanted to set the team up for success. He made it clear that this was his 'A' team and that he was committed to building upon the work of his predecessor. His number one priority was to ensure that the team would have the opportunity to become a high-performing team. Paul had been influenced by the insightful work of Patrick Lencioni in his five dysfunctions of a team model:

1. Absence of trust.

2. Fear of conflict.

3. Lack of commitment.

4. Avoidance of accountability.

5. Inattention to results.

Paul used this as a lens to look through with the team and stated his intent to address these areas so that eventually the team could work together in a climate of trust, have transparent conversations, and drive collective commitment, accountability and results. Paul shared the starting point for the executive committee, which was for each team member to see the executive committee as their primary team. This is usually one of the biggest wake-up calls for executive committees as they are often wired to think that their primary team is the one they lead, rather than prioritizing the team with their peers. Paul was clear: the role of the executive team was to lead the company, which meant it must be their number one team.

In our conversation, Richard Solomons, Chairman, Rentokil Initial plc, reinforced the importance of team, recounting his experience as CEO at IHG: 'For a CEO to succeed you must prioritize building the right team. Your ability to plan and execute will be in direct proportion to your ability to maximize the team. I made sure that I was surrounded by a diverse and brilliant team who challenged me. Ultimately your role is to leverage their capabilities to deliver outperformance, so I made sure to understand their strengths and weaknesses, and welcomed the fact that they were smarter than me.'

Another leader who emphasizes the significance of team is Wim Dejonghe, Senior Partner, Allen & Overy LLP: 'Your success as a CEO is dependent on the success of your team. A CEO needs to ensure that everyone understands what is expected of them, which includes having ownership of the strategy and being accountable for delivering their part of the plan.'

Emma Gilthorpe, COO, Heathrow, articulated how a CEO can embrace the power of teamwork: 'Probably the biggest watch-out as a CEO is having an inflated ego and operating with an individualistic mindset. If people seek to be CEO because they want to be number one, or they think it is a manifestation of their supremacy, they will ultimately fail because they won't create followership. You need to be ambitious for the company, your people and yourself, but when it bleeds into a view that you are "better" than others it becomes a derailer. As CEO you are surrounded by people who are better than you in many ways, with more skill, experience and capability. Being a team player and demonstrating humility are critical ingredients for engaging and inspiring others to follow.'

Back to Paul and forming his new team. He planted a seed by asking each executive member to recall a time when they were part of a high-performing team and to highlight one stand-out attribute. It was a revealing conversation as people shared experiences of being on teams in turnaround situations, crisis scenarios navigating financial recessions, mergers and acquisitions, and delivering organizational change. The attributes called out included trust, openness, clarity, focus, collaboration, consistency and fun. Paul challenged the team to rate themselves currently against these qualities. Scores were low. Paul took the opportunity to share that his initial priority was to build a high-performing team, however he appreciated the fact that everyone would need to think about it and to decide if they were on board and fully committed to the journey.

Paul followed up the meeting with intensive one-to-one conversations to understand individual preferences, needs and expectations. One executive member made it clear that working in a team environment was not for them. They derived their energy delivering functional objectives, which they had done on a consistent basis over the last few years, and had been recruited on that basis. Although it appeared that this individual was an indispensable member of the executive committee due to their experience and results, Paul made it clear that the approach was changing and the team came first. The exit of one of the highest-performing individuals in the company sent a symbolic message to the whole organization: team first, individual second. In Paul's other conversations with direct reports, a mixed picture emerged, including people having wanted to form as a team in the past, however any efforts had been quashed due to the dynamic of the previous CEO, which had resulted in silo working, competing for resources and lack of personal connection.

Paul asked me to conduct my first set of diagnostic interviews to be able to hold up an objective mirror for the team. A clear picture emerged of a highly talented group wanting to co-create a shared strategy, develop organizational capability, nurture talent and beat the plan. In order to accelerate the journey of becoming a high-performing team we agreed to start by building a relationship. No relationship, no team. We used storytelling to develop connection where each team member had the opportunity to share what had shaped their personal and professional lives and what was most meaningful for them through the lens of their personal values and sense of purpose. A strong glue was established which provided the foundation to schedule a series of strategy days, in close succession, to co-create and align on a new plan. The team worked diligently together to form a three-year plan consisting of four strategic pillars which they jointly owned. It is all very well to talk about team, however a genuine team emerges only once the team members do actual work together.

The team set up an engagement plan to involve all colleagues with the refreshed strategic direction and committed to developing a true team culture, including:

- Form an extended leadership team consisting of the executive committee direct reports. This team met on a monthly basis and took ownership for co-creating and delivering the one-year strategic plan. This freed up the executive committee to focus on the longer-term business and empowered the next generation of leaders to expand their impact and influence.

- Drive a high-performing team development programme where each senior team in the organization had the opportunity to form as a team using a simple framework agreed by the extended leadership team: trust one another; engage in great conversations to build and develop ideas; commit to decisions; hold one another accountable; focus on achieving collective results.

- Schedule regular all-hands company meetings to engage and inspire all colleagues with the strategic direction and team ways of working model.

- Align performance management with a balanced scorecard focused on how colleagues would deliver their objectives using team-based behaviours.

- Recognize team performance by shouting out wins and great behaviours across multiple channels.

- Provide cross-functional internal coaching and mentoring opportunities for colleagues to drive their technical and behavioural development.

Paul and the executive committee stayed consistent in their approach to create a great place to work based on high-performing teams. Multiple benefits were cited as a result, such as:

- retaining top talent
- increasing employee engagement
- embracing innovative thinking
- having an uplifting work environment
- feeling recognized.

The business was also able to demonstrate a clear linkage between better teams and better results through hard data with improvements to finance, attendance, safety, health and wellbeing, customer care and reliability.

I appreciate the perspective of Amy Edmondson, Novartis Professor of Leadership and Management, Harvard Business School, on the significance of teaming: 'A CEO needs to aim high for something meaningful and ambitious. They need to create and implement stretch goals that require innovation. However, the primary way innovation takes place is teaming across silos. The CEO needs to build an enterprise perspective where everyone shows up with the belief that our collective success is my personal success, as opposed to a silo mentality where people think my success is at the expense of your success. Although it is an obvious requirement to deliver company-wide innovation, it needs to be stated clearly because the traditional mental model is if I win, you lose. It is the role of the CEO to help everyone understand the model that when we win, we really win. Therefore, if you do well, it helps me and if we do well together it helps everything. This is an enterprise mindset which creates opportunity for colleagues to team up, get to know each other and make rapid progress when crossing disciplinary boundaries.'

Neil Jowsey, CEO, Cromwell, captured the significance of teaming: 'It is essential to surround yourself with great people, however it is more important to develop a strong sense of teamwork. I would take good talent and build into a great team, rather than have great talent who don't work together. Make it a priority to build cohesive teams based on a high degree of trust. When you have trust, you can go faster and get more done due to the fact that people are not trying to second guess each other. Trust is a magic ingredient and helps you to not waste energy.'

This point of view was reinforced by Jonathan Akeroyd, CEO, Burberry, who stated: 'Your success as CEO is about your team. A key priority is to develop a world-class team focused on the same purpose, vision, values and culture. Once you have your immediate team aligned with shared goals it will impact the whole company.'

Viviane Paxinos, CEO, AllBright, also emphasized the importance of teaming: 'CEOs lead the business through building a great team. It is impossible to achieve the organizational goals without the right people. The role of the CEO is to build a team you can trust with complementary skills to share the vision and passion for the business and who can deliver the plan.'

A great CEO has a clearly developed point of view about why high-performing teams matter, what great teamwork looks like and how to develop it. Most importantly, they don't just talk about it. They live and breathe teamwork with their leadership team. They make it a priority every day, rather than when they think they have the luxury of some time to focus on teamwork. Effective CEOs build teamwork into the fabric of the mindset, behaviour and actions of the company.

Define your approach, reflecting upon the characteristics of a high-performing team, including:

- Ensure team members know exactly what is expected of them.
- Think team first, individual second.
- Have open and transparent conversations about the company strategy, capability, talent and culture.
- Demonstrate alignment and one voice, once collective decisions have been made.
- Take collective responsibility for the delivery of the strategic plan.
- Have the necessary tools and resources to deliver and, if not, work together to make the right trade-offs for the good of the business.
- Ensure team meetings are informative, energizing and effective through the use of right governance, data and decision making.
- Discuss ways of working in team meetings to ensure the right focus on mindset, behaviour and business issues.
- Help team members to feel safe so that they can take risks and be vulnerable in front of each other.
- Enable team members to provide high levels of support and challenge to each other.
- Recognize that the work you do together as a team matters and helps make the world a better place.

I am not a big fan of translating sporting examples into business, however there is one parallel worth noting: practice. A high-performing sporting team spends the majority of its time on practice. Teams in business spend the majority of their time on work, with occasional moments of practice. One CEO I supported was a big advocate of what she called 'time off the pitch'. Elaine had done track and field at a high level and was fully bought into the concept of practice. Together we developed a systematic way of building high-performing teams focused on four key stages:

1. **Diagnostic**. Elaine was passionate about having a regular pulse about how her team was performing together, not just analysing the standard dashboard metrics. She asked me to conduct diagnostic interviews with her immediate team each quarter covering big topics like strategy, capability, talent and culture. We debriefed the insight with her CPO and shared it with the team to highlight key issues to address any outcomes to achieve.

2. **Design**. Informed by the diagnostic findings I brought together a draft agenda to drive the development of the team. There were standard agenda items such as:
   a. Check in to understand in depth what is on people's minds and how they are feeling about the business, team and their own learning and development.
   b. Review team progress, challenges and gaps to drive the business forward.
   c. Align on strategic direction and the required behaviours to deliver the plan.
   d. Give and receive feedback between team members to resolve any issues and ensure people are working together to succeed.

3. **Deliver**. Schedule an overnight session on a quarterly basis to develop the team, progress the strategy, strengthen relationships and drive high performance. It was imperative that any output emerging from the offsite was integrated into day-to-day business. In my experience leadership teams are so busy that any activity which falls out of the plan will simply not get done. We devised 90-day sprints focused on key priorities, messages,

behaviours and symbolic actions to reinforce the vital work to be done.

4. **Debrief**. It is vital to demonstrate the value of team development through aligning on some measures to evidence progress. These are usually linked with the employee engagement survey or an external body, like Great Place To Work. However, it's powerful if the impact can be linked with the delivery of the strategic plan. Working with Elaine's leadership team in the retail sector meant that they focused on metrics like customer centricity, sales, availability, digital as well as employee engagement.

As a coach it has been interesting observing the trends in team development. A few years ago, I found executives sceptical and resistant about investing in team building. However, as pressures have increased to accelerate growth, and new business priorities have emerged (such as EDI, ESG, health and wellbeing), combined with the crisis of a global pandemic, sentiments have changed and I am now finding CEOs hungry for the contact and time with their teams. Paul Dupuis, CEO and Chairman, Randstad Japan, takes this further by stating: 'Developing a high-performing team is the most important building block for growing a high-performing organization and starts by choosing the right people.' Paul referenced the seminal work of Jim Collins who in his book *Good to Great* developed the concept 'First Who, Then What'. Collins wrote: 'Those who build great organizations make sure they have the right people on the bus and the right people in the key seats before they figure out where to drive the bus.'

As Paul Dupuis reinforced: 'Attracting the right people to join the organization isn't enough. It is equally important to ensure each person is in a seat where they can shine.' He went on to say: 'Along my journey I discovered that high IQ does not necessarily equate to the highest performers. In fact, the common denominator among the highest performers I've observed is a strong value set, which is in line with the values of the organization and the leader. They value being natural team players, possess the humility to look in the mirror, and when they face a decision and aren't sure which way to go, they ask for help.'

Someone who has coached more leadership teams than most is Graham Alexander, founder, The Alexander Partnership. His perspective for CEOs: 'Co-create a plan that excites the team. It is essential to have a game worth playing for people and to constantly communicate about it to make it real. Be clear about why the team would work for you rather than anyone else. Make sure you develop an exciting, stimulating, purposeful culture at the top of the business.'

Graham recognized that one of the biggest challenges for CEOs is to create great relationships around the executive table. He said: 'It is difficult due to potential conflicts in the business, or personal issues. However, you need to set up the conditions for openness, honesty, support and challenge.'

Graham also advised: 'Figure out if you are going to create an inner team that will deal with certain issues within the business. This can be particularly useful in a crisis, for instance, working closely with the CFO, COO and HRD to move things faster. However, it can create tension with other members of the executive committee, so you need to be clear about why you are doing it and transparent about the process.'

I resonate wholeheartedly with Graham's final words: 'Build a strong executive team with a track record for running and delivering a business and you will succeed.'

> ### CEO NOTE
> Success as CEO is dependent on the quality of your team.
> Make it a priority.

Succession

As CEO one of your immediate objectives coming into role is to identify your successor. Ideally you want to have three potential internal successors whom you champion from your early days on the job. It is rare in my experience to come across CEOs who make this a priority, however it is the right thing to do in order to build a sustainable organization. When I challenge CEOs about why they don't prioritize CEO succession, I get comments about factors such as busyness, perceived lack of capability, readiness and not wanting to create favouritism. However, I suspect there are other concerns at play, including relinquishing control, accelerating the development of others, or risking being challenged for supremacy earlier than intended. Whatever the reason, it is your responsibility to provide robust succession plans for the organization. Doing it from day one in role sends out a powerful message about the importance of developing talent.

Amy Edmondson, Novartis Professor of Leadership and Management, Harvard Business School, takes a strong stand about succession: 'It is simple. As CEO if you don't put sufficient focus and thought into your succession you are not fulfilling one of the most important aspects of the role. The opportunity to develop others and leverage the tacit knowledge, skills and behaviours of existing colleagues usually outweighs the benefits of bringing in someone from the outside. On occasion it is the right thing for the organization to recruit an external successor; however, if this is the case, it is usually the result of failing to build up a robust pipeline and the necessary bench strength for internal succession to occur.'

When I asked Keith Barr, CEO, IHG, about what keeps him awake at night, his response struck a chord: 'How to attract and retain the best talent I need.' He went on to say: 'You cannot deliver the business yourself. To drive sustainable high performance, you need a great team in place, right succession plans and to have the right people in the right roles.'

Keith is deliberate in his approach to developing talent: 'When building your team, be clear about the mix of skills and styles required to be high performing and deliver the strategy. It's important to make the distinction between the jobs that need to be done really well versus having great people and putting them in the job. The job needs to come first. When I restructured the company, I told everyone that their job was at risk as we needed to change the operating model. I started with my top team. We designed the organization first and then put the right people into the roles. Be conscious about your top talent and where they fit in the business. Be methodical about ensuring your top talent go into the top jobs. Do it on a constant basis by understanding where your talent is and how you are going to develop it. Make sure that you have people in jobs who are more talented than their predecessors.'

Andy Mitchell, CEO, Tideway, shared his view on the matter: 'There is a tendency in the project world to bring your old team with you when you move organizations. I made a conscious decision not to do this as it is disempowering for the rest of the company. A CEO needs to recognize the fact that if you surround yourself with people like them, it is unhelpful. It is vital to have a range of disciplines and behaviours in order to have creative tension in the business and to enable neuro-divergent thinking. The blueprint for a high-performing organization is to have diversity even when it's uncomfortable. It's unavoidable to have preferences for people, but the goal is to be effective.'

Andy continued: 'In order to attract, retain and develop a strong talent pool it needs to be based on hard, practical reasons to be diverse and to ensure full representation. I have found that there is a strong argument that people in the organization should rep-resent the society they serve. When leading multi-billion-pound infrastructure projects, the main leadership representation tends to be white, male and older as a result of previous tenure and expe-rience. Therefore, it is important for a CEO to get out of the way. Don't wait for people to prove they have the talent. Give people the opportunity to stretch and grow faster than you did. In my experience very few people intentionally make mistakes. I believe that if you are not making at least two mistakes a year, you are not trying hard enough. Put people in positions where there is a high chance that they can get things wrong and be open-minded when you look at their progression. Give people a chance and keep an eye on them. Your intent is to reach the point where you are not needed any more.'

I found it heartening that every CEO I spoke with prioritized people. Will Stratton-Morris, CEO, Caffè Nero UK, had a clear approach about putting people alongside the strategic direction of the business: 'Alongside developing the plan, it is critical to build the right team around you to execute the strategy. You need to be aware of the many pitfalls that leading people brings. Some businesses have a culture of hiring and firing whereas others have a culture of no firing and accepting mediocrity. My approach is to ensure that I have the right people for the big roles and that I have enough people who could be successors for the CEO role. Whilst assessing people I consider four key criteria:

1. **Intellect**. Having the curiosity and right cognitive capacity to think ahead, problem solve and create innovative solutions.
2. **Energy**. Having the passion and drive to overcome challenges and execute the plan.
3. **Empathy**. Having deep compassion to understand others, appreciate difference and ensure everyone belongs.
4. **Values**. Having a cultural fit through shared values to create a great place to work where everyone can thrive.'

Will went on to say: 'When I spend time interviewing people, I don't waste time revisiting technical qualifications on the CV – instead I look for evidence of these four areas. That's what really matters.'

Paul Dupuis, CEO and Chairman, Randstad Japan, has led organizations across different countries and sectors and arrived at a similar conclusion: 'I have come to realize that what is more important than the service or product you offer is people. A primary mission as CEO is to find your replacement. Make it one of your top priorities to search and raise your successor from within. Look for people who have high potential and demonstrate high performance. I use great conversations as an approach to developing talent, which means that I have ongoing and fluid conversations about people's learning and development. It is vital to keep your finger on the pulse with your leadership team to identify potential successors for every role. Come up with a shared action plan to develop your people. At Randstad we call it the People Review, where we identify successors for every role and commit to an action plan to develop and mentor them.'

Paul gave more perspective about developing talent: 'I do believe that past performance is a predictor of future success.

When someone has a track record of delivering performance, over-coming obstacles and making courageous decisions, it is an indi-cator of future performance. I have found that, typically, people who deliver high performance with impact are consistent. In order to get to the next role, they need to demonstrate the desire to get there along with behaviours aligned with the organization and a reliable track record of performance. An important watch-out is to not push someone into a leadership role against their will. They must have the ambition to take on the role, otherwise they can crumble.'

When I asked Paul about his approach to attracting talent, he shared the following: 'When recruiting it is important to define what a high performer looks like. I believe it is a mixture of char-acter and track record. Find a way to measure attributes through a selection process. When assessing resilience, I ask candidates about their education. On one occasion a candidate described how whilst at university he worked four jobs. His father worked for the gov-ernment, his mother was sick, and they had financial difficulties at home. This individual had to support himself through university. I knew that he had resilience and self-reliance. This approach helps me understand if the candidate has the values to take the business forward. I have found that skills can be learned, however, values are formed in the past. At the end of the day my deciding factor for pulling the trigger on hiring people is a gut feeling. Once you have tested the evidence for performance, I believe it is an instinct based on wisdom and the battle scars of getting your selection right or wrong.'

Mike Mathieson, Chairman, NED, advisor and former founder and CEO, Cake, described his approach to getting succession right: 'Take the time to find the right people to work for you who are differ-ent to you. Initially I created mini versions of me. Hiring people like me led to failure. You need to hire people who are different to you to have the creative friction taking your business to another level. Take the time to hire the right people as when you get it wrong it's a big waste of resource and energy.'

I love the perspective of Javier Echave, CFO, Heathrow, about talent: 'People are born great. The role of a CEO is to remind them how great they are and to create the right environment for them to flourish. Watch out for creating processes and behaviours that cause people to forget how great they are. As CEO you don't have to be the best on every dimension. It is the role of your leadership team to cover all bases. Surround yourself with the best talent to lead and deliver the plan.'

An essential dimension as CEO is to codify your approach to attracting, retaining, developing and deploying talent in order to apply a thoughtful and robust plan. This could include:

- Make talent a key priority. Some CEOs make talent excellence their number one goal. This sends a powerful signal to the company about the importance of creating the right conditions for great talent to thrive, and recognizes that however strong your strategy, unless you have the right people in the right roles to deliver you are at risk of missing your targets.

- Focus your top team on talent. The CEO must ensure that the company has leading-edge analytics software that can help track the progress of key people, and even evaluate the likelihood of success in the next steps on their career paths. Use this data to have talent conversations on a regular basis. In our fast-paced world, relying on one or two structured talent reviews puts you at risk. Talent needs to be discussed on a monthly basis to ensure that you have the right people in the right roles performing at the right level. This also gives visibility and transparency about talent in the organization and helps to build a consistent approach to the talent agenda.

- Engage the Board with the talent agenda. CEOs who prioritize a talent-first organization work with the Board to leverage talent as a strategic differentiator for the company. Although it is difficult for a Board to have direct contact with the top talent in the business, they can make sure that the CEO and top team are held accountable for the recruitment, deployment and development of talent.

- Be a magnet for talent. Be clear about what it takes to become an employer of choice. If you are not in a position to provide financial rewards in the upper quartile, there can be a host of other factors that can make great talent want to join your company and encourage top talent to stay, such as:

o great leadership – provide inspirational, supportive, empowering leadership focused on development

o great company – have meaningful purpose, values and culture within a business that delivers high performance and makes a difference to society

o great roles – create valuable opportunities for growth and progression, with impact and influence

o great rewards – give recognition and benefits that go beyond financial metrics.

- Match talent to key roles. Get the best people into the most important roles. Take a systematic approach to identifying the roles that create the most value and how top talent contributes to the company success. Sometimes key roles are not prominent in the organization chart, yet they are critical to current performance and future growth. Be aware that important roles and performers can sit sometimes two or three layers below the executive committee and identifying them is hugely motivating for employees.

- Act decisively with those who are in key roles and underperform or undermine the company culture. Probably the biggest regret I hear from CEOs is failing to move swiftly on those who do not fit within the organization. The options are to move them out of important roles or exit them out of the business. It is vital to weigh up the potential drain on time, energy and attention given to managing those who are not in the right role, not performing at the right level, or not demonstrating the desired behaviours. The reasons for making changes quickly are, on a practical level, to ensure that the right leaders are in the right roles, and symbolically, to send the right message to the company that what you deliver and how you do it matter.

- Champion learning and development opportunities. With the rapid pace of change and the level of complexity to be navigated, it demands learning in real time to fuel an organization. The learning agenda ranges from longer-term areas like leading sustainable growth (ESG) and creating an environment of belonging (EDI) to shorter-term needs such as technology, digital, data and systems. Set the example by putting learning and development on the agenda for the executive committee. This means that the right mindsets, behaviours and tools are modelled from the top down and creates an inclusive culture where everyone takes ownership for building a better future.

I will give the last word on succession to Keith Barr, CEO, IHG, who offered a powerful sentiment: 'As CEO it is important to know when the right time is to go and to have robust succession plans in place. It is time to go if the following have happened:

- You have lost the vision, or passion for the business.
- You are in a status quo mode.
- You think the company is complete.
- You become complacent.'

Keith continued: 'You need to be driven by the highest levels of self-awareness and insight into the company to make it better. If there is any risk of these diminishing, set your successor up for success.'

CEO NOTE

Identifying and developing your successor demonstrates your commitment to championing talent.

Learning and Development

It was remarkable watching Suzanne in action. Despite her full schedule she would allocate a half-day to prepare her annual performance reviews for each direct report on her executive committee. However, measuring objectives was the smallest part of the conversation. Suzanne spent considerable time reflecting upon the ambition of each direct report, how they were progressing and the key opportunities they could focus on for the forthcoming year. She was very close to both the personal and professional aspirations of each direct report and prepared detailed feedback that covered both areas. The result was that team members thrived and recounted that their performance reviews were a career highlight.

This approach was not an accident. Suzanne had experienced the good, the bad and the ugly of line management. In her varied career she had experienced bosses who were genuinely committed to her success and took precious time to care. They sought to understand what success looked like for Suzanne both at work and in her life. They supported and challenged her in a way that brought out the best in her. They accelerated her career progression, giving her stretching opportunities to demonstrate her capability, and on one occasion protected her during her first maternity leave. Suzanne also had line managers who used her for their own gain, showing little regard for her career and wellbeing. Conversations were about task. Any reference to personal, leadership or career development was simply a tick-in-the-box activity. In one case the line manager made it perfectly clear that they had no interest in Suzanne's progression. In fact, they saw her as a threat and made her well aware of the fact that she would not be moving ahead unless it was 'over their dead body'.

As a consequence, Suzanne made a personal vow that if she made it to CEO, investing in her people would be a top priority. She started the process ahead of commencing her first CEO role. Suzanne requested a week's immersion in her new company before her official time in office. She scheduled one-to-one sessions with each direct report in which she asked for their views across a range of topics about the business strategy, organizational capability, talent and culture. She also took the opportunity to lay the foundations for meaningful development conversations. Suzanne asked each direct report to reflect upon their ideal vision, what great looked like for them in five years, both personally and professionally, and how she could help. She recognized that this would probably be unnerving for some, but she wanted to set the tone for how she would continue.

Suzanne led by example, sharing her own vision about what was most important for her, including obvious areas like growing the business, beating the plan, improving capability, as well as her passion projects including developing next-generational talent and being the best boss possible. With this in mind she wanted to understand how she could help her direct reports fulfil their potential. She created a psychological contract with them that a core part of her role was to champion their careers and lives where appropriate, and in return they would be transparent with her about their aspirations and concerns if they were not thriving in the company. Suzanne had one member who showed visible resistance to this approach. In her disarming way she inquired about the apparent scepticism. The team member explained that Suzanne's predecessor had little interest in their development, so it was an unusual first meeting, but they welcomed the change in approach.

Suzanne wanted to demonstrate her meaningful commitment to their development and followed up her initial conversation by dividing her first one-to-one meetings in the business between task and development. She asked each direct report to explain how they liked to be led and what engaged them from a development perspective. As expected, Suzanne received a variety of responses. Some preferred a formal approach including an annual deep dive to define and align on a meaningful development plan covering personal, leadership and career focus areas accompanied by milestones with a trackable action plan. Others preferred a more relaxed way by agreeing a key theme, which they would develop through mentoring conversations. Suzanne adapted her style accordingly. She then put development on the monthly executive committee agenda. This time was dedicated to progressing their collective understanding and approach to igniting and driving development within the business. Team members were initially uncomfortable with these conversations as they didn't appear to drive immediate decisions or actions. However, what emerged was a collective commitment to being a genuine learning organization where personal, leadership and career development was institutionalized and linked clearly with the progression and delivery of the strategic plan.

Each CEO I spoke with had their own unique experience of development, but there was no doubt that they shared common ground about the impact of learning and that their careers had been super-charged through multiple development opportunities and, as a result, they were committed to accelerating others' development. Amber Asher, CEO, Standard International, shared: 'My background as general counsel in the organization enabled me to interact with every department and develop a view about what worked and what needed improvement, which definitely prepared me for the role of CEO.'

She went on to say: 'It is critical to have a business mindset to deeply understand the organization, what makes it tick and where it can fail. As a consequence, having multiple experiences is a great help as CEO. My background in finance, strategy and general counsel, as well as being in a broader role as company president, gave me the required experience to become CEO.'

Viviane Paxinos, CEO, AllBright, fast tracked her success through an insatiable appetite to learn and grow: 'I have always had a passion for understanding all parts of business. I had high curiosity about what drove customers, consumers and different parts of a business. I developed my personal brand on being helpful, bringing people together and learning something new every day, which enabled me to acquire great organizational breadth, including product, technology, data, performance, marketing, finance, as well as my core skills of sales and marketing. I was always very open about wanting to be a CEO and believe that we shouldn't shy away from our ambition.'

As CEO of a global career network, Viviane is a personal advocate of blending your network with learning: 'It's important to nurture your CEO network. Find other first-time CEOs to develop a network where you can connect, share challenges and learn from each other. It can be isolating as a CEO, so having a broad and deep network is essential, as well as having an executive coach for support.'

Jonathan Akeroyd, CEO, Burberry, was also passionate about the importance of learning and development, both on a personal and an organizational level: 'It is vital to keep challenging yourself to grow. I took the role at Burberry to learn more. Coming into a bigger organization provided the opportunity for growth. Watch out for getting stale. You need new challenges to keep your energy levels up.' He went on to say: 'Organizations need to provide the workforce with clear pathways to grow in the company, which goes beyond financial reward. Make sure learning and development opportunities are in place to support employees to continuously improve.'

Helen Tupper, CEO, Amazing If, made a direct link between learning and success: 'You cannot afford to be a static CEO. The world is changing. Everything is evolving all the time. To be a successful CEO you need to be a successful learner. You need to create a learning culture for the company. You need to be learning as much as you are leading.'

Emma Gilthorpe, COO, Heathrow, reinforced this perspective: 'It takes time to ready yourself to be a CEO. The organic approach that many take is to give your best in every role, then most of the time you will build a reputation second to none. With that in mind it's important to be thoughtful about what you take on, balancing what's in it for you with what's in it for the business. Think beyond task to what are you going to learn, how is it going to broaden your experience and demonstrate new skills, and what you can give in the role to propel the business forward. Figure out the roles where you can outperform and then run hard with every opportunity. When something doesn't feel like a fit, listen to your instincts so you own and drive your career.'

Emma reflected: 'In the past people were bred to be CEOs and the path would have been laid way in advance. In today's world a good CEO has built up a range of experiences along the way in different contexts, with diverse challenges, successes and failings. It is the collective endeavour of your career that gives you the breadth of judgement to help you succeed. To become a CEO, luck and patience play an important role. Grab a CEO role which is not right and you will crash and burn. And sometimes great leaders can be overlooked for CEO because they hang on too long in a support role. You need a healthy dose of luck and patience combined with having excellent judgement about people, decision making and context.'

Justin Basini, CEO and co-founder, ClearScore, paints a compelling picture about the importance of championing development in a business: 'My founding belief about people is that it is our human right to achieve our potential. We are given a set of skills and talents, and in the right environment those skills and talents can do anything. My responsibility as CEO is to create an environment where people can succeed. One of the main challenges is to help them understand their self-limiting beliefs and to unleash their true potential. I ensure that leaders in the business use this type of language and have the right conversations to make this happen, which is relatively unusual in business.'

Justin takes a very broad view to development and breaks down barriers between work and life. He went on to say: 'I believe it is essential to take the whole person very seriously. In the business we might only see someone 8–10 hours in a day, however it's important to recognize the full 24 hours we all have. I don't believe in work–life balance. We have 24 hours in a day and everyone has their own scorecard of what they want to achieve across a day, week, month, year and decade, such as getting a promotion, singing a song, looking after a parent, attracting a partner or having a family. The modern workplace needs to understand that work is a part of life.

'As a CEO you need to create an environment where people can tick more of those boxes than elsewhere. I used to work in banking and the scorecard was simply to get to work before your boss and to leave after they left. My approach is to recognize that as long as a colleague gets their work done, I don't care where they do their job or how they do it. We are clear about the mission and objectives to deliver, but if people can do their work in their preferred time, good for them! It might mean that the business gives them a few more objectives to deliver, but flexibility allows people to feel better about ticking boxes on a balanced basis. We have people who choose to take their kids to school in the morning or exercise in the day. Trusting people and giving them the autonomy to thrive is an effective route for them to succeed more.'

Paul Dupuis, CEO and Chairman, Randstad Japan, has made it his mission to embed development into the organization. 'Create a culture where people aim to be better than yesterday. This starts with a mindset that reflects the intent, "Let's be better than yesterday." In order to make this happen it is essential to create the environment where ambitious people can feel part of a movement to be better. As a CEO you must prioritize learning and development. You need to generate a learning environment and allocate resource to it. For instance, taking learning and development from a lower priority to a top priority. Once you have defined the strategic direction for learning and development, set measurable goals about how many people will be attending the programmes and how they will perform as a result. Leverage the learning. Look for high potentials to be developed and turn them into growth opportunities.'

It is essential to have an informed and broad view about the role and return on investing in personal, career and leadership development. Research from the employee experience platform Culture Amp, conducted in the midst of the Great Resignation, with over 100,000 employees who exited companies between January and August 2021, showed that 'a lack of growth (in their career or development opportunities) was selected by one in three employees as a top reason for leaving at the time of exit'.

Having supported CEOs and organizations for nearly 30 years in the world of development, I believe that best practice for a company is to drive one primary collective development area each year championed by the CEO and executive committee. When John Holland-Kaye, CEO, Heathrow, started in role he was a passionate advocate for a leadership and cultural development programme entitled 'Leading with Purpose and Values', which I had co-created with Paula Stannett, Chief People Officer, and her team. The organization had shifted its cultural identity from infrastructure, where they invested several billion pounds each year in operating, building, maintaining and expanding infrastructure systems, to a service company, where they redefined their vision: 'To give passengers the best airport service in the world.'

The programme was influenced by John's personal experience: 'I have got the most out of work where my values have been aligned with the company I'm working with. On the other hand, I have found the most stressful times at work have occurred when my values were challenged by the organization. I appreciate that when you're working in a company it's harder to align personal and organizational values because you don't set the agenda, but it's often a deal breaker if they are too at odds. One of the priorities I have always set whilst working on executive committees, and now as a CEO, is to utilize the opportunity to shape the company values in order to create strong alignment with the people I work with, which makes work far more enjoyable. You can also get a sense of real achievement in terms of what matters beyond financial reward.'

John also recognized the significance of learning and development: 'My parents were both teachers and as a result I grew up in schools 24/7. One thing I learned is how education is a great leveller and allows people to fulfil their potential. In one of the first companies I worked for, the people who did the best were not necessarily those who went to the "top" schools. However, work gave them the opportunity to fulfil their potential which had not been nurtured by our educational system. I came to believe that it doesn't matter where you have come from because what matters is where you are going. It shaped my belief that my primary role is to help people unlock their talent and to achieve where they want to go.'

In order to design 'Leading with Purpose and Values' we engaged a cross-functional group of high-potential leaders in the organization who tested the ideas and approach. It was agreed that the programme should take people on a personal journey of self-discovery, as well as providing the opportunity to enhance leadership skills and the cultural climate. We piloted the programme with John and his executive committee, which accelerated the formation of his team, as well as ensuring that they could apply their learning back in the business and set the tone for the company. Over the next few years, every colleague had the opportunity to attend a version of the programme and make an authentic connection between their own sense of purpose and values and Heathrow. The emphasis placed on leading and working with purpose and values infiltrated the organizational system, including recruitment, onboarding, performance management and skills-based training, and was measured by the company's participation in Great Place To Work, as well as its internal employee engagement survey.

As well as aligning leadership and cultural expectations through development, one of the other key areas to address as CEO is the quality of line management. Research from the global analytics and advice firm Gallup states: 'The quality of a manager accounts for 70 per cent of the variance in team engagement.' The research goes on to say that poor line management is one of the main reasons employees don't leave companies, they leave managers.

Joel Burrows, CEO, Ghirardelli, believes strongly in the impact of line manager excellence and is championing the company to focus on continuously improving the quality of its management. Joel recognizes that great managers help to connect every part of the business, from purpose to performance to wellbeing. He has monthly one-to-ones with his direct reports in which he combines a mix of leading, managing and coaching in order to meet people's needs. Joel shared: 'Be conscious about what you're doing. I like to see how people have evolved, as well as managing the checklist. However, my drive is to only do the things I can do in order to have the right conversations focused on what's important, not urgent. If there isn't a burning platform, then I ensure we are able to have the conversations about the critical success factors for the long term and make sure we are setting up the conditions to deliver. Sometimes you are required to seek more clarity in the short term, otherwise I find people appreciate having meaningful conversations about the future and developing a shared understanding about how to get there.'

At the end of the day the majority of CEOs I speak with say that delivering the numbers and achieving big targets fade into the distance, but what is always constant is the impact of making a tangible difference in people's lives. Sophie Moloney, CEO, Sky New Zealand, captured this sentiment in our conversation: 'There is a real magic in asking great questions. When you ask a great question and truly listen, it's amazing what you can unlock. As CEO, recognize that you don't have all the answers and don't think for a second that you need to. When things don't feel quite right probe more. Ultimately, learn to be yourself with more skill, which will help others along the way.'

One of the greatest privileges and responsibilities as CEO is the value you can add by helping to develop others. Whether you do this directly through your own provision of leadership, management, coaching and mentorship, or more widely through ensuring the organization allocates sufficient resource and time to development activities, it lies at the heart of building a sustainable organization. I will leave the final word on the strategic impact of creating a culture of learning and development to Amy Edmondson, Novartis Professor of Leadership and Management, Harvard Business School: 'For a CEO to set the example for lifelong learning and development, what matters is to combine high levels of self-awareness about how they show up and the impact they have on others with the required depth of expertise to navigate the challenges of the industry. This means continuously progressing their general knowledge about strategy, organizational capability and financial requirements which lead to excellent decision making. The combination of developing technical and personal skills cannot be overstated.'

CEO NOTE

Champion learning and development as a fundamental
ingredient of your leadership agenda.

Be a Connoisseur of Talent:
Exec Summary

- Teaming: your success is dependent on the success of your team. Build the right team. Develop an exciting strategy together. Get out of the way and let them deliver.
- Succession: one of your key priorities is to identify and develop at least two successors. Be bold. Challenge yourself to align with your chair and Board about who can replace you and invest in their growth.
- Learning and development: create a genuine learning organization by embedding learning into the strategy. Recognize that in order to deliver a stretching plan, everyone will need to build the right capability to perform.

CHAPTER 6

Be an Architect of Culture

• • •

Climate

London has relied on a 150-year-old sewer system for a population less than half its current size. As a result, millions of tonnes of
raw sewage spills, untreated, enter into the River Thames each year.
Tideway is building a 25km Super Sewer under the Thames to inter-
cept these nasty spills and clean up the river for the good of the city,
its wildlife and people. If you were responsible for delivering such a
challenging project, you might be tempted to get immersed in the
technical requirements and spend the majority of your time solving
problems. However, Tideway's CEO, Andy Mitchell, takes a different view. In our conversation he said: 'As CEO your main responsibility is to be the architect of the organizational culture. Therefore,
it is vital to understand the culture in which you are leading, both in
terms of the external environment as well as your internal corporate
culture. It is valuable to bring and retain an independent point of
view in order to be most effective.'

Andy went on to say: 'At Tideway it was like a start-up. We had
a clean sheet of paper with no past baggage, therefore we had the
opportunity to develop and evolve our own culture. It was a great
opportunity to say: "how do we create the Tideway approach", and
to define how we behave rather than have written-down values.
I saw huge passion for the project to clean up the River Thames,
which went beyond a focus on engineering. However, the language
being used had its origins in legal or technical engineering speak,
rather than the emotional language that existed behind our passion.

I suggested that we explore questions like, "If you heard people talking about Tideway in the pub, what would you want them to say?" And, "If this was the best company in the world, how would it be?" The development of our culture focused on our lost love affair with the River Thames. We tapped into the emotion about what we are doing. For instance, we looked at why we no longer see people fishing in the river. The challenge was to go beyond our engineering capability to have the right conversations about how we do things, not what we do. This curiosity has underwritten everything we do and is at the heart of how we present the company now.'

Andy concluded: 'As CEO I recognize that I am the most influential person shaping the corporate culture, which in the case of Tideway is about looking after the emotional health of the company and how we can all be fit, healthy and creative as an organization. On a personal note, as an engineer I found that the more I spoke in emotive language, the more it helped me connect with others and feel authentic.'

Culture is simply described as 'the way things are done around here', which translates into the unique way that your organization lives out its company purpose and delivers on its brand promise to customers. Culture can appear intangible, yet a great company culture is a competitive differentiator for attracting, retaining and developing talent, as well as being a magnet for attracting customers and turning them into brand advocates. Culture can be measured in multiple ways, such as:

- Surveys: cultural surveys are a great tool to get honest feedback from your entire workforce. Most companies run periodic engagement surveys using internal indicators which help to understand overall employee sentiment and highlight any trends or issues that need to be addressed. It can also be valuable to use external surveys such as Great Place To Work certification, which uses a research-driven Trust Index™ to show what makes your workplace unique.

- Key performance indicators: an organization needs to correctly identify, measure and regularly monitor the company culture's relationship to key performance indicators such as safety, innovation, quality, revenue, profit, efficiency, diversity and inclusion, absenteeism, promotions, environment, sustainability and governance.

- Anecdotes: pay attention to anecdotal feedback to uncover patterns or common themes, for instance from exit interviews, Glassdoor reviews and social media posts. As CEO you can also set up a direct feedback loop where employees are invited to share feedback with you on an informal basis, either electronically or directly in writing.

- Tracking behaviours: there are different tools that can be used to understand the prevalence of the behaviours associated with the company values, which can be a useful indicator of your culture's strength. For instance, if ownership is one of your values, with associated behaviours like doing what you say you'll do and not walking past problems, you can ask managers and team leads to report on the frequency of colleagues taking ownership in the business. You can also use tools like Culture Amp, Humu and TINYpulse to increase communication and transparency, and improve and measure culture.

On one occasion I was coaching a CEO who, even before starting in role, could sense the complacency in the business. Originally the company had been number one in its sector for service, quality and efficiency. Growing from a family business it had a loyal customer base who went out of their way to shop with them. The larger the business became, the greater the disconnect became from its original values and ways of doing business. For instance, the company used to have a strong partnership with suppliers where trust played a big role in working together. This relationship had eroded to such an extent that during a recent economic downturn the company tightened the rope with suppliers, causing many to go out of business. Employees used to work across the organization, willingly leaning into company issues to solve rather than staying stuck in siloes which had emerged, causing bottlenecks to getting stuff done.

The CEO recognized the idea that culture is an outcome of leadership and in order to change the culture they needed to change the way the company was led. With this in mind I was engaged with a team of coaches to deliver a cultural development programme to build the right leadership capability to turn the business around. This involved a series of stages, including:

1. Conducting a deep-dive set of diagnostic interviews with the top 50 leaders in the business to get under the skin of what was going on culturally, what great looked like and what it would take to get there.
2. Redefining what great leadership looked like in the business and setting clear expectations about the desired behaviours to demonstrate.
3. Refreshing the company values to make them relevant and aligned with the leadership expectations.
4. Aligning the leadership behaviours and values with the company strategy, including the purpose, vision, priorities and key performance metrics.

The company formed an internal steering group to guide the work and act as a conscience for the business. We worked in partnership with the steering group, which was an essential element, to ensure all ideas had the best chance of working. At the outset we had a regular slot at the executive committee monthly strategy meeting to give the work the right priority and profile. The CEO took personal accountability for the programme and kept up a consistent narrative to the organization about each stage of the work to ensure visibility and buy-in. We involved colleagues to test all ideas and made changes to reflect the feedback.

Expectations grew. Energy increased. Eventually the company launched a new goal, values and set of leadership behaviours to help make the company great again. We delivered a leadership development programme for all 1,000 people managers in the business, designed to provide the opportunity to understand expectations and what it would take personally and collectively to make it happen. The CEO and executive committee set the tone by attending the first programme and then collectively ensured that they had presence at each programme going forward. What emerged out of the programme was an aligned set of expectations about the intended behaviours to reset the culture, such as taking initiative, working together and owning it, as shown in Table 6.1.

TABLE 6.1   JOINT PICTURE FOR GOING FORWARD

Take initiative	Work together	Own it
• Define common goals together for the good of the business. • Use the customer lens as the driver for high performance. • Consistently seek to improve shared services.	• Rebuild trust between the organizations. • Commit to being a partner of choice based on close collaboration. • Leave the legacy contract behind so that it is not referenced at every meeting.	• Ensure projects and deliverables are on time and on budget. • Have visibility and transparency of projects. • Recognize and reinforce great performance.

The CFO set a great challenge for everyone – to do one thing better every day to improve the culture. They saw the opportunity in having 1,000 managers taking personal accountability for the culture going forward and the ripple effect it would have across the company.

The company set up 'success walls' around the office where colleagues posted stories and examples of the improvements being made to build momentum. The refreshed strategy was referenced in every main leadership meeting, including both the 'what' (priorities, metrics) and the 'how' (values and behaviours). These were reinforced in one-to-one meetings where people managers had meaningful conversations with direct reports about how they were working to deliver the agenda, not just what they were doing. 'Shout-outs' were added to team meetings where evidence of the desired behaviours were recognized and celebrated. The changes in the internal culture soon began to spread externally. Meetings were set up with existing suppliers to reset relationships and to explore what it would mean to take initiative, work together and own stuff together. Behavioural charters were set up with new suppliers and included in contracts to give equal weighting to 'what' and 'how'.

As part of the rebuild with suppliers, I was asked to facilitate a workshop to help navigate a particularly difficult supplier relationship which was having a major impact on the overall culture. There was a legacy contract in place which no longer served either party, however it had to be fulfilled. I set up a strong psychological contract at the start of the session to ensure an aligned learning mindset was in place to allow the right conversations to be held. I gave equal time to both parties to share their experience of the working relationship, to challenge each other's perspective and ultimately to reset the relationship. There were some high-tension moments, however I asked each side to play back what they were hearing to ensure no assumptions were made and to deepen empathy. What emerged was a good intent from both sides, which had been diluted by years of mistrust and frustration. We now had sufficient goodwill to rebuild the partnership going forward. Focusing on what a great culture would look like evidenced by shared behaviours, we created a new joint picture of how they were going to work together going forward.

The CEO socialized the cultural change with the chairman and Board. Updates were made on a quarterly basis and made their way into the annual report to strengthen the importance of having the right culture to deliver the plan.

Mike Mathieson, Chairman, NED, advisor and former founder and CEO, Cake, is a passionate advocate for culture. He shared: 'Early on in my career I had the good fortune to work for Richard Branson. One thing I learned was his ability to build a brilliant team and culture. He had a work hard, play hard approach. Building a strong culture means people will go the extra mile for you every time. One way of doing this is to celebrate success. As CEO, if we won a pitch, I made sure it was a moment to remember. Celebrating success brings a team together and breeds a culture of success.'

As CEO it is vital to stay closely connected to the culture as there is a risk people only bring you what they think you want to hear. Mike had a clear way of managing this risk: 'As a CEO you can get removed from the day-to-day running of the business through the inevitable hierarchy which can get destructive to the culture.

In order to make sure I stayed highly connected to the "shop floor" each week, I scheduled time to walk the floors. I made it my business to get around the building saying hello, checking in with people and asking what was going on. I would also do it in an evening to check in with people who were still in the office to understand what they were doing and to make sure they had what they needed. On occasion if a team was pulling an all-nighter I would be there with the troops, which gave me a valuable pulse check about the organizational climate and sent a powerful message to everyone about how much I cared.

BlackRock is the world's largest asset manager, with $10 trillion in assets under management as of January 2022. Each year Larry Fink, CEO, BlackRock, writes an annual letter to CEOs on behalf of BlackRock's clients, who are shareholders in their companies. In his 2022 letter entitled 'The power of capitalism', Larry Fink writes: 'When my partners and I founded BlackRock as a start-up 34 years ago, I had no experience running a company. Over the past three decades, I've had the opportunity to talk with countless CEOs and to learn what distinguishes truly great companies. Time and again, what they all share is that they have a clear sense of purpose; consistent values; and, crucially, they recognize the importance of engaging with and delivering for their key stakeholders. This is the foundation of stakeholder capitalism.'

Consider having a culture based on a clear sense of purpose, consistent values, engaging with and delivering for key stakeholders. This is a simple and powerful way of thinking about what is at the heart of a great culture and translates as 'the way things are done around here'.

Being deliberate about the way things are done around here is vital to the success of a CEO. Amy Edmondson, Novartis Professor of Leadership and Management, Harvard Business School, stated: 'CEOs have an outsized impact on the company culture. It comes with the territory, as the more visible you are, the more your behaviour and words influence the sense-making of others. People will consciously and tacitly size up what works around here, including how to get ahead and learn to do what the cool kids do! As CEO you cast a large shadow, therefore it is part of your responsibility to be aware of your intentions and impact. The best CEOs are interested in knowing the impact they have on others and seek the relevant data through feedback to make sure their good intentions do not get lost in translation.'

In my conversation with Viviane Paxinos, CEO, AllBright, she echoed the impact of your actions: 'People act as you act. As a CEO, recognize that everything you do, even off the job, is an expression of your values and influences others. In a start-up culture it is really important to act in a certain way to set expectations. If you have someone who is not in sync with the company values, it will have a big impact on the culture and you need to act accordingly.'

Wim Dejonghe, Senior Partner, Allen & Overy LLP, is clear about his role and impact on culture: 'My role is to be the guardian of the business and the culture. I need to leave it in a better place and the next generation of leaders need to do a better job than me so that we continue to improve our global platform.'

The significance of the CEO's role on culture was highlighted by Emma Gilthorpe, COO, Heathrow: 'Spend time on what really matters to your business and you. For instance, if you say safety matters and you're not doing a safety walk every month, what signal does that send? If you say diversity and inclusion matters but you're not taking visible personal action to improve equity, how credible is that? Decide what you want to champion that is critical to the business, its culture and values and be resolute and consistent in how you drive it.'

Joel Burrows, CEO, Ghirardelli, echoed the sentiments about the impact of a CEO on culture: 'We live in a world where leading with humanity in the workplace is the fundamental ingredient to create the right environment for people where they can be engaged and resourced to perform at their best. I have found that actions speak louder than words. You need to lead by example, which means that whatever you say you must follow up with action. Focus on being a good human. Be clear on your own purpose in terms of what drives you and gives you energy. On a personal note, what's important to me is to help people be at their best and to have real relationships. This means that I put a lot of attention on making sure that colleagues are enjoying being in the company we are co-creating, which helps improve the culture and motivates me going forward.'

These points were reinforced by Graham Alexander, coach to CEOs and founder of The Alexander Partnership: 'A CEO is the role model for the culture. You have to live what you want in the business. If you want a culture of openness and honesty, you have to live it. Everything you say and do is interpreted in the business. If you are out of sync with what you want in the culture, you will be in trouble. Remember, as CEO you cast a big shadow.'

Graham continued: 'If you are coming in as a new CEO, find out about the existing culture. Once you have defined where you want to take the business – own the culture or change it so that the culture is fit to deliver the strategy. It will be individual to each business. A culture consisting of high pace and action may be inappropriate for some businesses which require a slower burn and more cerebral way of working.'

As the pandemic eases and organizations continue to recover from the aftermath of Covid, CEOs need to assess how their culture has changed. The global lockdown and travel bans have upended assumptions about the nature of work and corporate interactions. People have discovered that they don't have to be in an office, that they can get most things done remotely. They do not need to commute to work.

Stephen McCall, CEO, edyn, shared some of the impact from his viewpoint: 'From a cultural perspective we want to create a human company. We try to provide guidelines and principles rather than rules and regulations. We championed flexible working long before Covid made it the norm. We have tried to keep our structure flat and non-hierarchical, and have stressed the value of relationship in role effectiveness over deferred authority or decision rights. This has helped us to stay flexible, adaptable and informal but there is a cost – a degree of somewhat organized chaos, which is fine for those comfortable with ambiguity, but perhaps less so for those who are not. We ensure that our people are ready for this, for instance making cultural orientation a priority in our approach to recruitment. If you foster a culture where you are encouraging everyone to be curious, you have to expect that meetings can take longer and decisions can be harder to make. You have to be prepared to take the downside with the upside.'

> ## CEO NOTE
>
> The way you lead determines the way things are done around you. Be deliberate about the example you set.

Relationship

Business is relationship. The quality of relationships determines the quality of business. You can have a great strategic plan, organizational capability and talent, however in the absence of having great relationships with multiple stakeholder groups you will either fail to deliver superior performance or it will be an uphill battle. I would go as far as saying that the primary responsibility of a CEO is to build great relationships, out of which all the other requirements to develop a sustainable organization follow.

One CEO who goes out of their way to invest in relationship is Will Stratton-Morris, CEO, Caffè Nero UK. In our conversation he shared his rationale: 'As a CEO you need to be passionate about building relationship at every level in the organization, and externally. If you are not interested in people, it makes it really hard to run a business. I had a supplier share recently that they would have given up their business during Covid as it was so challenging, but it was the quality of our relationship which helped sustain them. On one occasion I learned an important lesson about investing in relationship. I led two teams who worked in the same office. They were situated in different parts of the office, and it just so happened that the kitchen and bathroom area were closer to one team than the other. For some time, I used the amenities and engaged with the team closest to them without consciously thinking about the impact on the other team. I had Ben facilitate a team-building workshop for both teams and what emerged in a feedback exercise was that the team further way from the amenities felt neglected by my actions. It was a significant moment for me to learn how to deliberately use office space – from entering the building, to riding in the elevator, to walking the floors in order to connect with colleagues and build relationship in real time. This really pays off when times get tough, and people understand you care. Make sure that the passion for people doesn't get squeezed out due to task.'

CEOs who prioritize relationships form genuine partnerships with diverse groups of people, internally and externally, seemingly without effort. They tend to have an infectious quality that evokes trust and good will. They have an ability to create followership which becomes a great asset for the business. CEOs with this skill have an intense curiosity about people. They spark up meaningful conversations every day by asking questions of the multiple people they meet and listen carefully to the answers. They remember personal points about people's work and lives which they can recall to powerful effect.

Steve was one of the most loved CEOs I have had the privilege to encounter. I use the word 'love' deliberately as everyone who encountered him had a personal reference based on a meaningful connection they had made with him, including colleagues, customers, consumers and shareholders. Even analysts warmed to his personable style. These connections often turned into long-lasting working partnerships and, on occasion, friendship. I was fortunate to deliver a leadership development programme in Steve's company. He would always join for an intimate 'fireside' chat with participants. Despite his full schedule Steve always showed up prepared. He had done his homework to understand who would be attending, what role they had in the company and a recent accomplishment they had delivered. Steve was an open book. He would start each chat by going around the group, referencing people's roles and achievements and inviting everyone to ask him any question, personal or professional. We would then be enthralled by his ability to share relevant stories, weaving in the questions as he went. Nothing went unanswered. On one occasion Steve was asked how he spent his time. His immediate response was to say, 'I do nothing.' He went on to elaborate that he believed his greatest value to the company was to build relationship, both internally and externally. Given Steve's natural propensity to being relational, this in his mind equated to 'doing nothing'. I would add that he had mastered the art of 'doing nothing with style'. Given Steve was leading a company with several hundred thousand colleagues and myriad stakeholders, he orchestrated his relationship building in very intentional ways to maximize everyone's time and have the biggest impact for the organization.

Focusing heavily on relationship is not every CEO's preference. However, as a CEO you need to have a strategic approach to relationships that adds value, particularly in this age where factors like building high psychological safety and creating a deep sense of belonging are fundamental requirements for a high-performing organization. You cannot afford to leave it to chance. One way of looking at the value of relationship is social capital – which in an organizational context is defined as the presence of networks, relationships, shared norms and trust among colleagues, teams and leaders, acting as the glue that holds the company together. Research by McKinsey on social capital shows that 'employees who feel more connected with people in their networks are two times more likely than those who feel less connected to report higher levels of sponsorship (or advocacy from a senior leader or colleague for their career advancements), and one and a half times more likely to report a sense of belonging at work, and one and a half times more likely to report being engaged at work'.

One of the most effective ways to build social capital across an organization is a company conference. I often see a conflict in companies where the CEO sees the conference as an investment, whereas the CFO clocks it as an expense. I would say that the days of blowing the company budget on a conference are virtually over, and there is no need. Simply the act of bringing people together and creating the environment where they can get to know each other is significant enough without having to go over the top! Joel Burrows, CEO, Ghirardelli, is a great believer in the value of building social capital across his extended senior leadership team, knowing the ripple effect it will have back in the business. He schedules two events each year in different locations and combines an effective mix of strategy, collaboration and fun. Joel spends initial time with his executive committee to clarify and align on the company strategic plan. Precious time is then spent in cross-functional working groups with his broader senior leadership team, understanding and challenging the plan. Joel champions purpose-led leadership and encourages relationships to be built on an understanding of people's deepest motivations, as well as scheduling sufficient social time for relationships to be built, knowing that it will strengthen collaboration back in the business.

Since the global pandemic there is a clear intent from CEOs to prioritize meeting in person, with the awareness that not everyone is going to feel comfortable travelling and mixing; however, contingency measures are put in place to ensure everyone has a sense of belonging. One CEO I coach places a high emphasis on relationship and ensures her executive committee meet on a quarterly basis, focusing with an equal mix on strategy and relationship. One of the primary tools they use to strengthen relationship is feedback. There is sufficient trust and understanding within the team to give and receive meaningful feedback, which makes a big investment in their relationship. The feedback can revolve around the creation or delivery of the strategic plan, or it can be behavioural focused on the company values, or the experience they have working together.

Relationships are like emotional bank accounts. It is essential to make deposits on a regular basis, which as a CEO has high leverage and could include:

- checking in regularly
- listening to understand
- asking reflective questions
- demonstrating objective empathy
- helping solve problems
- sponsoring career development
- making personal introductions
- providing recognition
- nurturing wellbeing
- supporting non-work aspirations.

Jeff Weiner, Executive Chairman at LinkedIn, demonstrates a high relational orientation, which is very appropriate when you have grown one of the world's largest business-related social networking websites. In a popular speech he gave at Wharton's graduation ceremony in May 2018, Weiner states how compassion builds better companies and that it's hard to make better decisions faster when a company's culture lacks trust and empathy. In Weiner's own words: 'I vowed that as long as I'd be responsible for managing other people, I would aspire to manage compassionately. That meant pausing and being a spectator to my own thoughts, especially when getting emotional. It meant walking a mile in the other person's shoes, and understanding their hopes, their fears, their strengths and their weaknesses. And it meant doing everything within my power to set them up to be successful.' He went on to say: 'I've now been practising this approach for well over a decade. And I can tell you with absolute conviction that managing compassionately is not just a better way to build a team, it's a better way to build a company.'

Great Place To Work has an extremely rigorous, data-based model for quantifying employee experience based on surveys with more than 100 million employees around the world. They have used those deep insights to define what makes a great workplace: trust. Within their Trust Model there are some important relational traits, including respect and camaraderie. It is nigh on impossible to build an effective relationship without respect. Given our wide range of differences, I don't believe it is possible or realistic to expect that you will like everyone at work. However, respect is about the appreciation of someone's ability, qualities or achievements. I observe that once a CEO has lost respect for an employee in the business, their tenure can be short-lived unless they are able to navigate a swift turnaround.

Stuart was a visionary chief information officer. He saw the big picture and was an effective communicator, generating excitement about the art of the possible. He was a popular figure and admired in the industry. However, he failed to deliver on the CEO's expectations and despite clear requests from the CEO about what was needed, performance did not improve. What was more significant than the actual results was the CIO's inability to be upfront and transparent with the CEO about delivery issues, which the CEO interpreted as a lack of respect. Unfortunately, once the respect eroded there was no turning back.

It is the CEO's responsibility to lay out clear expectations in order to manage relationships effectively. There is a useful model to remember about how to manage expectations:

Appreciation

Familiarity

Expectations

Disappointment

Grievance

Being right

Figure 6.1 Managing expectations

The model works in the way shown in Table 6.2

TABLE 6.2 HOW THE MODEL WORKS

Appreciation	At the outset in a relationship there can be mutual appreciation. This is often influenced by reputation or first impressions. A CEO needs to be mindful about the information they are given about people as not everyone operates with an objective agenda and can try to influence a CEO in biased ways.
Familiarity	After a period of time a relationship reaches a comfort zone. A CEO has to watch out for how behaviours show up at this stage as guards can come down and unconscious bias can be demonstrated.

(Continued)

TABLE 6.3 (*CONTINUED*)

Expectations	Many expectations in relationships are not communicated and therefore not met. It is a CEO's responsibility to set out clear expectations across multiple dimensions, including attitude, behaviours, performance and contribution. Effective relationships are the result of expectation management.
Disappointment	A CEO needs to recognize that if expectations have not been met, frustration can set in. Before acting on frustration, a CEO needs to understand if it was the genuine intent of someone to cause disappointment or an unintended consequence of mismanaged expectations.
Grievance	No one is perfect. Everyone has strengths and weaknesses. A CEO needs to adopt a clear approach to relationship management, otherwise it is all too common to write people off as incompetent, or not being the right fit, without having all the facts or sufficient understanding.
Being right	Watch out for having blinkered vision and wanting to be 'right'. A CEO must possess high self-awareness to manage their own triggers. Once the amygdala (the integrative centre for emotions and emotional behaviour in the brain) has been activated, it is vital to stay objective and fact based in relationships.

It is possible to move back up the sequence through expectation management. A relationship is a psychological contract. Make sure you lay out your dos and don'ts so that people understand your expectations and can navigate them accordingly.

I resonate with the sentiment of Andy Mitchell, CEO, Tideway, who as an engineer demonstrates an objective point of view about people: 'People want to do a good job and to see how good they are. Create safe environments where people can dare to be themselves. Help them make decisions that are important to them, with a clearly held view about how you do things around here. Make sure that they have the right technical competence and are empowered to do a great job. Very few people have the lack of competence to make critical mistakes.'

If as CEO you have taken these steps, built a strong relationship and someone chooses not to maximize the opportunity you have provided, then it is understandable that respect may no longer be present.

In terms of camaraderie, I would like to reference a quote from my last book, *LoveWork*, where my co-author Sophie Devonshire and I suggested that our ability to feel good about our work is linked to other people. One of our contributors, Paul Snyder, Executive Vice President Stewardship, Tillamook County Creamery Association, shared his perspective: 'Love is the most underused word in business. It seems to be incongruous that as human beings we carve out 8–10 hours of our day to live in environments where love is supposed to be absent! I believe that most people love some of what they do, but what's really important is to love who they work with. Can anyone say "I love my job" without loving who they work with? Love has been programmed out of business and we need to bring it back. Be open to loving the people you work with and letting them know as it would be very difficult to develop a mindset of loving your work if you can't share it.'

The best CEOs create environments where relationships thrive. They recognize that functional relationships are at the heart of effective collaboration and high-performing teams. They champion the most important relationship that employees have in organizations – the line manager relationship. They demonstrate exemplary line management with their own direct reports and hold line managers to account for essential line management skills, including:

- connecting individual objectives to the company direction, to ensure employees understand why they are doing their work and how it contributes to the bigger picture
- ensuring employees use their strengths on a daily basis to be energized and fulfilled in what they do
- coaching employees to continuously improve and develop the required mindsets, skillsets, behaviours and relationships to succeed

- providing honest feedback on different dimensions such as performance, impact, influence, commerciality and stakeholder management to become better

- recognizing and rewarding excellence – the majority of people thrive on genuine praise and encouragement for doing good work

- sponsoring career progression by understanding employees' aspirations and helping them shape a path to getting there

- caring beyond work – everyone has a life and life happens in ways that can have a major impact on work. A great line manager understands what is going on in team members' lives and provides the necessary support and guidance to help them navigate situations to the best of their ability.

The final area I will mention concerning the importance of relationship is the view that it is lonely at the top. In the words of John Holland-Kaye, CEO, Heathrow: 'People often talk about the loneliness of a CEO. This is not my experience. The reality is that you have a variety of people around you to support and it's vital to be able to lean on them. The only time I have found it lonely is when I have had to lead from the front and convince others to follow, however this has been rare. If you find that you are having to lead from the front on your own on a frequent basis, it probably means that you have failed to take people with you and will probably result in you getting fired!'

CEO NOTE

Build great relationships to be a great CEO.

Influence

'As CEO I do not control. I have never had it and don't want it. My primary function is to create the highest-performing company I can. One way I apply this function is to stay at the right level of decision making. I genuinely believe that I have made less than ten big decisions over an eight-year period. Adopting this approach means that as CEO you only get the major decisions coming your way. I have trained myself to step away from solving problems. It's not my job. I take the unavoidable decisions if I have to, but I only step in when I think that we are about to do something that is not right for the sustainability of the business. At times I have watched people make decisions that I don't think are right, however there is no point in stepping on their toes, as I will only get pulled into a level of detail that is not right for a CEO.' I applaud this approach by Andy Mitchell, CEO, Tideway. As an engineer, Andy is a trained problem solver and historically had roles that contained 'Control' in his title. However, Andy quickly realized that to succeed as CEO, being intentional about not taking on control is one of the most powerful ways to influence an organization.

This view was reinforced by Andy Cosslett, CEO, Chair, ITV plc and Kingfisher plc , who recounts the day he took over as CEO, IHG. Sitting in his office leading a global company consisting of several hundred thousand employees, as well as several thousand hotels over which he had no control, Andy realized that what he did have was influence, which he needed to master in order to create the conditions for others to succeed. In all my work with CEOs, making the shift from control to influence is one of the most profound requirements to step into CEO shoes. Before becoming CEO, the most common measures of success are usually evidenced through control, whether it is formulating a strategy, delivering numbers, managing a budget, driving efficiencies or improving systems. Some weight is given to the ability to influence senior stakeholders once a CEO is at the selection stage for role but, even then, the need to demonstrate the successful delivery of proof points takes precedence.

Once in role, influencing takes centre stage, which initially starts with communication. Keith Barr, CEO, IHG, gave his view: 'One of the key characteristics of a CEO is to be a clear communicator in order to build followership with all stakeholders. It is vital to understand where your messaging needs to be consistent and where it needs to change. Think about what resonates with your stakeholders. Understand what's important for them and their point of view. Be clear about what you want them to think and walk away with.'

Graham Alexander, CEO coach and founder of The Alexander Partnership, reinforced this perspective: 'As CEO you need to be the internal figure head, be visible and communicate with the business. As an outward-looking role, the priority is to communicate externally to the media, and investors.'

To validate the importance of communication to influence I turned to Simon Baugh, Chief Executive of the Government Communication Service: 'There is a variety of levers to achieve change as a CEO, including setting budgets, allocating resource and making critical decisions to shape the future. However, outside those types of areas the primary way to make things happen is communication. In the Government Communication Service I have 7,000 people to influence. The only way that I am going to reach them is through communication. It is the biggest single lever I have.'

Simon went on to say: 'The secret to effective communication is to simplify the message to such an extent that it feels embarrassing to share it over and over again. On one occasion when I was heading up a communication department, we had a high-energy CEO who pumped people up. His ability to motivate was fantastic, but the delivery in the organization didn't work. I then supported another CEO whose primary communication style focused on continuous improvement and meeting the deliverables for our customers. The results were spectacular. He had an ability to use communication which changed mindsets and drove behavioural change to improve the customer experience. He also had an ability to create an environment where people could speak up and be honest. He recognized that communication is two-way. It's about listening as well as talking. He would get out to the front line and listen to people. I have modelled that practice and spend one day a week in different parts of the country listening to what people are thinking, understanding their concerns, and spotting the things that are holding them back from doing their job. In a diverse organization such as Government Communication Services with over 300 departments around the country, it is vital to be visible, understand what's going on and make sure that you are not just spending time at number 10 Downing Street.'

Joel Burrows, CEO, Ghirardelli, shared his experience: 'Influencing requires different approaches with different stakeholders. With my team I have a consistent focus about the strategy and priority projects. If we are drifting away from what's important for the long term then I bring the team back to where we are, where we are going and what it will take to get there to ensure clarity about key deliverables and who is doing what. We have a game plan with defined metrics which I can see any time, however I need my team to be thinking 3–5 years ahead. I reinforce the need for them to equip their teams to deliver the short term so that we can shape the longer term.'

Joel also acknowledged the dynamic of leading in a global company across, upwards and downwards: 'With CEO peers in a global company, we need to build relationship across the organization so that we get to know each other, which then helps in terms of influencing and getting things done. One of the secrets to influencing upwards is knowing when to push. You can't get everything you want all the time. I believe in the sentiment, "Don't get even, get what you need to deliver your plan!" When it comes to influencing the next generation, it's important to find the right hook to be relatable. On one occasion I was engaging with a group of next-generational female leaders. I thought about how they could make an authentic link with a middle-aged male CEO. I shared a story about my daughter who played at a mixed sporting event where initially none of the boys passed her the ball. I encouraged her to keep going until finally she got the ball and was able to help the team perform. Given the fact that many of these female leaders had needed to break through glass ceilings to reach their position, it was an analogy that built connection. In order to influence, it's essential to make sure you know your audience, their objectives and how they like to receive information.'

Back to Simon Baugh, Chief Executive of the Government Communication Service, to strengthen this view: 'As CEO it is critical to understand the key relationships you need to influence. In government it is with the secretary of state and politicians, which are comparable to a Board in an organization. I believe that the starting point is to immerse yourself in their agenda. I have found that if you are not successful it's probably because you haven't asked the probing questions to understand what your key stakeholders really want and what drives their decision making. You must be able to demonstrate that you are delivering their agenda.'

Simon went on to explain: 'I have multiple stakeholders to influence. The trick is to make each person feel that you are spending the majority of time on their agenda, whilst staying true to your vision. You need to achieve what you want in role whilst presenting it in a way that represents their agenda. Part of my learning when I came into role and did my original pitch was that I realized people nodded their heads, however my message didn't really land. Now with the challenges we have faced with our prime minister position, I have flipped my approach. I am investing time with key stakeholders and asking them: "How can we help you achieve your priorities? What is your vision for government?" I am offering some ideas about what could help deliver their objectives, but the priority is to get agreement on the plan and track it relentlessly to demonstrate progress. Effective CEOs get alignment and track the plan so that they can show what they focused on and the difference it has made.'

In my role coaching executives, one of my main observations about influencing is that you cannot leave it up to chance, or to simply be good at what you do. On the way to the top, I often hear leaders exclaim how their results should speak for themselves, but they don't! Metrics are not enough. High performance is a given. Therefore, it is critical to be thoughtful and astute in the way you plan your stakeholder management and to think ahead. On one occasion I collected feedback on behalf of an executive committee member who was aspiring to the CEO role. Peter had a track record second to none. He had traversed several senior roles in the organization across different disciplines and had delivered success every time. However, when I asked Board members and the existing CEO about their view of Peter, there was very little commentary about the delivery of results, but there were common themes linked to the importance of influence, including:

Identity:

- If Peter became the CEO, what would it look like? How would he spend his time? Develop his identity before getting the title.

- Be Peter. Define his own identity rather than becoming some-one else.
- Peter should use the time he's got in his existing role to demon-strate change and to become a brilliant communicator. Get in the limelight.

Impact:

- Find the optimal point for being compassionate and assertive. Peter runs the risk of becoming overlooked. I want to see the edge. He does a great job, but he can be deferential. Be prepared to challenge and push back.
- Show strong leadership with the CEO and Board. Manage up more. Connect with gravitas and impact. Peter needs to demon-strate he is the right person with the right vision for the future to convince the Board. Board members look for leadership, ideas and drive.
- Peter should focus on his own profile for owning outcomes. Demonstrate more visibility for results so others can't ignore him.

Influence:

- Peter needs to be vocal about the key drivers of value. Be factual, be clear. Deliver his elevator pitch. Peter doesn't need to justify the detail as he has credibility.
- Speak truth to power. Have the confidence in his own ability and advice. It can feel risky when you've worked your way up the organization, however he has earned the right to be at the top.
- Peter can improve his ability to demonstrate clear articulation. Be concise. Have the ability to succinctly describe strategy to come across as focused and passionate.

Peter took this feedback to heart. It provoked him to create a robust stakeholder plan to act swiftly on what he was hearing. He used the feedback as a platform for going back to the Board, personalizing his approach to understand what success looked like for each of them in a future CEO, and developing his campaign accordingly. With some Board members that meant keeping up a consistent dialogue about business developments and seeking their counsel on specific issues. For others it meant a lighter touch, however Peter sought relevant opportunities to meet in person within the business context in order to keep influencing alive. Peter also focused on having more transparent conversations with the existing CEO about succession. Understandably it is a sensitive topic to look at influencing a CEO while in role, however it is the responsibility of a CEO to create the right conditions for others to influence them in constructive ways which are right for the business.

Amber Asher, CEO, Standard International, reinforced the need to influence wisely: 'You can only succeed by having the support of others. In my case that meant being supported by my predecessor, as well as the Board.'

Joel Burrows, CEO, Ghirardelli, shared his experience: 'The best way to get buy-in is to show a strong ability to grow the business in order to get the alignment for investment. If you are influencing upwards, keep it simple and focus on the success criteria you need to unlock.'

Keith Barr, CEO, IHG, built upon this view: 'Make sure you invest the time to build relationships with Board members in order to understand how they want you to add value and to get the necessary benefits for the business. Don't treat Board relationships as a transactional process.'

Neil Jowsey, CEO, Cromwell, strengthened this perspective: 'The Board is important in the creation of the right culture for a company. Often business challenges are driven out of how the Board operates. It can have a profound impact on the organization subject to how close they are to the business. CEOs need to think about how the Board is going to enable them to deliver and how they can influence accordingly.'

Another critical relationship to influence is the chair. Keith Barr, CEO, IHG, recounted a story about a fellow CEO: 'The biggest mistake they admitted to making was to not spend enough time working out who they needed to have as their chair for them to be successful.' Keith went on to say: 'Although the CEO doesn't make the chair decision, they can influence it and therefore it is important to think about what type of chair is needed for the company and how to be able to work well together.'

Keith also pointed out that once in role as CEO: 'Beyond the chair make sure you have what you need to get the best out of the Board and for the company. Define the experience, style and skills needed. If you end up with a poor fit, it can be a risk to the business. Sometimes it is better to have Board members with functional expertise that can advise on specific areas, whereas at other times it can be more appropriate to have members with high levels of C-suite experience.'

I have witnessed a variety of chair and CEO partnerships with varying degrees of success. In one highly effective dynamic there was a very complementary fit. The chair had vast business experience sitting on numerous Boards and could bring an informed and relevant external lens to the organization. The CEO had deep sector and company knowledge, having worked in the field for many years. The chair was extroverted and a compelling communicator in public settings. The CEO was introverted and had their biggest impact in smaller settings. They evolved a plan to use each other's strengths across multiple stakeholder groups to maximize their influence. With the Board they agreed to both step back in order to enable Board members to have voice, which provided them with diverse views and supported alignment in decision making. With the executive committee they gave each exec member a platform to showcase their agenda with the Board and to have sufficient exposure in order to support engagement and buy-in. With shareholders and investors, they devised who would lead on different topics subject to the outcome they were trying to achieve. With the media they shared a profile for the good of the business.

Sneh Khemka, former CEO, Simplyhealth, shared his experience of influencing: 'Success as a CEO is heavily influenced by character. Being an extrovert means that I am able to use my style to broach a wide range of stakeholders, from those who are supportive to those who are highly challenging. I am able to play a strong commercial bat with customers, colleagues and community. It is vital to understand and include all stakeholders so that you can create a business narrative that helps everyone buy into the strategy and to put their hearts and minds into the journey.'

Sneh also highlighted the need to simply be human: 'As a CEO it's important to expose vulnerability in the right way. You need to allow people to see your humanity to build trust, empathy and followership.'

I will bring back Andy Mitchell, CEO, Tideway, to have the final say on influencing: 'I have learned to be totally authentic and human with people. This approach runs the risk of baring your soul in sharing where you are coming from and how you are feeling. However, my commitment is to help people be as clear as possible about where I am coming from, which means exposing my innermost thoughts. The biggest influence you can have is your example.'

CEO NOTE

Move from control to influence to have
the right impact on the organization.

Be an Architect of Culture: Exec Summary

- The CEO is the architect of the organizational culture, so be very intentional about the way you do things as it sets the tone.
- Invest in your relationships as they are the currency to make things happen.
- Become a master influencer as it is the primary lever to travel in the direction you want to go.

STAGE III

Performance

Let's check in with our journey so far. In Stage 1: Purpose, we explored the importance of aligning your personal North Star with the company direction you want to go:

- Chapter 1 looked at how to be yourself with more skill so that you can adapt your authentic self to the job at hand.
- Chapter 2 challenged you to create a compelling vision and define your big bets in order to unlock brilliant performance.
- Chapter 3 encouraged you to invest in the necessary preparation to set the organization up for success with the right capability and to remove any barriers.

We then moved on to Stage 2: People, challenging you to put talent at the heart of your value proposition:

- Chapter 4 invited you to lead with humanity and create the conditions for everyone to have a sense of belonging and be their best selves.

- Chapter 5 inspired you to prioritize the talent agenda, build high-performing teams, create robust succession, and ensure development becomes embedded in the fabric of the organization.

- Chapter 6 suggested that as the cultural architect of the company, you set the climate in which relationships can thrive and have the mandate to influence others.

We now move on to the final part, Stage 3: Performance, which is where the rubber hits the road and is the ultimate test for a CEO.

CHAPTER 7

Be an Enabler for Sustainable Growth

• • •

Deliver Results

As a new CEO for a global company, Jane was responsible for the overall performance in more than 70 countries, with main hubs in Singapore, New York and London. On the outside results looked good. There appeared to be a growth trajectory based on metrics such as market share, sales revenue, net profit margin, gross margin, customer loyalty, retention, profit, net promoter score and employee engagement. However, as Jane dug into the detail, the veneer of success began to peel away. She had a gradual awakening that the results had been manipulated to paint a glossy picture to shareholders, however they didn't tell the whole picture. Jane brought her executive committee together for an extraordinary meeting to address the facts. She set the context by creating a safe environment for the truth to be put on the table. The dawning realization hit each executive member in turn. The minor adjustments of numbers added up to a brutal reality which needed to be addressed immediately.

Call me naïve but my starting point is that people show up at work with good intent. If behaviours and actions don't match the good intent, then there will be a reason. I often find that once discovered, these reasons are not deliberate ways to undermine a company, cause failure or damage a reputation. Having witnessed different corporate failures I believe that often the causes have their roots in fear. The fear of speaking up when a fundamental operational flaw is known, but no one wants to take accountability for it and potentially get fired. The fear of presenting bad news and getting hauled over the coals. The fear of going over budget or being late on a deliverable so coming up with excuses to delay the inevitable conflict with the powers to be.

Jane had sufficient awareness to understand that the only way she would be able to make the necessary changes and take people with her was to give people the benefit of the doubt and to collectively find a solution. She recognized that the previous culture had created an environment where people needed to present everything as 'good news', which meant results getting manipulated to fit the message. Jane was a firm believer in the power of psychological safety and put the steps into action. To set expectations and ensure everyone had voice, were prepared to take calculated risk and admit to mistakes, Jane took accountability for failing to dig into the detail sooner. She explained her preferred leadership style was to give people autonomy and to stay out of the detail, but recognized that given her time in role she should have moved faster. Jane's humility set the tone. Team members came forward with their version of reality, explaining how the need to deliver positive results meant painting over cracks. Jane responded to this level of participation with the focus on looking forward and finding solutions together.

The starting point was to review the key metrics being measured. The team aligned on a refreshed dashboard consisting of ten success metrics to deliver, which boiled down to three main areas – colleagues, customers and cash. Beginning with the end in mind, the team identified the outcomes for each metric, from which point they were able to align on vital priorities to drive. They broke these down into major projects, which if delivered on time and budget would move the business in the right direction. Each executive team member took accountability for key areas and agreed to work in 90-day sprints to provide absolute transparency of outcomes and activities.

The next step was to define the required behaviours to deliver the plan. The team agreed it was vital to keep them real given the previous dilemma. They agreed on three primary expectations:

1. Talk direct – be open, honest and transparent.
2. Own it – take accountability for actions and outcomes.
3. Make it happen – ask for help, give help.

The team devised a collective approach to communicating the plan, developing the right mindsets and behaviours, and embedding what they called a 'performance culture' in the business. Jane fronted the shift in focus by delivering a clear and compelling message in the next company town hall. She presented the facts in the most transparent way possible so that people could understand the severity of the situation without creating unnecessary anxiety. Jane laid out the future direction through the new performance plan. Each executive member then brought to life their chosen priorities with the associated behaviours required to be successful. They personalized each request in order to match the human factor with the business challenge.

On the back of the town hall, the executive committee quickly mobilized a system to engage their immediate teams with planning sessions to deliver the results, and made sure everyone was resourced for success. These planning sessions rippled through the organization. The 'performance culture' began to create its own currency. The behaviours 'Talk direct, Own it and Make it happen' were referenced in everyday meetings and conversations. Rather than delivery simply being seen as a transactional effort, the 'performance culture' captured hearts and minds. It broke down previous silos. Teams started collaborating across boundaries. New partnerships were formed and accurate results were delivered.

Jane was deliberate in how she positioned the approach and narrative with her chair and Board. She was concerned about undermining her executive committee as she knew she was under massive time pressure to turn around the status quo. Jane decided to take her chair into her confidence about the past ways of doing things. The chair recognized that the Board was also collectively responsible for creating an environment where the pressure to present 'good news' drove unintended consequences. Thankfully the chair's support meant that Jane was able to present the historic results with the solution to fix stuff at the next Board meeting. Agreement was reached to sponsor the 'performance culture' method. Bringing this message back to her executive committee gave a confidence boost and reinforced the actions being taken.

Research from *Harvard Business Review* echoes Jane's approach. In an article entitled 'Leaders don't have to choose between compassion and performance' (February 2022), the authors said that for leaders to achieve a balance of compassion and performance over the long term, they require data, prioritization, proper setup, and collaboration. I found their recommendations of figuring out what matters, making time for compassion, increasing transparency and co-creating solutions mirrored insight from the CEOs I interviewed. In the words of Justin Basini, CEO and co-founder, ClearScore: 'It has been difficult to separate being CEO from being the founder of the business. As a founder of a company, it is a different role to leading an established big business. One of the most important requirements is to set your team up to perform. In the early days of the business, the focus was about not giving up. The easy option would have been to quit. You need to keep faith whilst understanding where value is really created in order to extract it. I found it important to use analysis and passion to keep going. Performance is about combining head and heart in order to keep everyone focused and energized. In a start-up you will have as many losses as wins. As a founder it is your energy that makes the difference. I have found the successes thrilling, but the failures hurt more. As CEO you need to manage people through the ups and downs of the performance cycle.'

With an organizational purpose focused on *soulful hospitality*, Stephen McCall, CEO, edyn, is mindful about what it takes to deliver results aligned with the company culture: 'The CEO needs to find a rhythm to manage performance. We have dashboards and scorecards across the business and have a systemized approach focused on review, oversight and escalation. I need to see the business at 30,000 feet, but I want to know that people are looking at the business performance at all levels. It's not the job of a CEO to manage performance all the way through the business, however it is the job of a CEO to set up a governance system to ensure that any enduring underperformance does not go unaddressed. It is critical that everyone in the business understands in their role what is going well, what isn't and has a plan in place. As a CEO, develop an approach that means you don't have to devote every hour interrogating the business. It is not the job of the CEO to solve performance issues. It is their job to make sure that those accountable are supported to do it. As a CEO you need reassurance that people's fingers are on the pulse, however I know many

CEOs who stare most of the day at business performance, which is not the best use of time.'

Jan Smits, CEO and Deputy Chair, APAC, Pro-invest Group, has spent many years refining how to deliver results across the world: 'As CEO it is essential to have absolute clarity and alignment about what you are going to deliver and how you are going to deliver it. This starts by clarifying your strategic plan and designing the right organizational structure so that you have the right people in the right roles for delivery.'

Jan always links purpose with performance to deliver optimal results: 'To build a performance-driven culture requires having a clear purpose, setting up delivery targets, measuring milestones, communicating progress and celebrating wins. It is vital to have an environment where people can provide open and honest views about ongoing performance and to encourage each other along the way.'

Jan emphasized the need for a CEO to be visible in how they manage performance so that people can see what is important. He stated: 'The principle, what gets measured gets done, is timeless. I firmly believe that everyone wants to do a good job and therefore the CEO role is to enable people to perform. If you have them set up for success and they are not able to deliver, they are in the wrong role. One of the biggest mistakes you can do as CEO is to tolerate under-performance as it sends the wrong message to the business.'

Jan also acknowledged the importance of having the right structure in place: 'Make sure your organizational design is aligned to what you are trying to do. The way you will know if you have the right organizational design is if you are running a smooth operation. If not, employees will be suboptimal in their performance and eventually burn out. You can also understand the effectiveness of your organizational design through measuring employee engagement, which will show your pinch points and what you need to address in order to be fit for purpose. To ensure successful delivery you must get the right balance between the teams who go out and win the work and the teams who deliver it.'

Jan's approach was reinforced by Dr Sam Barrell CBE, Deputy CEO, The Francis Crick Institute: 'To manage performance against the company ambition it's vital to be clear about how it translates for all individual functions. At the Crick, every team has their own objectives that are set on a three-year horizon and against which they create their KPIs. As an organization this means we can make decisions in the context of the overarching scorecard. To track and monitor performance we initially had multiple software systems, which were not set up to produce centralized data. We changed this to enable us to have a view about how the business was performing as a collective. We benchmarked against each service and created a heatmap about where we were and how well our services were landing with our scientists.'

Sam went on to say: 'Performance matters. It is essential to have a clear view of the organization's operation with an evidence-based approach. Understanding performance affects where you prioritize and put resource. To achieve this, we created our "Crick Data World", a company dashboard, created from the bottom up, which enables us to see relevant data to help drive our performance. At Board level we create our top 10 metrics against which our performance is measured.'

Will Stratton-Morris, CEO, Caffè Nero UK, emphasizes the need to have the right processes in place to maximize results: 'As CEO you need to assess how the organization operates and if the right processes are in place proportionate to the business needs. It's important not to be afraid to reduce or add to them. Even if you have a compelling strategy based on a differentiated truth with a clear framework and a great team, unless you enable the business by putting in the right processes to drive the right decision making and optimize the business, your efforts will be compromised. Getting a clear RACI (responsible, accountable, consulted and informed) model and making it stick is very difficult. You will need to invest time in constructing, aligning and setting everyone up to implement. In big companies the role of the centre can overlap with the role of the region. You need to understand the overlaps to avoid unnecessary tension. When I worked at Disney we had two regular meetings – a policy meeting and an execution meeting. The creation of two-matrix-structured meetings broke down barriers. They provided the right forum to challenge perceived tensions. The discipline of mandatory meetings forced participants to discuss issues, which yielded better outcomes.'

The role of the CEO to enable performance was clearly articulated by Wim Dejonghe, Senior Partner, Allen & Overy LLP: 'As CEO, you need to have the overview about the drivers of performance to make sure people take the right opportunities and have a clear understanding about how the strategic plan fits together, combined with ownership of individual objectives across the business whilst knowing where people can collaborate together to succeed.'

This perspective was reinforced by Justin Basini, CEO and co-founder, ClearScore: 'A critical differentiator between low- and high-performing organizations is the way standards are set and met. This starts at the top. One of the most important roles a CEO plays is to set high standards and hold yourself and others to account. There is no question that if something is being well run, it is led from the top. You see it all over, from schools to hospitals to businesses. The head of the organization sets the tone and the standards. To deliver results you need to ensure there is sufficient data to create fast feedback loops. In the early days, our COO put in a data system which gave a high level of transparency across the organization about performance in the business, including our revenue, profit and product. When you democratize data, people are able to self-diagnose problems and take appropriate action. My approach to delivering results is to set high standards and then provide the right data with transparency. By empowering people to make decisions at the front line, whilst knowing where to go for advice, speeds up delivery and allows you to achieve superior results.'

Another advocate of setting people up for success is Jamie Bunce, CEO, Inspired Villages: 'To deliver great results you need to create a culture where people are empowered and free to own and partake in more than the delivery of task. Results need to be linked back to the company purpose so that, when people are in task mode, everyone can understand how their role impacts the business, from frontline cleaners, cooks and housekeepers to the Board.'

Jamie concluded: 'Make sure people have personalized objectives and key results in order to understand the role they play in delivering the big company targets. To be successful, people need to feel successful. If someone feels like it is their result to deliver, you stand a much better chance than if it feels imposed on them. Celebrate delivery with rewards which are beyond monetary. Understand what gets endorphins flowing. Make sure roles are more than just about having a job and receiving a pay check. As CEO enable people to understand their value in helping the business perform.'

Graham Alexander, founder, The Alexander Partnership, coaches CEOs to ensure there is a clear strategy broken down into clear deliverables for the business so that everyone has defined and monitored KPIs. Graham shared: 'The role of the CEO is to unlock the potential of the business to grow and perform. This involves having great people running the business who are excited about where you are trying to get to and having a clear and aligned strategy translated into KPIs. The CEO then needs to monitor performance, stir the pot when necessary and celebrate success along the way.'

To bring in the perspective from the world of finance, Javier Echave, CFO, Heathrow, stated: 'The CEO is the performance driver of the business. Organizations need to deliver for investors, colleagues and the community in a sustainable way.' Javier uses the fable of the golden goose as an analogy: 'Set up the business to collect the golden eggs without killing the goose.'

One CEO who is renowned for the delivery of results is Jonathan Akeroyd, CEO, Burberry, who shared: 'To create the right conditions for delivery, make sure everyone knows what is expected of them. Find the right cadence in terms of meetings and check-ins to stay connected. It is vital to free teams up to execute. When things don't go your way, and they won't, stay focused and calm. Being focused is about having clear and aligned goals in place, enabling the right mindset to recognize that it's not a rigid plan and that you have the flexibility to make it work. As CEO, keep communicating about the strategic goals, focusing on what is most important. Repetition is essential to keep everyone on the same path.'

John Murray, CEO, Sonesta International Hotels Corporation, gave a range of valuable points linked to delivering results: 'Make sure you have accomplished people in your key roles as they will hold themselves accountable to high standards and set the tone for the business.'

John echoed a point all CEOs I spoke with shared: 'Set clear goals and targets and make sure everyone is aligned and held accountable.'

He went on to say: 'Make sure people have the right tools to perform. If they have the right tools and underperform, address it immediately. You need to have the whole organization hitting on all cylinders.'

John also shouted out the need to recognize the achievements of others: 'Nobody succeeds as CEO without the hard work of a lot of people. In the hotel business, if colleagues are not getting our service right then guests aren't happy and stop staying. Make sure you recognize everyone who is contributing to your success.'

Neil Jowsey, CEO, Cromwell, described his approach in the following way: 'As a CEO your accountability is super clear – the company results. I have learned that my focus has to be the success of the company, which I combine with other elements I love like seeing people thrive and contributing to customer happiness. At the end of the day your success is measured by the performance of the company.'

Neil also advocates the power of planning for performance: 'In one business I spent 26 days with my executive committee co-creating our business plan. This ensured alignment, as well as mitigating the risk of any cracks at an executive level becoming gulfs in the organization. Once developed, you need to translate the business strategy into functional plans. I suggest creating a compelling visual on a page which can be used as a communication tool in the company. Make sure that people are continuously involved in the evolution and execution of the plan so that they feel listened to and have ownership.'

Neil concluded: 'Once the plan is in place, the performance of the business demands relentless and disciplined focus on execution and the delivery of results. As CEO you need to move boldly and stay focused on what really matters. I call it acting with intent. Highly effective CEOs provide exceptional leadership, build great teams and ensure that the right resources are available to drive brilliant results.'

CEO NOTE

Delivering great results is a prerequisite for being a great CEO.

Lead Today

As I write about leadership today, in the autumn of 2022, the challenges for CEOs continue to multiply. On a global scale many businesses have had to stop, start, reassess and reconfigure on a daily basis. As stated by the World Bank (2022): 'The global economy continues to be weakened by the war through significant disruptions in trade, food and fuel price shocks, all of which are contributing to high inflation and subsequent tightening in global financing conditions.' The World Health Organization (2022) predicted that 'rapidly escalating Covid-19 amid reduced virus surveillance forecasts a challenging autumn and winter in the WHO European Region'. In the UK the combination of Brexit and the political uncertainty caused by changes in party leadership and policies led to Shevaun Haviland, director-general of the British Chambers of Commerce, saying that the next prime minster needs to 'return both political and economic stability' (2022). Other issues include:

- New, unpredictable and unplanned scenarios mean CEOs having to diversify or adapt their product or service in real time. For instance, in response to Heathrow Airport maybe needing to limit passenger numbers for Christmas, John Holland-Kaye, CEO, Heathrow, told the BBC's Today programme the airport wanted to 'get back to full capacity as soon as possible. We don't want to have a cap at all. The reason for having a cap is to make sure we keep supply and demand in balance' (2022).

- Lack of resources, including people, finance and supplies, can cause projects to be put on hold, slow down or stop. The combination of the Great Resignation, spiralling costs and supply shortages is putting extraordinary pressures on companies to deliver, requiring CEOs to make tough choices for the good of the business.

- Fear is often systemic and is experienced throughout an organization when impacted by local or global uncertainty. Colleagues can be afraid of losing their jobs or have concerns about organizational change, which impacts engagement and productivity.

CEOs need to be highly attuned to the emotional climate and provide sufficient clarity, humanity and transparency to counteract anxieties.

- Increased emphasis on colleague wellbeing might look like a drain on a business, but prioritizing mental health and physical wellbeing is a vital investment for the company culture and performance. CEOs must address this at all levels in the organization. Data shows the C-suite are struggling alongside Gen Z employees. Deloitte reported around 70 per cent of high-level executives are seriously considering quitting their jobs, largely to improve their emotional wellbeing (2022).

I appreciated the view of Phil Bayliss, CEO, Infinium, about how to navigate this type of agenda: 'As a CEO you need to be a visionary and have the ambition to change the world. You need to be able to inspire exceptional behaviour and performance in others, creating a culture and environment for them to be at their best while maintaining an unwavering belief that you will succeed. You need to develop a big strategy that inspires people to be part of something extraordinary. One of my current company's prime areas of concentration is the creation of a new sustainability-focused asset class, which brings together commercial real estate and electric vehicle infrastructure to drive efficiencies, create a better working environment for last-mile delivery service providers and combat climate change. We have the opportunity to be bigger than all the existing oil companies combined. The traditional indicator of success as a CEO is to put down a scorecard and deliver it, driven by messages like "measure what matters" and "get after a clear set of objectives and outperform them". However, reflecting upon my various roles, the flashing green scorecard is in fact a lag indicator. Our world today is so dynamic that you need to measure success differently. For instance, if you made the measure of success about driving growth and size, you could end up a busy fool.'

Phil went on to look at the relationship between thinking big, acting small and balancing both in today's age: 'I have unlimited energy for the top-line, exciting, big-picture thinking. However, I have had to learn how to dive deep into the small stuff and do it well, such as having individual conversations or focusing on small operational matters. As CEO it's important to be able to drop like a stone into detail and then come back out to help people perform strongly. It's important to learn the skills of being a balanced leader. I have seen most CEOs needing strong understanding in finance, marketing and business planning, alongside operational delivery, executing revenue budgets and driving back-of-house functions. Making high-quality, informed decisions is the realm of a brilliant CEO. You need to take informed risk, which is not about taking risk at any cost but creating the environment for others to do the same. It is essential to keep making the small, incremental gains that build a sustainable future for the business, whether it is managing the finances right or building deeper personal connections. As a CEO it is essential to walk the floor and make real connections with employees at all levels, engaging on family and personal interests. It is vital to use your behaviour to set the standard for the expectations you have of others.'

Phil shared: 'Upon awakening it can feel that I have conflicting priorities, both big and small. For instance, I need to discipline myself when going into a meeting by thinking about the desired outcome. I ask myself, "What am I here to do? Is it to sit down with a team and show I care, or is it about setting exciting new priorities?" They can sometimes appear to be competing characteristics; however, I need to operate at both levels.'

Sneh Khemka, former CEO, Simplyhealth, reflected on the ongoing shifts for CEOs in today's unpredictable world: 'The cultural and societal expectations for CEOs today are very different to the past. Historically, the primary role of a CEO was to run the P&L, and to lead with a command-and-control style producing profit for shareholders. Now a CEO has to demonstrate true humanity and to lead in a conscious way across a range of topics far beyond the P&L. A CEO needs to understand the political, demographic and changing needs of the workforce and customer base. They need to be a rounded individual who can deal with the socio, political and economic environments to progress the business.'

Sophie Devonshire, CEO, The Marketing Society, recognized the impact of the global pandemic: 'We are playing catch-up from Covid. There is tension and tiredness across the business. However, wellbeing has to be balanced with the delivery of business needs. Within this environment we decided to give people time sovereignty and to focus on outcomes, rather than hours worked. We are building it as a culture based on an acceptance that the way we drive performance has changed in the workplace.'

Sophie also acknowledged the need to celebrate success along the way: 'What we sometimes forget is the thrill of achievement. It's vital to show people the progress they have made, which also boosts energy. It is very motivating to be part of a team that delivers and to have pace driven by progress.'

Managing pace was a theme also addressed by Viviane Paxinos, CEO, AllBright: 'Unless you are starting a company it's important to remember that the business existed before you. If you are inheriting an organization with a culture and a set of relationships, it takes time to grow. It is unlikely that you will turn the business around overnight, therefore your focus should be on what you can influence going forward. I use the analogy with my team that our goal is to reach base camp, not Everest. As CEO it's easy to come up with big ideas. The challenge is to solve problems one step at a time to drive the next phase of business growth. This involves the real skill of deciding what to say no to. We have three clear strategic pillars and if things don't fall into them, we say no. You need the right mental capacity to focus on the right areas.'

The challenge of leading today was clearly articulated by Amy Edmondson, Novartis Professor of Leadership and Management, Harvard Business School: 'As CEO you must hold the dual focus of value creation and delivery. You create value by investing in innovation and deliver it through operational excellence. You need to be willing to invest in the uncertain work of innovation and be prepared to experiment with new ideas and markets. You then need to rally people to deliver.'

Jan Smits, CEO and Deputy Chair, APAC, Pro-invest Group, brought in a combination of strategy, capability, people and performance to succeed: 'As CEO these are some of the most challenging times in which I have led. It is like white water rafting and having to navigate the rapids as they come at you. You can't influence the geo-political issues going on, so your best bet is to clarify what winning looks like, translate it into your strategy, focus on building organizational capability, nurture talent and execute.'

He went on to say: 'One of the biggest challenges at the moment is the change in the working environment. Boundaries are changing. The next generation coming into the workforce have a very different view of the world and what work looks like. Many people are now clear that unless they can work from home at least some of the time, they don't want that job. It is a disruptive environment where people are also focused on the cost of living. As CEO you need to listen and take the next generation on a journey to manage expectations and set them up for success. Be balanced and compassionate in your approach. Provide greater transparent communication about what you are trying to do and where you are going.'

Emily Chang, CEO, Wunderman Thompson West, reflected upon what daring CEOs from across industries and the globe are doing to create extraordinary impact in today's rapidly changing world, and the difference between East and West: '1) The way we define failure. There's a fine line between failure and learning. In the West, we set clear milestones to ensure a high likelihood of success. In the East, we prioritize speed to market, getting something launched quickly so we can learn and iterate. 2) How we embrace the "and". In the West, we often think in terms of "either/or". Even the construct of AB testing assumes an either/or approach. However, in the East, a company may concurrently launch two products and monitor purchase intent. In setting up this construct, the company learns quickly and immediately produces the more desired product, launching with a high degree of certainty in purchase intent.'

Will Stratton-Morris, CEO, Caffè Nero UK, provided his point of view about leading in today's evolving environment: 'It is essential to take the complexity of a business and create a simple narrative to tell the story so that people quickly get what's going on. Simplifying complexity is a real skill to master. You need to have a framework to build the narrative. I use a structure based on a house which builds the story consisting of the vision, purpose, priorities and culture. To create the framework, be immersed in the business, stand back and ask, "What are we about? What are our key focus areas? What are the strategies we need to focus on?" Develop a clear and simple framework. Make sure that the level of detail is the same for a non-executive member as for frontline colleagues. When engaging the Board, headline key points supported by a pack with the depth. If you have done the narrative well, the Board won't need to dig into the detail and will appreciate your clarity and rigour.'

Will continued: 'Accept that people will look to you for the macro and micro view of the business. The best CEOs know when to stay high level and when to get into the detail on the right things. There is an interesting paradox that as you evolve up the chain, you tend to not get your hands dirty in the detail, however you need to be ready to plunge. Sometimes it's only you who can ask the right question. You might have an intuition based on experience and need to test and validate it. Other times, through your listening and sensing when something is lightweight, you will need to push down to see if there is anything of significance to unearth.'

Justin Basini, CEO and co-founder, ClearScore, shared a clear message about leading ambiguity: 'As a CEO, leading in today's age of uncertainty requires a real commitment to a meaningful mission both personally and for the business. ClearScore is a business dedicated to helping our users improve their financial wellbeing. People rally to our mission, especially the next generation who self-select companies based on what they stand for. It is vital to be able to bring everything back to the mission. Each time we focus on revenue targets with the team we also talk about how this revenue is millions of positive actions for our users and sales for our partners. We talk about user first, partner next and revenue last. The result of our customers being happy is a healthy business.'

Justin went on to say: 'One of the challenges in today's climate is navigating the need for diversity and creating level playing fields where everyone can learn and unlock their potential. In an environment where you need to set high standards it can get difficult quickly. I want an environment where everyone can succeed, an organization packed full of people committed to ClearScore and who build our culture. We need to make sure that we connect with people who believe in what we believe, irrespective of background. I find that the best companies create a set of standards where a diverse set of talents can perform and belong within a clearly defined culture.'

One of the most important roles that a CEO plays to impact performance is in creating the right conditions for effective decision making, particularly when a company needs to make important trade-offs in the short term which can impact the longer term. Andy Mitchell, CEO, Tideway, put it across in the following way: 'As CEO it's important to work hard to be clear about the delegation of decision making and authority. In the early days of the business with my leadership team, we used the analogy of red buttons to define the key decisions we were accountable for, and if anyone was going to press the red button it would be us. We couldn't have everyone in the business making the big financial decisions. However, outside of the hard final decisions, we needed to agree how many other things we wanted to be brought up to the exec level. Initially we had a long list. We challenged each other and boiled it down to a few vital areas. It wasn't a hard list as there is no such thing, but we agreed that unless it was a decision with massive implications, and it was not fair to let someone else make it, then the decision would sit with us. We established an effective decision-making governance and worked within it. We agreed not to meddle and to stay out of people's way. Over time it has become second nature. People still try to bring decisions to the Exec because they want comfort, so we talk through the rationale for the decision in order for them to own it.'

Graham Alexander, founder, The Alexander Partnership, has coached more CEOs than most on how to enable effective decision making: 'A CEO focuses on what only they can do. They are brilliant at delegating and letting others get on with delivering the business. A CEO should only do what they can uniquely do, including:

- know what's going on
- be as open and honest as possible to create an environment of high trust
- be available to support and challenge when needed
- have a constant process of raising your self-awareness through getting input from others about how they think you're doing.'

Graham went on to say: 'We live and work in challenging times where many of our political, cultural and ecological systems are broken.

Leading a business by breaking it down into a set of component parts is a limiting approach. To thrive as CEO today you will need to think differently, including how you can collaborate with competitors and who are your key thought partners to help you think creatively and see things differently. It is essential to have a place for blue-sky thinking and scenario planning to think about the future in a deeper and broader way.'

Another thoughtful perspective about the role of the CEO in decision making came from Jonathan Akeroyd, CEO, Burberry: 'To make effective decisions you need to balance information and instinct. I am a commercial specialist, which brings a natural instinct about running a business, such as flexing costs and other ways to supplement the company. It's important to have a select group of people around you to partner and help make the right decisions. It is not about you as CEO being the decision maker. It is about making sure others have a voice and that you have the right team with you when critical decisions arise.'

John Murray, CEO, Sonesta International Hotels Corporation, shared his experience: 'Once you have enough information, be prepared to make quick decisions. Trust your instincts, knowledge, and watch what happens. You can't let your ego get away from you. If you make the wrong decision, own it, take time to course correct and go in a different direction. It is important to recognize and correct mistakes.'

Each leader I spoke with had their own way of navigating the current climate, providing clarity for the organization and enabling people to perform. Amber Asher, CEO, Standard International, draws upon her strengths to stay energized and have maximum impact: 'I am skilled at coming up with a plan, getting everyone aligned, bringing the team together and delivering together. I am highly effective in a crisis and will always come up with an answer. I have an ability to do deals and stabilize the business to drive performance.'

Emma Gilthorpe, COO, Heathrow, reinforced the need for CEOs to demonstrate these types of characteristics: 'To be a CEO you need to evidence that you can think through complex problems and navigate ambiguous strategic situations, give teams what they need to thrive in difficult circumstances and execute the plan, and in modern business you need a high level of emotional intelligence.'

Emma's executive colleague Javier Echave, CFO, Heathrow, stated: 'As CEO you need to create a plan in an ambiguous environment and make the big choices. It's useful to have a framework to ask the right questions. One simple model I have seen work well to structure thinking is the following:

1. What does success look like? What are the objectives to achieve?
2. What options are available?
3. What the opportunities, threats and mitigations for the options?
4. Execute the plan and review based on new information.'

Jonathan Mills, CEO, EMEA, Choice Hotels, started in role during turbulent times: 'My baptism of fire coming into a new business as CEO in a Covid environment was not straightforward, however it forced me to be even more diligent in my initial interactions:

1. Listen to stakeholders directly. I made sure that I understood things first hand. Do not rely on others' opinions. I started by engaging with senior executives across the company and then drilled through the layers of the company to understand the business and the marketplace. I went outside the business to a variety of stakeholders, in my case this included customers (franchisees) and partners (online travel agents) to understand their perspectives and needs.
2. Experience the experience. I made sure to regularly experience the customer journey. In my world this involves making hotel bookings through different channels and staying in different hotels.
3. Understand the competitor and parallel industry organizations so that you can benchmark your business and learn from the great work of others.'

Keith Barr, CEO, IHG, offered sound advice when there are so many variables to your agenda: 'When something goes wrong, get to the root cause of the issue. You have to accept the fact that you are constantly going to be disappointing someone about something. Everyone has a point of view about what you should do, however you are the decision maker. Make sure you look across the entirety of the landscape. Decide how you will prioritize and sequence, and be comfortable that not everyone is going to agree with your choices.'

Keith continued: 'I believe that doing the right thing and being resilient is a good formula. You can't do everything. Be clear about why you are making the right decisions and mobilize others to deliver.'

I appreciated the perspective of Jamie Bunce, CEO, Inspired Villages, who recounted: 'I will never forget the day my father said to me, "Without data you're a loudmouth with an opinion." Ever since that moment I have developed a thirst for data to help me understand what things mean. I have a variety of sources which inform how I shape my response to today's climate, including what is happening in the land market, construction, colleague engagement and customer sentiment. All these various data points go to frame my view about how to lead today. In particular I look at the key modes that can make a massive difference and help us deliver our results. As I speak, we are in the middle of massive uncertainty. We operate in the building sector. The open housing market is down 50 per cent just in the last month. I am looking at what happened in the last recession and assessing what happened to our sector of the open housing market. I am then facing into the reality now by understanding the sentiments of our residents. These data points shape my understanding of our customers' behaviour, for instance how to respond to the cost-of-living crisis by creating an incentive package to help our residents release more income.

'My approach is to let data be a foundation to help shape decisions. I come to my own conclusions and socialize them with my management team so that we arrive at an aligned decision. We then disseminate our decisions across the business through co-creating objectives and key results with colleagues. A dictatorial approach doesn't drive performance in today's world.'

Neil Jowsey, CEO, Cromwell, was cognisant about the need to strike a balance between operating in the present and tomorrow. 'A CEO must balance time, energy and resources for now and the future. Having a clear process to create a strategic plan forces you to think about the future, where you are heading and how you are going to get there. The planning process is a key part of spending time in the future, however in today's dynamic environment it has to be matched with the ability to see round corners. You need to interpret information from all sorts of places, e.g. the market, customers, suppliers and external predictions. Once assimilated you must decide what it is telling you and where to go. Your ability to predict the future in ways that are not obvious will be a key differentiator. Be bold about where the business needs to go when it's not obvious to everyone else.'

Being bold is a major obstacle for many organizations. Wim Dejonghe, Senior Partner, Allen & Overy LLP, shared his dilemma: 'One of the biggest challenges I face is the appetite of people to take risks. Lawyers are paid to identify risk. However, given the nature of our business, we can't stop at identifying risk. We need to be able to take them as well.'

Wim also described the challenge of needing to move fast when an organization is at risk: 'Our business is based on having an inclusive approach. However, our scale makes it challenging to ensure all 630 partners have a sense of ownership. In a law firm, I recognize that creating ownership is the opposite of a corporate culture, which tends to adopt a top-down approach. In times of crisis, I implement a top-down approach as there is a business-critical need to take hard decisions. However, in my whole career I have only needed to do this on a few occasions. People expect you to do it when the going gets tough. An effective CEO has to be prepared to stand up, act at pace and get on with what the business needs to do.'

Dr Sam Barrell CBE, Deputy CEO, The Francis Crick Institute, echoed Wim's sentiments about taking risks: 'In these current times my focus is to build long-term financial sustainability, given the ongoing inflation and energy crisis. It's obviously challenging but also offers opportunity to think big and be ambitious. We cannot tinker around the edges, which drives stimulating conversations about where we want to go and how to get there.'

Justin Basini, CEO and co-founder, ClearScore, reinforced the need for visible and symbolic leadership in challenging times: 'As CEO you have to give a shit. I think that is easier as a founder of the business, but perhaps harder if you are a non-founder CEO, but demonstrating how you much you care for the customer and the team will be critical.

It comes down to not what you say but the symbolism of where you spend your time and effort. We survey our financial institution customers every quarter around the world. If any of these partners say they aren't satisfied with our service, then I reach out personally to speak with them and understand their issues. They are often surprised to get an email from me, but it is a signal that their business, our company and our services are critically important, and we listen.'

CEO NOTE

Leading today is a paradox of thinking big and acting small. Galvanize people with the big picture and connect them in human ways to ensure clarity and alignment.

Develop Tomorrow

Probably the most important role of a CEO is to build a sustainable organization that helps leave the company and the world in a better place. This can cover multiple levels, including the creation of a long-term growth strategy, building enduring organizational capability, developing a robust talent pipeline and enabling an inclusive culture. Korn Ferry published a fascinating report entitled 'Future of work trends in 2022: A new era of humanity'. They set the context for organizations in the following way: The future holds a mix of opportunities and challenges, including climate change, digital acceleration, supply chain issues, and ever-changing customer preferences. To thrive, businesses must prioritize customer needs, adapt their models, and implement flexible production methods. Emphasizing people and technology to enhance productivity is vital, along with fostering a strong sense of purpose and interconnectedness within the organization. The journey ahead is both exciting and daunting, but success hinges on embracing continuous change.

As CEO you need to be at the front end of anticipating and creating a sustainable future. In his foreword for Heathrow Airport's strategic brief, John Holland-Kaye, CEO, states: 'This Strategic Brief document brings together everything that we represent at Heathrow, creating a clear set of aspirations for a future Heathrow in 2040. It will provide the basis to guide, inspire and evaluate our business plans and, in particular, the expansion programme over the next 15 to 20 years.'

In such unpredictable times it is a big undertaking to focus on shaping the future, however it is a vital part of the CEO role.

I resonated wholeheartedly with the way Keith Barr, CEO, IHG, assesses the value of a CEO for delivering sustainable success: 'It is important to recognize that there are certain things only you can do. At the top level there are four key areas to lead:

1. Strategy: have crystal clarity about the plan.

2. Capability: have the right machine to deliver the plan.

3. Talent: have the right talent to deliver the capability.

4. Culture: have the right culture to deliver the strategy, based on an environment of openness and transparency, to enable you to move quickly.'

Keith continued: 'Develop real clarity of purpose and strategy. You need to be very articulate about the direction and take people on the journey. When I took over the company, I had developed a clear picture about what we needed to do in five years which included buying and launching brands, transforming our cost base, technology, loyalty programme and owner proposition. As a result, we are hiring people today who wouldn't have considered working for us in the past and we have owners working with us who wouldn't have worked with us before.'

In terms of the personal challenge for a CEO to develop tomorrow, Keith commented: 'Be a good strategic thinker. You need the ability to take a complex set of data and synthesize it down to what matters. It's important to understand where the noise is and what really makes a difference. You need to be able to see around corners. It's relatively straightforward for executives to think about what they have to do next year. However, as CEO you need to think longer term and have the ability to anticipate the future without having clarity about all the moving parts. You need to ask yourself big questions like, in 15 years from now, what will success look like? Where do we want to be? How could we get there? You need to think bigger, longer term and help your team to expand their thinking about the future. Recognize that the decisions you make today will impact the company in five and ten years. You have to manage the short and long term. As a public company I have to manage the delivery each quarter, each year, as well as steering the long-term growth.'

Jan Smits, CEO and Deputy Chair, APAC, Pro-invest Group, gave a telling picture about the challenge for CEOs in developing the future: 'No one can tell what tomorrow will look like, however it will look very different from the past. A CEO needs to look five years ahead, but plan in shorter cycles. Tomorrow will have an even greater focus on people and the need to build capable and aligned teams. Given the scale of what we will face, having a capable team puts you in the best possible place to overcome challenges and make the most of opportunities. Make sure you prioritize succession and have the right depth and diversity of talent in the organization. As CEO I am constantly learning how to use technology for our advantage and take the noise out of the system.'

Justin Basini, CEO and co-founder, ClearScore, reinforced the focus on people: 'A CEO needs to help lay out a sequence of processes and experiences which take the organization forward, have a plan for the long term while solving the first problems first. We are currently investing in leadership and training to ensure we get the best out of our amazing talent. This was less important in the past when we were smaller and the senior and most experienced leaders were managing most people. Now we are bigger and we have the high-class problem of how we scale our management and leadership. We are democratizing the translation of our strategy to help everyone understand the business and be empowered. If we get it right, the company has a better chance of succeeding in the long term and can deliver real progress against our mission, irrespective of if key people leave and move on in their careers.'

I was intrigued by the approach of Paul Dupuis, CEO and Chairman, Randstad Japan, who also took a people-centric approach to developing tomorrow: 'My philosophy to building a sustainable organization is People + Growth = Output. For instance, Japan is the second largest business in what we do. We are growing at an unprecedented growth rate on our top line. What I notice is that when a CEO talks about growth in a business, the typical expectation is that it will be about the numbers. However, I had an 'a-ha' moment in the India business. We were losing budget. I chose to change our approach. I brought great people together and gave them a clear purpose focused on creating an environment where everyone could be the best version of themselves. We redefined growth and moved it to the following definition: An environment where everyone can shine, be enabled and equipped with the right tools to grow.'

Paul went on to say: 'With a clear formula we agreed that meetings needed to start by focusing on people, not the financial outputs. We set up our time to discuss how we were developing people and providing the tangible evidence to demonstrate what we were doing. At the end of meetings, we focused on the financial output. It was a challenging concept for colleagues, like when the Finance team got together it took time for them to adapt to starting meetings by discussing people rather than the numbers! However, doing it persistently and consistently meant that it became part of the company culture where people knew that they would finish with the output.'

Paul also shared in our conversation: 'I believe that the measurement of CEO effectiveness is what happens when you leave. I watch with deep interest what happens to organizations when I leave and find that my reward comes when I witness that what we worked on together has been taken to new heights. The ultimate contribution of a CEO is to build a sustainable organization and do good in the world.'

Joel Burrows, CEO, Ghirardelli, invests considerable time with his management team to develop tomorrow. He stated: 'As CEO you need to develop a shared understanding and alignment through the organization of the future you are trying to create and the challenges and problems to solve.'

Joel's principles centre on the following: 'As a CEO it's critical to focus on three key areas to set and deliver the strategy:

1. Where have you been? Immerse yourself in how the business has developed. Take time to uncover the amazing stories and people in your company's history and how that story has evolved.

2. Where are you now? Make a very honest assessment of where you are right now. Understand what is working, what needs to improve and if the company is measuring the right things to determine progress.

3. Where are you going? Be clear about where you want to go. Identify the key success factors for sustainable, long-term growth and what resources you need to get there, such as cost, quality, time and people.'

Top of the agenda for developing tomorrow is the sustainability agenda, and not just the environment. As Stephen McCall, CEO, edyn, put it: 'The ESG agenda needs to be one of the top things to focus on. You cannot get away without scrutiny. In the future the impact of CEOs will start with sustainability and end with performance. The social context is key for the business. Elements like employee wellbeing, EDI and integration in the community are fundamental. We have a super inclusive environment, but I get called out for being a white, straight, middle-class guy. Most people will ask you about inclusion and you need to have a thoughtful answer.'

Jonathan Akeroyd, CEO, Burberry, shared the importance of having an intentional approach to the ESG agenda: 'As a purposeful, values-driven brand, we are committed to being a force for good in the world. As CEO it's important to make sure your customers are aware of how your product connects with the ESG strategy and that you get the right balance between governance and execution.'

This is how Andy Mitchell, CEO, Tideway, addressed the topic: 'We need to live in a more sustainable way, therefore as CEO make sure your focus on sustainability is within the broadest context through the lens of ESG. You need to understand the societal benefits, as well as the environment and governance ones. I firmly believe that if you do things in the right way, you will get good business performance, which is a major investment for the future. We have made decisions that cost us a lot of money. When we awarded our initial contracts, we needed to move things by river. It was the right thing to do. But to create a more vibrant and commercial movement on the river cost us £50 million. We didn't need to do it, but it has paid back massively with our shareholders as it signified what we stood for. We had to raise £4 billion to deliver the project. At the time it didn't matter if as a company you had a good sustainability story. You could borrow money cheaper if people knew that you could make money. Now if you don't have a good sustainability story, you might not be able to borrow money. The markets have caught up. Do the right thing and the right things will happen. You need to recognize that at some point the right decisions will pay off.'

Andy also commented: 'We are a single-project company. Our remit is to do ourselves out of a job, which means that we have delivered. However, we still always try to do more. I don't have a long-term career to offer anyone, but I can develop people to be stronger and better for their next role. Although we are a time-limited project, the best thing I can do is to help others be the best they can be.'

To develop the future success of an organization, a CEO needs to think about the long term. By creating a picture of what they want to see happen and making a strategy that is a representation of the big picture, CEOs have the ability to step back and make important decisions in the direction they want to go. The risk of operating with a short-term focus is that the amygdala, best known for its role in fear and threat detection, takes over, preventing you from being able to think clearly and reducing your ability to tap into your long-term prefrontal cortex to think longer term. Going into the future and beginning with the ultimate outcome means that you are able to figure out what things have to happen for that future to occur. Whether it's a bold vision about sustainability or some other large issue you want to solve, developing and articulating tomorrow's future, and recognizing the milestones it will take to get there, is what helps you plan for a better tomorrow.

Emily Chang, CEO, Wunderman Thompson West, blended the idea of thinking long term with the value of consistency: 'No one likes being called "predictable". It feels boring – a predictable CEO may be seen as someone who doesn't stand out. But what's the other side of this coin? A predictable CEO eliminates the disruptive churn that comes from trying to guess how the boss is feeling today. Someone predictable can be counted on. Developing expected routines and exhibiting predictable behaviour creates a sense of comfort and safety. And when a CEO is predictable, people know what to expect. This reduces the emotional investment that goes into trying to guess after, adjust around, or manage the boss.'

Emily gave more insight about what being a predictable CEO looks like, which goes to help develop a better tomorrow, including scheduling regular:

- one-to-one meetings to set clear expectations and check progress on a regular basis
- team meetings with a clear agenda, attendee list, location and timing expectations
- town halls for broader groups, so people know when they will all come together
- aligned updates or escalation paths, which give people a clear route to resolution
- consistent leadership visibility that enables regular connects that break down the walls of hierarchy.

Jamie Bunce, CEO, Inspired Villages, spends considerable time looking into the future and trailblazing new paths: 'I am blessed to work in a sector where the demographics clearly indicate that things will get better. We have new investors interested in the sector of later living, with existing investors who are inquisitive and supportive. To reach this point we needed to build the foundations to have our business engine running well through our team. We have invested in radical thinking to make a positive transformational change in how people age in the UK and the world. If we continue to do it right and approach growth in a systematic way, I believe that in the future people will have the opportunity to think differently about aging. As CEO you need to think ahead of the organization. Make sure you are connected with colleagues in each part of the business. As CEO I look at the horizon and take soundings on the basis that we will hit our goal to be the world-leading retirement community operator. Somebody has got to do it and I my preference is that it is us.'

Francesca Lanza Tans, CEO, The Alexander Partnership, reinforced the need to be bold: 'When thinking about future-proofing the business, an easy trap CEOs can fall into is to avoiding making the wrong calls at all costs. As CEO your job is not to play safe. You need to think like an entrepreneur, question the status quo, stick your neck on the line and understand the unspoken rules. Experiment. Have a fail-fast mentality. You learn most from the mistakes you make. If you plan the future based on what has worked in the past, you may preclude yourself from exploring something entirely new. But if you allow yourself and others to be driven by curiosity, openness and the courage to try something different, you might come up with a game-changer. You won't always get the result you expected, but pick yourself up and start again. Foster a culture that is open to the outside world. Read as much as you can and learn from others. Acquire knowledge from peers, competitors and organizations in other sectors. Understand others' mistakes. Be outwards facing, and resist the temptation to navel gaze too often.'

The ability to think differently and innovate was a consistent theme for future success. Mike Mathieson, Chairman, NED, advisor and former founder and CEO, Cake founder and former CEO, Cake, shared: 'The key to building a sustainable business is reinvention. If you rest on your laurels today, you will be history. The perfect model is to have people in the company who are innovating on a consistent basis. Constant change is a necessity, particularly in the service industry. Consumers are changing all the time. You need to make sure you have digital natives around you to challenge and move the business along. You need a brilliant executive team to develop the culture, and to live and breathe the core purpose of the business. Everyone in the business needs tangible KPIs to ensure responsibility and accountability. Be at the forefront of ESG principles. If you shine from within, consumers will buy into your passion.'

A CEO needs to be plugged into tomorrow. Ensure you are attuned to different ways of thinking, different ways of working and different networks to establish a clear and compelling way to develop the future. One movement to be aware of is B Lab: 'A non-profit network transforming the global economy to benefit all people, communities, and the planet.' As B Lab states: 'There's no Planet B. Our international network of organizations leads economic systems change to support our collective vision of an inclusive, equitable, and regenerative economy.' As CEO you could go down the route of seeking B Corp certification to measure your company's entire social and environment impact.

Another resource to note is Conscious Capitalism, whose philosophy encompasses the following intent: 'We believe that business is good because it creates value, it is ethical because it is based on voluntary exchange, it is noble because it can elevate our existence, and it is heroic because it lifts people out of poverty and creates prosperity. Free enterprise capitalism is the most powerful system for social cooperation and human progress ever conceived. It is one of the most compelling ideas we humans have ever had.'

To develop tomorrow, build a solid company foundation consisting of a clear strategic plan, robust organizational capability, great talent and an inclusive culture so that the company delivers superior performance today, which allows you the space to lift up and chart a compelling future enabling you to do good for the world and do good for the business.

CEO NOTE

Probably the greatest privilege of being a CEO is to help create a better tomorrow for all stakeholders.

Be an Enabler for Sustainable Growth: Exec Summary

- Don't wait to be a CEO.
- Every day you have the opportunity to deliver great results which will be a blueprint of your success.
- Every day you have the opportunity to lead through today's complex world, which will equip you to think big and act small.
- Every day you have the opportunity to build a better tomorrow by being a leader of the future.
- Think like a CEO today.
- Put your company agenda first.
- Help make sure the strategy is fit for purpose.
- Evolve the organizational capability.
- Unlock talent.
- Contribute to an environment of belonging.
- Make being a CEO an act of service to create a better world.

Epilogue

• • •

Acting upon the lessons in *How to Be a CEO* can help in your quest to be a CEO, however no amount of books, advice, skills, knowledge or experience can prepare you fully for the reality of being a CEO. It is similar to parenthood. For those who have been fortunate enough to experience the nine-month pregnancy period where you try to cram in as much preparation as you can, the actual reality of having a new-born in your arms is indescribable. As CEO, no matter how ready you are, it takes at least the precious first 100 days to acclimatize. Recognize that there is no such thing as the perfect CEO – similarly there is no perfect parent. Immersing yourself in the principles from *How to Be a CEO* will accelerate your journey and, most importantly, challenge you to create your own framework to being the best CEO you can be.

One of my biggest learnings from coaching and working with multiple CEOs is that it is rare for them to have codified their CEO plan and approach before coming into role. Would you go on a journey without a map? I do know some people who relish the opportunity to leave a vacation unplanned and love to wander. However, even setting aside a specified amount of time to travel on a whim is an outcome. Start with the end in mind. Have a clear intent to become a CEO. Whether you ultimately achieve this outcome is a different matter. Developing a mindset to be a CEO is essential to testing whether it is genuinely the right destination for you. Mapping out your route to becoming a CEO will give you the best possible chance.

There is no right plan to make, however using the 21 steps in *How to Be a CEO* will give you a robust path for the way ahead:

1. **Purpose**. Be clear about your big why and the difference you want to make in the world. Combining this with the ability to

build and lead a purpose-led organization will be a competitive differentiator as a CEO.

2. **Values**. Take a stand for what matters beyond financial profit. People will want to understand your personal brand and, if it is something that is meaningful, it will inspire them to follow.

3. **Strengths**. Understand where you add the most value and have the biggest impact. Being a CEO demands extraordinary grit and drive, so using your strengths will help you be on top of your game and sustain you for the long run.

4. **Vision**. Develop the ability to think big and differently. The role of a CEO is to provide clear direction, therefore it is essential to lift people up by painting a compelling picture of a desired future state.

5. **Strategy**. Become brilliant at combining insight and data with judgement and courage to create a roadmap for an organization to follow. Ensure everyone can translate the strategy to their personal objectives to create a golden thread from individual to company targets.

6. **Energy**. A CEO is the weather setting the climate for infectious positivity and performance. Make sure you are the type of CEO who lights up a room when you walk in, not when you walk out!

7. **Preparation**. Mastery takes practice. It is uncommon to stumble into becoming a CEO. Be clear about the capability required to be a CEO in your specialism. Do you need to build huge credibility in your existing domain, such as law? Do you need to become a brilliant generalist covering commercial, operational, strategic and financial areas? Once you are in the fortunate position of landing a CEO role, be ahead of the curve with a robust 90-day plan containing a proposition of the initial big bets you will take.

8. **Capability**. Learn what great looks like to build an organization fit for delivery. Have sufficient understanding about the company machine, including data, technology, procurement, process and systems, to be able to assess and develop the organizational capability required to succeed.

9. **Blockers**. The success of an organization is equal to its potential to perform minus interference. From an internal perspective this can include factors like unclear priorities and plans, broken systems and technology, turnover, lack of productivity or limited innovation. External factors can be political instability, market conditions, recession or global pandemics. You will need to be equipped to navigate blockers in agile ways to ensure the company drives performance at pace.

10. **Safety**. In a climate of uncertainty and anxiety, learn how to create an environment of psychological safety where everyone has voice and contributes ideas without the fear of negative consequences. In an age of humanity this will set you apart from leaders who do not deliberately orchestrate the opportunity to invite participation, encourage risk-taking and champion continuous learning.

11. **Belonging**. Your strategic and technical competence needs to be balanced with your awareness and expertise in creating the conditions where everyone has a sense of belonging and can be themselves. Championing the equity, diversity and inclusion agenda is the foundation for creating a highly functioning and performing organization.

12. **Thrive**. As CEO you need a deep appreciation of the physical, emotional, mental and spiritual capacities for people to be the best version of themselves at work. This means being at the leading edge of managing health and wellbeing, working patterns, learning and development, and enabling people to do the work they love and love the work they do.

13. **Teaming**. The only way you will succeed as CEO is to build your own super-team, as well as breaking down any organizational silos so that all teams can work together across boundaries in agile ways. The majority of company agendas require cross-functional teamwork to combine the required mindsets, skillsets and tools to deliver at pace.

14. **Succession**. The success of a CEO can be directly linked to the depth and breadth of the company succession plans. Championing the talent agenda through recruitment, retention

and development is a major priority of a CEO and needs to be treated accordingly.

15. **Learning**. The ability of an organization to learn faster than its competitors is a sure-fire recipe for success. The number one quality that people need to embody is curiosity. This needs to be role modelled as a CEO through being present, asking questions, listening to understand, requesting feedback, being prepared to say 'I don't know', and showing a willingness to make mistakes and adapt at pace.

16. **Climate**. A CEO is the cultural architect of a company. It is essential to understand how to develop the right cultural conditions to enable the delivery of the strategic plan, and to stay highly attuned to the reality of the way things are done so that behaviours match the cultural intent.

17. **Relationship**. Your success as CEO will be significantly determined by your social capital. In other words, to maximize your relationships with multiple stakeholders including the chair, board, shareholders, colleagues, consumers, customers and community. Draw upon a network of shared values and resources to enable people to work together to achieve a common purpose.

18. **Influence**. As CEO you have a relatively small circle of control, however your circle of influence determines your success. Your ability to understand others' agendas, meet them where they are, take them on a journey to align needs and put the company first is a competitive differentiator.

19. **Delivery**. Demonstrating consistent delivery is point of entry for becoming a CEO. However, the big shift to make once in role is to create the conditions for excellent execution. This will require you to have your finger on the performance pulse in real time so that you can pull the necessary levers to drive it forward when needed.

20. **Today**. We are living in unprecedented times of complexity, ambiguity and unplanned scenarios, which demands CEOs to combine a mix of thinking big, understanding the detail, having

conviction, acting swiftly, and mobilizing people to demonstrate extraordinary levels of resilience, agility, drive and optimism.

21. **Tomorrow**. The test of CEO greatness is to build a sustainable organization. This means ensuring the four fundamental areas of a company – strategy, capability, talent and culture – continue to improve. The ideal scenario for a CEO is to spend 80 per cent of their time focused on the future. The best way of making this happen is to do what only you can do.

Now is the time to reflect upon the formation or evolution of your CEO plan. Different scenarios I encounter are:

- *Aspiration*: Next-generational CEOs who have genuine ambition and drive to progress into the role.
- *Succession*: CEOs on the company succession plan, performing in role and positioning themselves for a future opportunity.
- *Transition*: CEOs who have secured the dream role and are preparing themselves for a great start.
- *Established*: CEOs in role who want to challenge themselves to become better and/or strengthen succession plans.

Whatever your situation, the proven methodology of *How to Be a CEO* will provoke your thinking and planning.

Purpose, People and Performance are timeless parts of leading a sustainable organization. Every CEO I spoke with shared the privilege of being in a role where they have direct impact on significant environmental, societal and economic issues. In their hands lie the following opportunities:

- Creating cultures of belonging and elevating individuals traditionally underrepresented in business.
- Sponsoring learning and development opportunities to grow employees and cultivate future leaders.
- Contributing to a world where people make a sustainable living and have prospects for betterment.

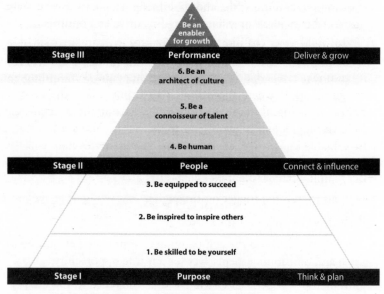

Figure 8.1

- Prioritizing the physical, emotional, mental and spiritual health of employees and their families through education and quality care.

- Championing sustainability practices and combating climate change to ensure a thriving planet for generations to come.

- Engaging local communities to support development and growth where we live and work.

Alongside the above, a CEO is accountable for defining purpose, vision, values and corporate culture; setting and executing organizational strategy; building the senior leadership team; and making capital-allocation decisions. Combining these is a potent mix and as CEO you can integrate life-changing scenarios with robust company plans. However, you are not an island. Another key insight in writing *How to Be a CEO* was the recognition that you will succeed only through engaging others. Starting with your chair and board, extending to your executive committee and rippling out to colleagues, consumers, customers, community, shareholders, investors, governments, regulators and the media, you will need to generate followership to succeed.

To build your coalition, be highly attuned to your stakeholder agendas. Everyone will have a different nuance. Have the humanity to understand what is important for them and demonstrate your commitment to where they are coming from. Make the necessary trade-offs to appeal to the majority while putting the company first. By investing in your network you are not alone. You are surrounded by valuable knowledge, experience and capability to help you navigate the organizational climate and to make the big decisions. Have the humility to seek the right advice to test and evolve your thinking. Be bold to pull the trigger on the highest-level calls. Stay vigilant to progress made and adapt at pace when needed. Keep listening. Keep learning. Keep leading.

Being a CEO is one of the most privileged opportunities in the world today. I sincerely hope that wherever you are on your own journey, *How to Be a CEO* will make a difference to the quality of your thinking, approach and impact. My purpose is to develop *better leaders for a better tomorrow*. If this book nudges you in this direction, I am sincerely grateful.

References

Accelerating sustainable and inclusive growth. 2021 ESG Report, available at www. mckinsey.com/about-us/social-responsibility/2021-esg-report/overview

Ackerman, Courtney E., What is neuroplasticity? A psychologist explains [+14 tools], 25 July, 2018, available at https://positivepsychology.com/neuroplasticity/

Amazon, Who we are, available at https://www.aboutamazon.com/about-us

Amire, Roula, The top 5 things millennials want in the workplace in 2022. Great Place To Work, 18 July, 2022, available at https://www.greatplacetowork.com/ resources/blog/top-5-things-millennials-want-in-the-workplace-in-2022

Amos, Owen, Boris Johnson resigns: Five things that led to the PM's downfall, BBC News, 7 July, 2022, available at https://www.bbc.co.uk/news/uk-politics-62070422

B Lab, Make business a force for good, available at www.bcorporation.net/en-us

Barsade, Sigal G., The ripple effect: Emotional contagion and its influence on group behavior, Yale University, 1 December, 2002, available at https://journals.sage-pub.com/doi/abs/10.2307/3094912?journalCode=asqa

Boyatzis, Richard, Smith, Melvin and Van Oosten, Ellen, *Helping People Change*, Harvard Business Review Press, Illustrated edition, 2019.

Brené Brown, The power of vulnerability, available at https://www.ted.com/talks/ brene_brown_the_power_of_vulnerability/c

Bryant, Adam, In sports or business, always prepare for the next play, *The New York Times*, 10 November, 2012, available at https://www.nytimes.com/2012/11/11/ business/jeff-weiner-of-linkedin-on-the-next-play-philosophy.html

Buckingham, Marcus, Defining strengths, 29 January, 2020, available at https:// www.marcusbuckingham.com/defining-strengths/

Buckingham, Marcus, Chumney, Dr. Fran, Hayes, Dr. Mary and Wright, Dr. Corinne, The Global Study of Engagement, ADP Research Institute, available at https://www.adp.com/-/media/adp/ResourceHub/pdf/ADPRI/ADPRI0102_ 2018_Engagement_Study_Technical_Report_RELEASE%20READY.ashx

Business Roundtable, Business Roundtable redefines the purpose of a corporation to promote 'an economy that serves all Americans', 18 August, 2019, available at www.businessroundtable.org/business-roundtable-redefines-the-purpose-of-a-corporation-to-promote-an-economy-that-serves-all-americans

Calic, Goran and Wu, Andy, Does Elon Musk have a strategy?, *Harvard Business Review*, 15 July, 2022, available at https://hbr.org/2022/07/does-elon-musk-have-a-strategy

Cameron, Kim and Seppälä, Emma, The best leaders have a contagious positive energy, *Harvard Business Review*, 18 April, 2022, available at https://hbr.org/2022/04/the-best-leaders-have-a-contagious-positive-energy

Chen, Natalie, IHG offers rising stars quick way to the top, Travel Weekly Asia, 29 March, 2016, available at https://www.travelweekly-asia.com/Travel-News/Hotel-News/IHG-offers-rising-stars-quick-way-to-the-top

Cisco, Overview, available at https://newsroom.cisco.com/c/r/newsroom/en/us/company.html

Clifford, Catherine, Bill Gates took solo 'think weeks' in a cabin in the woods – why it's a great strategy, CNBC, Make It, 28 July, 2019, available at https://www.cnbc.com/2019/07/26/bill-gates-took-solo-think-weeks-in-a-cabin-in-the-woods.html

CliftonStrengths, Don Clifton's desire to change the world through empowering human development, available at https://www.gallup.com/cliftonstrengths/en/253754/history-cliftonstrengths.aspx

Collins, Jim and Porras, Jerry I, Building your company's vision, *Harvard Business Review*, September–October 1996, available at https://hbr.org/1996/09/building-your-companys-vision

Collins, Jim, First who, then what: Excerpts from *Good to Great*, Random House Business, 4 October, 2001, available at https://www.jimcollins.com/concepts/first-who-then-what.html

Conscious Capitalism, We believe that business is good, available at www.conscious-capitalism.org/

Covey, Stephen R., *The 7 Habits of Highly Effective People*, Simon & Schuster, 2020.

Cowen, Alan S. and Keltner, Dacher, Self-report captures 27 distinct categories of emotion bridged by continuous gradients, The Proceedings of the National Academy of Sciences (PNAS), 5 September, 2016, available at https://www.pnas.org/doi/abs/10.1073/pnas.1702247114

Craig, Nick and Snook, Scott A., From purpose to impact, *Harvard Business Review*, May 2014, available at https://hbr.org/2014/05/from-purpose-to-impact

Cranston, Susie and Keller, Scott, Increasing the meaning quotient of work, McKinsey & Company, 1 January, 2013, available at https://www.mckinsey.com/business-functions/people-and-organizational-performance/our-insights/increasing-the-meaning-quotient-of-work

Devonshire, Sophie and Renshaw, Ben, *LoveWork*, John Murray Press, 2021.

Dewar, Carolyn, Hirt, Martin and Keller, Scott, The mindsets and practices of excellent CEOs, McKinsey & Company, 25 October, 2019, available at https://www.mckinsey.com/business-functions/strategy-and-corporate-finance/our-insights/the-mindsets-and-practices-of-excellent-ceos

Dixon-Fyle, Sundiatu, Dolan, Kevin, Dame Hunt, Vivian and Prince, Sara, Diversity wins: How inclusion matters, McKinsey & Company, 19 May, 2020, available at https://www.mckinsey.com/featured-insights/diversity-and-inclusion/diversity-wins-how-inclusion-matters

Duckworth, Angela, *Grit: The power of passion and perseverance*, Scribner, 3 May, 2016, available at https://angeladuckworth.com/grit-book/

Edmondson, Amy C., *The Fearless Organization*, Wiley, 2018.

Edwardes, Charlotte, Universal Music CEO David Joseph: Why I'm standing up for difference, *Evening Standard*, 24 June, 2019, available at https://www.standard.co.uk/news/uk/universal-music-ceo-david-joseph-why-i-m-standing-up-for-difference-a4174601.html

Ellis, Sarah and Tupper, Helen, *The Squiggly Career*, Portfolio Penguin, 2020.

Fink, Larry, The power of capitalism, Letter to CEOs 2022, available at https://www.blackrock.com/corporate/investor-relations/larry-fink-ceo-letter

Fisher, Jen, Hatfield, Steve and Silverglate, Paul H., The C-suite's role in well-being, Deloitte Insights, 22 June, 2022, available at https://www2.deloitte.com/us/en/insights/topics/leadership/employee-wellness-in-the-corporate-workplace.html

Future of work trends in 2022: The new era of humanity, Korn Ferry Insights, 2022, available at https://www.kornferry.com/insights/featured-topics/future-of-work/2022-future-of-work-trends

Gardner, Heidi K. and Mortensen, Mark, Leaders don't have to choose between compassion and performance, 16 February, 2022, available at https://hbr.org/2022/02/leaders-dont-have-to-choose-between-compassion-and-performance

Globescan, Reinforcing the need for long-term purposeful business in a capitalist society: Analysis of Larry Fink's annual letter to CEOs, available at https://globescan.com/2022/02/17/analysis-larry-finks-annual-letter-ceos-2022/

Great Place To Work, Trust model, available at https://www.greatplacetowork.com/our-methodology

Hasson, Uri, This is your brain on communication, TED2016, available at https://www.ted.com/talks/uri_hasson_this_is_your_brain_on_communication?language=en

Heathrow's Strategic Brief, available at https://www.heathrow.com/company/about-heathrow/company-information/heathrows-strategic-brief

Holford, Patrick, Mental health, available at https://www.patrickholford.com/topic/mental-health/

Jackson, Fresia, Why your best employees are leaving and how to stop it, Culture Amp, 27 August, 2021, available at https://www.cultureamp.com/blog/why-your-employees-are-leaving?

Kluge, Dr Hans Henri P., Rapidly escalating COVID-19 cases amid reduced virus surveillance forecasts a challenging autumn and winter in the WHO European Region, World Health Organization, 19 July, 2022, available at https://www.who.int/europe/news/item/19-07-2022-rapidly-escalating-covid-19-cases-amid-reduced-virus-surveillance-forecasts-a-challenging-autumn-and-winter-in-the-who-european-region

Lauricella, Taylor, Parsons, John, Schaninger, Bill and Weddle, Brooke, Network effects: How to rebuild social capital and improve corporate performance, McKinsey & Company, 2 August, 2022, available at https://www.mckinsey.com/capabilities/people-and-organizational-performance/our-insights/network-effects-how-to-rebuild-social-capital-and-improve-corporate-performance

Lencioni, Patrick, *The Five Dysfunctions of a Team*, John Wiley & Sons, 2002.

Loehr, Jim and Schwartz, Tony, The making of a corporate athlete, *Harvard Business Review*, January 2001, available at https://hbr.org/2001/01/the-making-of-a-corporate-athlete

Mackey, John and Sisodia, Raj, *Conscious Capitalism*, Harvard Business Review Press, 2014.

McKinsey & Company, Help your employees find purpose – or watch them leave, 5 April, 2021, available at https://www.mckinsey.com/business-functions/people-and-organizational-performance/our-insights/help-your-employees-find-purpose-or-watch-them-leave

McKinsey & Company, Making a daily 'to be' list: How a hospital system CEO is navigating the coronavirus crisis, 23 July, 2020, available at https://www.mckinsey.com/business-functions/strategy-and-corporate-finance/our-insights/making-a-daily-to-be-list-how-a-hospital-system-ceo-is-navigating-the-coronavirus-crisis

McKinsey & Company, Network effects: How to rebuild social capital and improve corporate performance, 2 August, 2022, available at https://www.mckinsey.com/capabilities/people-and-organizational-performance/our-insights/network-effects-how-to-rebuild-social-capital-and-improve-corporate-performance

Nanji, Noor and Thomas, Daniel, Patagonia: Billionaire boss gives fashion firm away to fight climate change, BBC News, 15 September, 2022, available at https://www.bbc.co.uk/news/business-62906853

Nohria, Nitin and Porter, Michael E., How CEOs manage time, *Harvard Business Review*, July 2018, available at https://hbr.org/2018/07/how-ceos-manage-time

Pendall, Ryan, 8 behaviors of the world's best managers, Gallup Workplace, 30 December, 2019, available at https://www.gallup.com/workplace/272681/habits-world-best-managers.aspx

Press release, Russian invasion of Ukraine impedes post-pandemic economic recovery in emerging Europe and Central Asia, The World Bank, 4 October, 2022, available at https://www.worldbank.org/en/news/press-release/2022/10/04/russian-invasion-of-ukraine-impedes-post-pandemic-economic-recovery-in-emerging-europe-and-central-asia

Race, Michael, Heathrow passenger limit may return for Christmas, BBC News, 26 October, 2022, available at https://www.bbc.co.uk/news/business-63396810

REFERENCES

re:Work, Guide: Understand team effectiveness, Google, 2012, available at https://rework.withgoogle.com/guides/understanding-team-effectiveness/steps/introduction/

Sainsbury's, About us, available at https://www.about.sainsburys.co.uk/about-us

Schwantes, Marcel, LinkedIn's CEO just gave some brilliant life advice. Here it is in 1 sentence, Inc. September, 30 September, 2017, available at https://www.inc.com/marcel-schwantes/linkedins-ceo-just-gave-some-brilliant-life-advice-here-it-is-in-1-sentence.html

Segal, Troy, 5 most publicized ethics violations by CEOs, Investopedia, 7 July, 2022, available at https://www.investopedia.com/financial-edge/0113/5-most-publicized-ethics-violations-by-ceos.aspx

Smith, Fred, Lessons from a decade of 'conscious capitalism', 11 November, 2016, available at https://www.forbes.com/sites/fredsmith/2016/11/11/lessons-from-a-decade-of-conscious-capitalism/?sh=59618f162e0c

Strategy&, Part of the PwC network, 2018 CEO Success Study: Succeeding the long-serving legend in the corner office, available at https://www.strategyand.pwc.com/it/en/insights/ceo-success.html

The Dalai Lama, *The Art of Happiness*, Hodder Paperbacks, 1999.

Thomas, Daniel, UK businesses plead for political stability as economic conditions worsen, *Financial Times*, 20 October, 2022, available at https://www.ft.com/content/212a0a7f-f94b-4695-9a2d-4c1203482a90

Watkins, Michael D., *The First 90 Days*, Harvard Business Review Press, 2013.

Weiner, Jeff, Be compassionate – Wharton Undergraduate Commencement Speech, 2018, LinkedIn, 14 May, 2018, available at https://www.linkedin.com/pulse/compassionate-wharton-undergraduate-commencement-speech-jeff-weiner/

Weiner, Jeff, LinkedIn's Jeff Weiner: How compassion builds better companies, Knowledge at Wharton, 17 May, 2018, available at https://knowledge.wharton.upenn.edu/article/linkedin-ceo-how-compassion-can-build-a-better-company/

Zak, Paul, J., The neuroscience of trust, *Harvard Business Review*, January–February 2017, available at https://hbr.org/2017/01/the-neuroscience-of-trust

Zak, Paul J., Why your brain loves good storytelling, *Harvard Business Review*, 28 October, 2014, available at https://hbr.org/2014/10/why-your-brain-loves-good-storytelling

Zohar, Danah, *Spiritual Intelligence*, Bloomsbury Publishing, 2001.

About the Author

Photographer: Noel Yeo,
Nudge Photography

Ben Renshaw is one of today's foremost leadership thinkers. Speaker, executive coach and author, Ben's innovative work with leading organizations, senior executives and entrepreneurs has brought him international acclaim. Formerly a classical violinist, Ben now plays a different tune, getting the best out of people. He writes about how to lead and be successful in today's volatile world and is the author of 11 popular books, including *LoveWork*, *Being*, *Purpose*, *Lead!* and *Super Coaching*. Ben's leadership development programmes include 'Leading with Purpose', 'Leading Change' and 'Leading Sustainable Growth'. As an executive coach and leadership consultant, Ben has worked with clients including Allen & Overy LLP, Aman Resorts, Barclays, Britvic, BT, Choice Hotels, ClearScore, Diageo, Entrepreneurs Organization,

Ghirardelli, Government Communication Service, Heathrow, Heinz, Henley Business School, HSBC, Hyatt, Imperial Business School, Inspired Villages, InterContinental Hotels Group, KPMG, Lindt Canada, M&S, National Highways, P&G, Sainsbury's, Sky, The Standard Hotels, Transport for London, UBS, Unilever, Virgin Media and Warner Bros.

To find out more about Ben Renshaw's speaking, executive coaching, team and leadership development programmes, or for media requests, please visit benrenshaw.com

Email: hello@benrenshaw.com

LinkedIn: www.linkedin.com/in/ben-renshaw

Acknowledgements

I am blessed to partner with inspiring leaders who, through our work together, constantly challenge me to learn and grow. *How to Be a CEO* is a direct result of the generous insight of all the contributors recognized at the start of the book. However, I do want to shout out to Amy C. Edmondson, Novartis Professor of Leadership and Management, Harvard Business School; Andy Cosslett, CBE, Chair ITV plc and Kingfisher plc; and John Holland-Kaye, CEO, Heathrow, who graciously wrote the foreword.

Thank you to my mentors who have been a rock in my own leadership development: Andreas Thrasyvoulou, Chairman, New World Hospitality; Graham Alexander, Founder, The Alexander Partnership; and Simon Woodroffe, Founder YO! Sushi.

Thank you to the brilliant team at Nicholas Brealey Publishing, an imprint of John Murray Press, for their expertise and commitment: Jonathan Shipley (commissioning editor); Meaghan Lim (project editor); Matt Young (marketing manager).

Thank you to my father, Peter Renshaw, for his generous support in reading the manuscript, and to my amazing children, India, Ziggy and Zebedee, who make it all worthwhile.

Would you like your people to read this book?

If you would like to discuss how you could bring these ideas to your team, we would love to hear from you. Our titles are available at competitive discounts when purchased in bulk across both physical and digital formats. We can offer bespoke editions featuring corporate logos, customized covers, or letters from company directors in the front matter can also be created in line with your special requirements.

We work closely with leading experts and organizations to bring forward-thinking ideas to a global audience. Our books are designed to help you be more successful in work and life.

For further information, or to request a catalogue, please contact:
business@johnmurrays.co.uk
sales-US@nicholasbrealey.com (North America only)

Nicholas Brealey Publishing is an imprint of
John Murray Press.

LoveWork: The Seven Steps to Thrive at Work

BY BEN RENSHAW AND SOPHIE DEVONSHIRE

Life provides a unique opportunity to do great things and help make the world a better place. Given that a staggering 90,000 hours of our lives (on average) will be spent working, how many of those precious hours will be meaningful or memorable?

Authors Ben Renshaw and Sophie Devonshire believe it's possible to make the time you spend at work more rewarding and enjoyable. In LoveWork they share seven simple steps to help you find new ways to build a more positive relationship with your work.

This book is for you if:

- You are moving up through your work or moving on to a new role
- You'd like to move faster or go further
- You want to find, rediscover or nurture your love of work.

You'll learn how to unlock your thinking to trigger a renaissance in your work experience, to embrace dynamic working and to discover, develop and then deliver new ways to thrive at work. If you want to love life, you'll need to LoveWork. It's time to stop counting the hours and start making those hours count.

"LoveWork offers a step-by-step framework for doing the work you love and loving the work you do. It is filled with illustrative scenario-based examples to nurture the free expression of ideas and help you thrive."
From the foreword by Amy C. Edmondson, Novartis Professor of Leadership and Management Harvard Business School

Hardback 978-1-52936-853-6
Audiobook 978-1-52936-856-7

Ben Renshaw

Developing purpose-led organizations to deliver sustainable performance & growth

Speaking | Leadership Development | High Performing Teams | Executive Coaching

hello@benrenshaw.com

www.benrenshaw.com